A Crisis in Leadership

Edited By Mike Willis

Truth Magazine Annual Lectures

June 21-24, 2010

© **Truth Publications, Inc. 2018. Second Printing.** All rights reserved. No part of this book may be reproduced in any form without written permission from the publisher. Printed in the United States of America.

ISBN 10: 1-58427-299-6

ISBN 13: 978-158427-299-1

First Printing: 2010

Truth Publications, Inc.
CEI Bookstore
220 S. Marion St., Athens, AL 35611
855-492-6657
sales@truthpublications.com
www.truthbooks.com

Table of Contents

Foreword, Connie W. Adams v

Part One — The Evening Lectures: Leaders in the Church
Simon Peter: "Everyman as Leader," Steve Wolfgang. 9
Leaders in the Church: Paul, Bruce Key. 36
Leaders in the Church: Barnabas, Steve Niemeier 44

Part Two — The Day Lectures
The Family Qualifications of an Elder, Bobby Graham 53
The Work of Elders, Sherrel Mercer. 65
Training Men to Serve, Gary Watt 76
The Non-Family Qualifications of Elders, Bobby Schrimshire 83
The Elders' Relationship to the Church, Jesse Flowers 100
The Terms Used to Describe Elders, Mike Vierheller 109
The Qualifications as They Relate to the Work, Randy Blackaby . . . 123
When Elders Abuse Their Authority, Jerry Blount 143
The Work of Deacons, Terrell Bunting. 154

Morning Classes
Historical Controversies over Leadership, Ron Halbrook 167
Women in Business Meetings, Tom Roberts 195
The Authority of Elders, Tom O'Neal 208

Ladies Classses
Qualifications of Elders and Deacons' Wives, Sherelyn Mayberry . . . 229
Women's Role in the Church, Kate Mitchell 238
Great Women I Have Known, Bobby Adams. 263

Addenda
The Process of Appointing Officers, Ron Halbrook. 277
Elders and Communication, Ron Halbrook 283

Foreword

When Jesus ascended to the throne in heaven, he "gave gifts unto men" so that "he might fill all things." What he gave were the necessary functions "For the perfecting of the saints, for the work of the ministry, for the edifying of the body of Christ." And what were these functions? "He gave some, apostles; and some prophets; and some evangelists; and some, pastors and teachers" (Eph. 4:7-12).

The apostles and prophets provided for the foundation work. We are "built upon the foundation of the apostles and prophets" (Eph. 2:20). They laid the foundation when they preached Christ (1 Cor. 3:11). That foundation still stands and we still build on it.

Evangelists made provision for the extension of the kingdom. They are to "preach the word" doing "the work of an evangelist" (2 Tim. 4:2-5).

Pastors and teachers provided for the spiritual growth and development of every Christian. They are to "feed" or "tend" the flock (1 Pet. 5:2). Paul taught brethren to "know them which labor among you and are over you in the Lord, and admonish you; and to esteem them very highly in love for their work's sake. And be at peace among yourselves" (1 Thes. 5:12-13). This work, and the proper response to it, is necessary to being at peace.

The Holy Spirit revealed the qualities which fit men for this noble work. 1 Tim. 3:1-7 and Titus 1:5-9 state the qualities of character, leadership and ability to teach required for the work. These qualifications are as stringent as God meant for them to be, but no more than that. On the one hand, many have erred through time in appointing men to serve who did not measure up to the standard given. Churches have suffered because of that. On the other hand, some have read more into the qualifications than the Lord stated. This has been the cause of endless disputes and has sometimes kept churches from having the leadership they needed.

Foreword

It does not take a Solomon to know that many churches are suffering a crisis in leadership. Some congregations have existed for years with no elders to lead or deacons to serve and with none in sight. Something is wrong when that situation prevails. Some churches have good and capable elders but are not working to train and develop men to continue that good work. It takes time for men to grow and mature to the point they can serve in leadership roles. They must choose godly companions and train their children in the way of the Lord. There are cases where some men have grown in their knowledge and ability, but their wives or children prevent them from being qualified. When a congregation only has two elders, they are one heartbeat, or one job transfer, away from having no elders.

There are some who have supposed that the church is like a business and needs skilled managers to lead them. One who successfully runs a business may learn some things which will be useful in interacting with members of a congregation, but the work of shepherding a flock, of nourishing, protecting and guiding each lamb may go begging.

Sadly, there are churches without elders and deacons, which are content to work through business meetings indefinitely. Sometimes there are men who do not meet the necessary qualifications, who take an active role in leadership and who fear they will lose their clout if elders are appointed. Some churches have been split for this very reason.

Some churches have suffered because elders have not been vigilant as to who does the teaching and preaching. Inept or worldly teachers have sometimes been employed to the dismay and discouragement of those who want to do what is right. Weak preaching has been allowed, if not actually encouraged.

All of these things create a crisis in leadership. That is why we have decided to devote the Truth Lectures in 2010 to this theme. Capable and qualified speakers have been invited to give us the benefit of their study and experience on the subjects assigned to them. The publication of this lecture book gives more permanent form to this needed material and extends its impact far beyond the actual presentation of these timely subjects to a limited audience. We thank those who have spent hours in study (not to mention years of experience which they have gained) for their work. Several speakers presently serve as elders, some have served in the past, and one is a deacon. This material needs to be in the hands of leaders and those who will, in time, take their place filling the ranks of those who must lay their armor by and go to give an answer to the Chief Shepherd. If you think this material is profitable, then why not purchase some extra copies and give them to elders and deacons you know or to younger men who show promise for the future. We welcome you to the Seventh Annual Truth Lecture Program.

Connie W. Adams
February 3, 2010

�# The Evening Lectures

Simon Peter: "Everyman" as Leader
Steve Wolfgang

"Of all the human personalities whom Jesus remade, Simon Peter is the one (next to Paul) about whom we know the most, and the man who seems most like ourselves." To quote one memorable phrase, the Lord "transformed a nature as unstable as water into the consistency of a rock."[1]

"Depart From Me, Lord, For I Am a Sinful Man" (Luke 5:8)

Simon Peter's tempestuous character is perhaps nowhere more clearly seen than in that dark betrayal night, vacillating from loud assertions of

---

[1] William Steuart McBirnie, *The Search for the Twelve Apostles* (Carol Stream, IL: Tyndale House, 1973), 17.

James Stephen Wolfgang was born 8 December 1948 in Indianapolis, to James H. and Jean Wolfgang, who still reside there. Steve's father and grandfather were elders in several Indianapolis congregations for more than fifty years. Steve's brother John, is an elder for the East County church in Portland, OR. His sister, Janet, is married to Mike Hardin, who preaches for the Bath Road church in Huber Heights, OH. Steve attended Florida College, where he met his wife, Bette (Ashworth). They married in 1969 and have two married daughters, Lesley and Lindsay. Bette is a board-certified psychologist now in private practice. Steve has preached in Marion, IN; Atlanta, GA; Franklin, TN; Louisville, KY; Danville, KY; and Downers Grove, IL (2008-). Steve served as an elder at the Danville congregation from 1999 to 2008. He has preached the gospel in nearly forty states and a dozen foreign countries, primarily in Eastern Europe, Russia, and China. He and Bette have conducted weekend or week-long marriage seminars in churches and other venues in various places in several states and in Australia.

Steve graduated from Butler University and earned an M.Div. at Southern Baptist Theological Seminary, as well as an M.A. in American Intellectual History from Vanderbilt University, and a Ph.D. in the History of Science and Medicine from the University of Kentucky. Steve taught history at the University of Kentucky (1993-2008). Over the years he has engaged in radio and television news broadcasting at CBS and NPR affiliates.

loyalty to his Lord, to impulsive physical violence, to cowardly denials and bitter tears of remorse. Yet only a few weeks later, Peter stands boldly before an audience of thousands, confidently proclaiming the good news: "Let all the house of Israel know for certain that God has made Him both Lord and Christ – this Jesus whom you crucified" (Acts 2:36).[2]

Understandable tendencies to recoil against attempts by Roman Catholic churchmen to exalt Peter to a status of "primacy" have unfortunately driven some to an opposite extreme which avoids the obvious. It cannot be denied that Peter plays a prominent role in the gospels. Despite a somewhat "scrambled" order in the listing of apostles (Matt. 10:2-4; Mark 3:16-19; Luke 6:14-16; and Acts 1:13), Peter's name is always first – indeed, Matthew begins his list by identifying him as "The first, Simon, who is called Peter." As Barclay points out, in this text "the word for first is '*protos*' [which] means 'first,' but it also means 'chief'; and it may well be that Matthew is not merely setting Peter's name first in the list, but that he is saying that Peter was the leader of the apostolic band."[3] Whether or not the evidence warrants the conclusion that Peter was "the" leader, it is beyond dispute that he was "a" leader even among the apostles.

Despite our modern tendencies to "democratize" or equalize the early disciples, Peter clearly is a defacto "spokesman" for the apostles in texts such as Matthew 15:15 and 16:16; Mark 8:29 and 10:28; and Luke 9:20, 12:41, and 18:28. The simple, understated fact that the temple tax collectors approached Peter in Matthew 17:24 may well be indicative of his leadership role. Peter is the one who asks the meaning of difficult sayings of the Lord (Matt. 15:15; Luke 12:41). It is Peter who asks how often one must forgive (Matt. 18:21), and what will be the reward of those who leave all to follow Jesus (Matt. 19:27). It is he who inquires about the withered fig tree (Mark 11:21) and who is listed first among the disciples seeking the explanation of the Lord's predictions about the destruction of Jerusalem. Peter is the one who attempts to answer the Lord's question about who touched Him in the midst of a crowd (Luke 8:45), and it is Peter who is still following the Lord with questions even after the resurrection (John 21:20-22).

Any notion that the apostles were somehow "equal" and the lists are "flat" or uni-dimensional is belied by the undeniable fact that Jesus Himself repeat-

---

[2] All biblical quotations are from the New American Standard Bible or the New Kings Version unless otherwise noted.

[3] William Barclay, *The Master's Men* (London, SCM Press, Ltd., 1959), 21.

edly selected three as an "inner circle" of sorts. In that select group, Jesus includes Peter repeatedly, with James and John, to see, hear, and experience things other disciples did not. It is Peter, along with the beloved disciple John, whom Jesus dispatches to prepare for the Lord's last Passover (Luke 22:8). Even in this elite group, Peter is prominent – if only as the one most frequently singled out by our Lord for correction, criticism and censure. That includes his identification with the Evil One (Matt. 16:23 – striking in its contrast with the commendation of 16:17). Even this jarring inconsistency cannot erase the stunning clarity of Peter's correct perception that Jesus is "the Christ, the Son of the living God" – a declaration reinforced by Peter's blurted protest of a question when His Lord asks if the halting, faltering disciples will abandon Him like everyone else: "Lord, to whom shall we go? You have the words of eternal life. We have believed and have come to know that you are the Holy One of God" (John 6:68-69).

Peter's unpredictable impetuosity – vacillating repeatedly between faith and folly – is also clearly on display in other incidents such as his failed attempt to come to the Lord by walking on water (Matt. 14:28-31), his imprudent suggestions at the Transfiguration (Matt. 17:4, Mark 9:5, Luke 9:33), and the Lord's correction of his misguided attitudes regarding the washing of the disciples' feet in John 13:4-11. Peter not only is the one initiating the inquiry into the identity of the Lord's betrayer (John 13:21), but is identified as the one whose act of bravado severs the ear of the high priest's servant, Malchus. That same night, Peter is singled out for criticism by Jesus for sleeping on watch – despite similar sloth by James and John (Matt. 26:40, where Peter is addressed – perhaps indicative of his role as a leader in the group?).

"Even Though All May Fall Away, Yet I Will Not" (Mark 14:29)
It has often occurred to me that I and others may be too hasty to judge Peter for his shortcomings. His impulsive, quick-tempered, emotional, misguided, quarrelsome, impetuous nature is perhaps simply the exaggerated distortion of a personality characterized by vigorous commitment, emotional devotion, resolute conviction, and fierce loyalty which typifies, in varying degrees, many of us who inhabit the modern world. In his limitations and deficiencies, and in his strengths and positive characteristics, Simon Peter is, indeed, *Everyman*. Some may view Paul as the model apostle and ideal evangelist, but it is Peter who, despite his numerous flaws, ultimately overcomes them and develops abilities which span the spectrum of service not only as an apostle and evangelist, but as a shepherd under the Chief Shepherd.

Even the shame of Peter's denial of the Lord must be tempered by our understanding of the circumstances. True, when Peter's Galilean accent betrayed him, he then, with cursing and an oath, betrayed the One who called him to be a fisher of men. But condemnation may be easy until we pause to ponder that Peter's denial occurred only because he was the only disciple in a position to do so – the other disciples having already fled in terror much earlier (Matt. 26:58, Mark 14:54, Luke 22:54). Barclay reminds us that "Peter's failure was the kind of failure that could have happened only to a brave man. He alone was in a position to fail."[4]

More significantly, even though Peter must have been pierced to the heart by his own self-fulfillment of the Lord's prediction (even before the Lord "looked at him" – and what a look that must have been!), the paramount consideration is that Peter was able to recover spiritually and rebuild his shattered life into a vessel useful for service to his Lord. In this, as in so many other ways, Simon Peter – Cephas the stone – becomes a model for all of us who must overcome our many imperfections, failures, and sins, forsaking all to follow the Lord. If we reach a point in our spiritual lives where we feel we are forever ruined by some shameful act or monumental transgression (as if there are "mortal" and "venial" sins), Peter can serve as a "role model" of sorts, teaching us that no misbehavior is so terrible that one cannot truly repent and be returned in some way to usefulness in the Lord's kingdom. The Lord Himself said to Peter, "when once you have turned again, strengthen your brothers" (Luke 22:32). If perhaps we become prideful – and pride may be the major downfall of modern Christians – because we may not yet have "sinned mightily" (or as publicly) as have others (thus imagining ourselves superior to other mortals), Peter's pre-denial hubris is also instructive. If we sing too loudly, "I'll Be a Friend to Jesus" or allow ourselves even to think, with Peter, "Even though all may fall away because of you, I will never fall away" (Matt. 26:33) – we may, like Simon, discover truly that "Pride goes before destruction, and a haughty spirit before stumbling" (Prov. 16:18).

"Peter, Taking His Stand with the Eleven, Raised His Voice" (Acts 2:14)

In Luke's history of the early church, Peter, of course, plays the most prominent role in the first half of Acts. His is the only recorded sermon on Pentecost. Even though the other apostles were speaking in languages understood by Jews from at least fifteen different nationalities (Acts 2:16),

---

[4] Barclay, *The Master's Men*, 22.

all we know of what was preached on Pentecost comes from Peter. Even so, what he preached was not of his own creativity – it was a product of faithful obedience to the Lord who told him to "go into all the world and preach the gospel to every creature," admonishing them that "he that believeth and is baptized shall be saved" (Mark 16:15-16).

Peter's prominence in the book of Acts begins in the very first chapter, before Pentecost, and his eminence extends through the first half of Luke's history of the early church. It is Peter who urges the replacement of the traitor Judas, having remorsefully repented of his own public denial of the Lord (Acts 1:17)), and who then exposes and rebukes the sins of Ananias and Sapphira (Acts 5:1-11). Peter demonstrates the Divine power of Almighty God by healing multiple individuals on various occasions – a lame man at the Temple's Beautiful Gate; Dorcas, and Aeneas (Acts 3:1-11; 9:32-43) – even as Jesus had predicted (Mark 16:14-20). The same Simon Peter, who ashamedly recanted in the presence of religious authorities in the night of betrayal, now boldly and powerfully confronts and challenges the presumptive "authority" of these same false religionists. It is Peter, empowered by the Spirit, whose defiant words rebuked the religious establishment who pretended to speak for God (Acts 4:5-17) when the Sanhedrin arrested and imprisoned Peter and John. After Herod murdered James and again had Peter imprisoned, Peter's singularity is again reinforced by the miraculous angelic liberation recounted in one of the most amazing and dramatic stories in all of Scripture (Acts 12:3-17).[5]

Furthermore, Simon Peter is the apostle singled out to expand the apostolic preaching of the cross to Gentiles. This singularity was neither incidental nor accidental. As he later reminded his fellow apostles, they well knew that "God made a choice among you, that by my mouth the Gentiles would hear the word of the gospel and believe" (Acts 15:7). In that great gathering of apostles, deliberating one of the most significant "issues" facing the early church (the relationship and relative worth of Jewish and Gentile converts to the faith), Peter's is one of three speeches recorded (again, the first recorded – Acts 15:6-11). Indeed, it is Peter's discourse here which

---

[5] Indeed, so prominent is Peter in the Gospels and the first half of Acts that even Roman Catholic authors have found it curious that more has not been written about Peter. To quote one example, "For many years I have wondered why there were so few books about Saint Peter, compared to the vast number on Saint Paul" (William Thomas Walsh, *Peter the Apostle* [London and New York: Scepter Publishers, 1948, 2005), 7.

decisively demonstrates that knowledge gleaned inferentially, by conclusions drawn from precept and precedent, is every bit as authoritative as those precepts and precedents (or commands and examples, as they are commonly described).[6]

"We Have Left Everything and Followed You" (Mark 10:28)

But Cephas abruptly disappears from Luke's narrative of the early Christians, to go to "another place" (Acts 12:17). Yet, in order that we may "call to remembrance the things previously written (2 Pet. 1:21), Peter wrote not only the epistles which bear his name, but, as many have long contended, quite possibly is the source of the earliest of the gospels. A very strong linkage between Simon Peter and Mark is revealed in Scripture, as Peter refers to him as "Mark, my son" (1 Pet. 5:13).

Eusebius – the "father of church history" – cites Papias of Hierapolis (ca. A.D. 120-140) as saying,

> Mark having become the interpreter of Peter, wrote down accurately whatsoever he remembered. It was not, however, in exact order that he related the sayings or deeds of Christ. For he neither heard the Lord nor accompanied Him. But afterwards, as I said, he accompanied Peter, who accommodated his instructions to the necessities [of his hearers], but with no intention of giving a regular narrative of the Lord's sayings. Wherefore Mark made no mistake in thus writing some things as he remembered them. For of one thing he took especial care, not to omit anything he had heard, and not to put anything fictitious into the statements.[7]

Irenaeus wrote (in *Against Heresies 3.1.1*): "After their departure [of Peter and Paul from earth], Mark, the disciple and interpreter of Peter, did also hand down to us in writing what had been preached by Peter." Of course, since Irenaeus had read Papias, this is not considered independent confirmation.[8]

---

[6] The development of the importance of statements (precept), examples (precedent), and necessary conclusions (implication and inference) is perhaps best explicated by David Koltenbah in a three-part series of detailed articles in several issues of *Truth Magazine* (1967), and in the *1974 Florida College Annual Lectures*.

[7] Eusebius, *Ecclesiastical History* (Book III, Chapter 39). This quotation is available in several print sources but probably most easily accessed online. This version is derived from *http://www.earlychristianwritings.com/mark.html* – one of several useful resources for early church history.

[8] *Ibid.*

Other external evidence tending to confirm that the author of the Gospel of Mark was a disciple of Peter comes from Justin Martyr, who quotes from Mark as being the memoirs of Peter (*Dial. 106.3*). Others have argued that Peter's speech in Acts 10:34-40 serves as a good summary of the Gospel of Mark, describing what occurred "throughout all Judea, starting from Galilee, after the baptism which John proclaimed" (v. 37).

While many modern scholars have tended to reject the contention that there are demonstrable connections between Peter and the gospel of Mark,[9] recently British scholar Richard Bauckham has argued from internal evidence (convincingly, I believe) that Mark's gospel is strongly rooted in Peter's eyewitness testimony of the Lord's life and teaching. In Bauckham's words,

> the Gospel of Mark itself, by means of the literary device of the inclusion of eyewitness testimony, indicates that Peter was the principal eyewitness source of this Gospel and that the authors of the Gospels of Luke and John understood Mark to be making this claim.[10]

Peter is, of course, mentioned both first and last in the gospel of Mark. If indeed it is the case that Mark's gospel is based upon Simon Peter's own eyewitness testimony, it is to his credit that there is no effort to conceal his shortcomings. Peter's own egregious blunders, and his Master's stern rebukes, even his own dreadful disloyalty, are on display. In Barclay's words, such stunning honesty demonstrates "the lengths to which the forgiving love and the recreating grace of Christ had gone for him."[11]

Mark's gospel contains references, sometimes in passing, even to the daily life and circumstances of Simon Peter's earthly existence. To cite only one example, Peter's house in Capernaum – where Jesus began his ministry in the town synagogue (Mark 1:21), recruited his first disciples (Mark 1:16-20) and became renowned for his power to heal the sick and

---

[9] See, for example, Pheme Perkins, *Peter: Apostle for the Whole Church* (Edinburgh: T&T Clark, 2000), as well as many other modern commentators. Perkins' comment is representative: "Scholars today recognize that Mark is not based upon memories of the apostle Peter" (53).

[10] Richard Bauckham, *Jesus and the Eyewitnesses: The Gospels As Eyewitness Testimony* (Grand Rapids, MI: Eerdmans, 2006). See especially Chapter 7, "The Petrine Perspective in the Gospel of Mark" (155-182), and the section "Mark as Peter's Gospel" (235-239).

[11] Barclay, *The Master's Men*, 15.

infirm (Mark 3:1-5) – has been a leading topic of discussion and debate among contemporary archaeologists.[12] Indeed, the question of the location of the house of Peter, where the Bible suggests Jesus stayed while in Capernaum (Matt. 8:14-16), is perhaps one of the "hottest topics" in recent archaeological fora.[13]

"On This Rock I Will Build My Church" (Matt. 16:18)

Of course, none of these incidents of Peter's "primacy," as impressive as they may be when considered collectively, indicate that Simon Peter became a "pope." Whatever authority Peter possessed derives not from his own rank, stature, or accomplishments, but rather from his association with the Lord Jesus Christ. Jesus Himself reminded Peter and the other apostles, "You did not choose me, but I chose you" (John 15:16). In his own words, Peter and the other apostles were "eyewitnesses of His majesty . . . when He received honor and glory from God the Father" (2 Pet. 1:16-19). Peter's authority, like that of the rest of the apostles, derived from his having been personally selected by Jesus (John 15:16) to accompany the Lord from the beginning of His ministry (John 15:27), and to continue the revelation of the Divine word even after Jesus' departure – guided by the Spirit of God (John 16:13). As a consequence of Jesus' choosing His closest disciples to become apostles of His message and teachings, receiving Peter and his teaching – and that of the other apostles – was tantamount to receiving Jesus Christ Himself (John 13:20). This divine commission gave Peter and his fellow apostles standing as ambassadors of Christ (2 Cor. 5:20). Paul's words, endorsed by Peter as authoritative as "the rest of the Scriptures" according to the "wisdom given him" (2 Pet. 3:15-16), describe the apos-

---

[12] See, for instance, James F. Strange and Hershel Shanks, "Has the House Where Jesus Stayed in Capernaum Been Found?," *Biblical Archaeology Review* 8:6 (November-December, 1982), 26-37. Controversies such as this frequently find their way into articles in the popular press regarding "Top 10 Finds" of such-and-such an era. See, for example, Shanks, "Ten Top Discoveries: Favorite Finds Throughout the Years," *Biblical Archaeology Review*, 35:4 (July-October 2009). For a differing, dissenting list, see Keith N. Schoville, "Top Ten Archaeological Discoveries of the Twentieth Century Relating to the Biblical World," *Stone Campbell Journal* 4:1 (Spring 2001).

[13] For the broader archaeological background of such questions, one may consult Vassilios Tzaferis, *Excavations at Capernaum, 1978-1982* (Winona Lake, Indiana: Eisenbrauns), 1989, and Jerome Murphy-O'Connor, *Oxford Archaeological Guides: The Holy Land* (Oxford, 1998), 217-220.

tolic message "not as the word of men, but for what it really is, the word of God" (1 Thess. 2:13).

"He Departed and Went to Another Place" (Acts 12:17)

Except for his brief re-appearance in Jerusalem in Acts 15, Peter disappears from Luke's narrative in Acts 12. Did he go to Pontus or Galatia, perhaps Cappadocia or Bithynia – provinces of Asia Minor whose residents are addressed by Peter (1 Pet. 1:1)? While it may stand to reason, the simple fact is that no one can say definitively. Was it to Babylon – an important center of the Jewish diaspora (1 Pet. 5:13)? This is certainly an intriguing possibility – but we cannot know with certainty. Or perhaps Babylon is meant to be a figurative reference to Rome itself. Many who have studied the evidence conclude that this is the likeliest possibility.[14]

Of course, even if it could be established definitively that Peter visited Rome – even if it were undisputed fact that he was crucified there (as tradition has it, inverted) – none of this would make the case for his being the "first pope" or "head of the church" or "the vicar of Christ on earth." None of the events of Peter's life lend a shred of credibility to any claim that he was infallible.[15] Even informed Roman Catholic advocates acknowledge hat early Roman Catholic scholars did not maintain such contentions.[16]

---

[14] Consult the sections, "He Departed and Went to Another Place" and "Peter in Rome," in Jack Finegan, *Handbook of Biblical Chronology* (Peabody, M: Hendrickson Publishers, 1964; rev. ed., 1998), 370-389. See also Daniel William O'Connor, *Peter in Rome: The Literary, Liturgical, and Archaeological Evidence* (New York: Columbia University Press, 1969), and, for an interesting journalistic interpretation of the evidence, see Aubrey Menen, "St. Peter's," *National Geographic* (December 1971, 140:6), 872-72.

[15] For an interesting discussion of such matters by an historian trained as a Roman Catholic but afterward turning to "evangelicalism," see William Webster, "Did I Really Leave the Holy Catholic Church? The Journey Into Evangelical Faith and Church Experience," in Alister McGrath, Harold O.J. Brown, et. al., eds., *Roman Catholicism: Evangelical Protestants Analyze What Divides and Unites Us* (Chicago: Moody Bible Institute, 1994), 269-293. Another useful volume exploring similar themes is Keith Fournier, with William D. Watkins, *A House United: Evangelicals and Catholics Together* (Colorado Springs: NavPress, 1994).

[16] Of course, works advocating and refuting Roman Catholic dogma are legion. One may profitably consult debates on such subjects including the Campbell-Purcell debate in the 19th century to the Gatewood-Farnsworth debate a century

While Luke's narrative shifts from Peter to Paul in the second half of Acts, Peter's prominent presence in the New Testament is re-emphasized when we encounter his epistles. Written in a much more mature period of his life, and inspired by the Spirit whom Jesus had promised would enable Peter to recall what the Lord had taught, they contain all the truth the Lord wished revealed, but which Peter could not bear at an earlier stage of his spiritual development (John 14:25-26; 15:26-27; 16:12-15). Because of his experience with the Lord, and empowered by the Helper, the Spirit of God, Peter could write about "everything pertaining to life and godliness, through the true knowledge of him who called us by His own glory and excellence" (2 Pet. 1:2). Even a brief analysis of the Epistles of Peter reveal the following significant themes (beginning with 1 Peter): the Christian's living hope in the midst of suffering (1:3); fixing our hope fully on the grace coming (1:13); the necessity of holiness (1:15); cognizance of the nature of being aliens in exile (1:17); our role as "living stones" (2:10) as we are changed from illegitimate children ("not my people") on whom God has no mercy, to adoption as children who have experienced God's grace (using the imagery of the prophet Hosea and his unfaithful wife Gomer).

Paramount in Peter's epistles are themes of Christ as the Cornerstone and pattern in all things (2:21). Other important themes include the Christian's obligation to be able in presenting a ready answer and defense of the faith (3:15), as well as the necessity to suffer as a Christian, and to let good works refute false accusations of the adversaries (4:4).[17] Behavioral matters, including social drinking and drunkenness, are addressed, as well as practical matters such as submission to civil authorities (2:13-17); relationships between servants and masters (2:18-25); domestic relationships between husbands and wives (3:1-7), as well as with fellow believers (3:8-12), stressing the need to love each other earnestly from the heart (1:22) as an expression of unfailing love for one another (4:7-11) – and even to those who persecute Christians, reacting as the Lord did (3:13-22). Relationships

---

later. For several other works written on a popular or non-technical level for intelligent "lay-persons," one may consult William F. Buckley, *Nearer, My God: An Autobiography of Faith* (New York: Harcourt Brace and Company, 1997); or Garry Wills, *Why I Am A Catholic* (New York: Houghton Mifflin, 2002), and *Papal Sin: Structures of Deceit* (New York: Doubleday, 2000).

[17] For a sobering example of "suffering for righteousness' sake," see the letter of the governor, Pliny the Younger to the Emperor Trajan, *Epistulae X.96* (accessible from the Ancient History Sourcebook at *www.Fordham.edu*).

Simon Peter: "Everyman" as Leader

among Christians are addressed in the instructions regarding elders (5:1-4) and their relationship with younger Christians, that there be no "generation gap" (5:5). Merrill Tenney makes the interesting observation that there are thirty-four (34) commands in this one relatively short epistle.[18]

"Baptism Now Saves You" (1 Pet. 3:21)

Indeed, Peter's strict compliance with his Master's instructions is as clearly perceived in what he did *not* say, as in what he did tell the Pentecost audience. He did not command them to "pray through," or respond to an altar call. Peter did not enjoin upon them the lighting of candles or the counting of beads while reciting soothing phrases. He did not answer that they were already saved by grace only and should do nothing, or that they should simply believe in order to be saved by faith only, or that they had been saved by "Christ plus nothing" and therefore could do absolutely nothing to be saved. Peter never suggested that they explore the "Four Spiritual Laws," pray the "Sinner's Prayer," or "accept Christ" as a "personal savior."[19]

The same apostle who commanded the first hearers of the gospel to repent and be baptized for the remission of sins, and who likewise commanded the Gentile household of the centurion Cornelius, here reiterates the essential nature of this aspect of humble submission to the Almighty's commands. Peter's comments in 1 Peter 3:21 could not be clearer regarding the nature of baptism – while a physical act, it has nothing to do with cleansing the body or removing physical dirt from one's flesh. It is not "water salvation." In this regard, it is interesting to note Wayne Grudem's comment on 1 Peter

---

[18] Merrill C. Tenney, *New Testament Survey* (Grand Rapids, MI: William B. Eerdmans Publishing, 1961), 351f.

[19] A recent work which contains trenchant criticism of substituting for baptism such practices as the "Sinner's Prayer" or "accepting Christ" as one's "personal savior" is Frank Viola & George Barna, *Pagan Christianity? Exploring the Roots of Our Church Practices* (Carol Stream, IL: Tyndale House/Barna, 2002, 2008). While I cannot wholeheartedly recommend this book due to its high concentration of very wrong and dangerous concepts, it contains good material on several isolated points. It is one of those books which is at once intriguing and infuriating – stunningly correct on some fundamental points – including its main thesis, which is that many of the practices of modern evangelical churches are borrowed from the pagan culture around us rather than from the New Testament – yet amazingly misguided on others. It is also a good object lesson on how it feels to have some cherished beliefs challenged by a smug, condescending opponent – an error we dare not repeat as we attempt to win some to Christ.

3:21 regarding Peter's understanding that baptism in the New Testament was immersion, expressed in the statement regarding washing dirt from the body: "note how incongruous the mention of 'removal of dirt from the body' would be if Peter thought that only a few drops of water were sprinkled on the head."[20]

"It Is Written, You Shall Be Holy, For I Am Holy" (1 Pet. 1:16)

Peter's exhortations here echo the Old Testament expectations God had of His people Israel. Those accepting the challenge of entering a covenant with Almighty God must dare to make the attempt of living in a manner reflecting God's own personal character. As many have observed, it is at this very point of holy conduct in our personal lives that many of us who inhabit the modern world have failed as spectacularly as the earliest Christians. It therefore is entirely appropriate – indeed, absolutely necessary – that we pay particular attention to Peter's warnings and admonitions regarding such matters.

That we "modern" (or "post-modern") Christians are living in an era of conflict between biblical standards and those of the world is beyond dispute. So did first century Christians; in many ways, our modern struggles are the same as their ancient conflicts. This is obvious enough that many, even within the wider religious world, have recognized such dangers and are addressing them with alarm. To cite only one such instance, consider the concerns of a leading "evangelical" author, Robert Gundry, who frames the issue in these words:

> By worldliness I mean not merely the disregard of fundamentalist taboos against smoking, drinking, dancing, movie-going, gambling, and the like, but more expansively such matters as materialism, pleasure-seeking, indiscriminate enjoyment of salacious and violent entertainment, immodesty of dress, voyeurism, sexual laxity, and divorce...[21]

Gundry is a modern "evangelical" – like many in denominational church-

---

[20] Wayne Grudem, *First Epistle of Peter*, 162. A stimulating recent examination of this and other New Testament texts relating to baptism is Ben Witherington III, *Troubled Waters: Re-Thinking the Theology of Baptism* (Waco, TX: Baylor University Press, 2007).

[21] Robert H. Gundry, *Jesus The Word According to John the Sectarian: A Paleo-Fundamentalist Manifesto for Contemporary Evangelicalism, Especially its Elites, in North America* (Grand Rapids, MI: William B. Eerdmans Publishing Company, 2002), 73-74.

es which still claim some sense of allegiance to Christ as the divine Son of God (not simply a profound ethicist) and to the Bible as God's revelation (not just a collection of pithy moral aphorisms). An emeritus professor at Westmont College in Santa Barbara, CA, Gundry has been controversial at least since the publication, decades ago, of his commentary on Matthew. Many "evangelicals" felt he was too comfortable with the methodologies of redaction criticism, even disputing Gundry's personal claim to believe in the inerrancy of Scriptures. But let us not be so distracted that we miss the larger point, or so focused on someone's methodology or errors in one area that we ignore plain truths – whoever the spokesman may be.

Nor are "evangelicals" the only ones Gundry disturbs. Some of our brethren among "churches of Christ" have reacted strongly to Gundry's description of worldliness when they have heard me recite it in sermons and lectures. Apparently it is precise enough to cause these brethren (who evidently feel stung by his depiction) to confront me. Usually they are indignantly intent upon informing me that they "preach about those things on my list" (or at least plan to, at some point in the future).

Of course, it's not MY list – it's Gundry's (though I like it well enough). Nor am I the Chief of the Brotherhood Morality Police, nor Chairman of the Watchdog Society, any more than Gundry is the Watchpup of Evangelicalism. But if it causes some brethren enough discomfort to voice concerned agreement, or to induce an outbreak of preaching on such subjects, why, *mirabile dictu* – "how marvelous to say." Gundry, however – not content with mere description – also identifies some causes of the erosion of allegiance to Biblical morality which he bemoans. His concern is that

> the sense of embattlement with the world is rapidly evaporating among many evangelicals, especially evangelical elites, among them those who belong to the 'knowledge industry.' In the last half century they have enjoyed increasing success in the world of biblical and theological scholarship. They reacted against the separatism of the fundamentalist forebears, who precisely in their separation from the world knew they had a sure word from God for the world . . .[22]

And how was this sense of alienation from the larger culture, the world, lost? Gundry explains: "With non-evangelicals' increasing recognition of our contributions to biblical and theological scholarship and with the consequent whetting of our appetite for academic, political, and broadly cultural

---
[22] *Ibid.*, 66.

power and influence are coming the dangers of accommodation, of dulling the sharp edges of the gospel, of blurring the distinction between believers and the world, of softening – or not issuing at all – the warning that God's wrath abides on unbelievers (John 3:36), in short, of only whispering the word instead of shouting him, speaking him boldly, as the Word himself did."[23]

"Grow in Grace" (2 Pet. 3:18) – Peter as a Leader

The purpose of studying the life of Peter and other biblical worthies is not simply to learn the facts of their interaction with Jesus, or the Holy Spirit, or God the Father – it is to be able to better equip us to grow in grace and knowledge so that we become ever more useful in our service in the kingdom of God. In a lectureship themed around "leadership," and given the evident lack of leadership apparent in many congregations, this seems a primary area to which we should turn our attention.

"Servant Leadership" is a modern management/leadership concept popularized by Robert Greenleaf (former AT&T executive), endorsed and referenced by Stephen Covey (best known for his *Seven Habits of Highly Effective Leaders*), Ken Blanchard (developer of the *One-Minute Manager* concepts), and others who have devoted themselves to a study of "leadership" and what it means to be a leader.[24] Jesus models leadership through service – washing the feet of His disciples, as a demonstration of the selfless manner in which they were to serve others (John 13: 12-15). Our Lord also urges His followers to be servants first, contrasting service in His kingdom with worldly "leadership styles":

You know that the rulers of the Gentiles lord it over them, and their high

---

[23] Gundry's use of terms like "sectarian" (especially in contexts or with nuances different from those in which many Christians are accustomed to hearing such terms) may be disturbing to some. But one need not use his language, nor agree with all of his conclusions or solutions, to acknowledge that his "insider perspective" on modern evangelicalism has the "ring of truth" – especially when he observes that "it is sectarians – those who have separated from the world, who see only in black and white – it is they, rather than reformers, accommodationists, and assimilationists who speak with the most controlling authority. Sectarians know the truth, the whole truth, and nothing but the truth; and they know it most assuredly" (77).

[24] Robert Greenleaf, *Servant Leadership: A Journey Into the Nature of Legitimate Power and Greatness* (25th Anniversary edition, ed. Larry Spears, Foreword by Stephen Covey; Indianapolis: Robert Greenleaf Center, 1977; Mahwah, NJ: Paulist Press, 2002).

officials exercise authority over them. Not so with you. Instead, whoever wants to become great among you must be your servant, and whoever wants to be first must be your slave—just as the Son of Man did not come to be served, but to serve, and to give his life as a ransom for many (Matt. 20:25-28; also Mark 10:42-45).

Greenleaf's classic essay, *The Servant as Leader*, describes the concept of "servant-leader" in these terms:

> The servant-leader is servant first.... It begins with the natural feeling that one wants to serve, to serve first. Then conscious choice brings one to aspire to lead. That person is sharply different from one who is leader first, perhaps because of the need to assuage an unusual power drive or to acquire material possessions.... The leader-first and the servant-first are two extreme types. Between them there are shadings and blends that are part of the infinite variety of human nature.
>
> The difference manifests itself in the care taken by the servant-first to make sure that other people's highest priority needs are being served. The best test, and difficult to administer, is: Do those served grow as persons? Do they, while being served, become healthier, wiser, freer, more autonomous, more likely themselves to become servants? And, what is the effect on the least privileged in society? Will they benefit or at least not be further deprived?[25]

Those who have developed a full-grown philosophy of "servant-leadership" have identified ten characteristic of servant leaders, as derived largely from Greenleaf's writings: listening, empathy, healing, awareness, persuasion, conceptualization, foresight, stewardship, commitment to the growth of others, and building "community." Servant-leaders achieve results for their organizations by giving priority attention to the needs of their colleagues and those they serve. Servant-leaders are often seen as humble stewards of their organization's resources (human, financial, and physical).

While some might see such principles as merely management "buzzwords," they trace in theory a pattern of leadership which has been demonstrated to be highly effective in many contexts. Sometimes those in "the world" may demonstrate more insight into the fundamentals of human nature than the "sons of light" (Luke 16:8, NASV).

---

[25] Robert Greenleaf, *Servant as Leader;* Larry Spears, ed., *Insights on Leadership: Service, Stewardship, Spirit, and Servant-Leadership*; Ken Blanchard, *Servant Leader* (Nashville: Thomas Nelson, 2003).

Exhorting as a Fellow Elder (1 Pet. 5:2)

While it may be unpleasant to do so, it is necessary to ask some pertinent and penetrating questions about leadership – or the lack of it – in present-day churches of Christ. To begin with, why are there so many churches without elders? While it may be impossible to quantify exactly, in my experience – limited though it may be[26] – at least 2/3, possibly as many as 3/4, of present-day congregations operate without benefit of elders. Why is that? Many churches not only do not have elders presently, many have not had any for years or decades, and many more have never had elders. Many of those congregations without elders have no discernible prospects of having elders in the foreseeable future, if ever. Why is this case in so many places?

To speak candidly, sometimes it has appeared as though churches do not really want to have elders. In other cases it is obvious that godly men who might be qualified in many ways have no desire to serve, or have lost that desire, because of the disrespectful and rebellious treatment they have seen inflicted on other men who were trying to do their best to serve as shepherds under the Chief Shepherd.

Of the minority of churches which are overseen by elders, why are there so many which have only a minimal number (two, or maybe three – and thus, as the saying goes, are only a heart attack or a transfer – or a heart attack and a transfer – away from no eldership at all)? And perhaps the most sobering question of all is: why are there so many marginally, minimally, or "technically" qualified men occupying the office – one-child elders, or men woefully ignorant of much of the Bible, or barely able to teach, or ill-informed about dangerous gainsayers and the doctrines they bring, or minimally hospitable, etc? In short, why are there so many churches which have are forced to wrestle with such issues, nibbling around the margins, rather than there being a multitude of churches which have an abundance of clearly and unquestionably qualified men willing and able to shepherd the flock?

Unqualified elders are unquestionably one of the greatest dangers facing the churches. This is not merely my opinion – the apostle Paul exhorts elders in Acts 20:28-31, sternly warning them of the dangers they themselves may

---

[26] By this I mean only a few hundred meetings in only about 200 or so of approximately 2,000 "conservative" churches – there are about 1800 I have NOT spoken at – over forty years and nearly that many of the United States.

pose to believers. Peter himself exhorts his fellow-elders to be mindful not to exceed their "authority" (1 Pet. 5:1-4). Recent experience testifies to the truth of and need for such warnings. Many who experienced the division of the 1950s over institutional "issues" can testify to personal experiences of maltreatment, treachery, and perfidy by unqualified and/or self-serving elders who hijacked congregations and turned them to their own agendas and perversities. It staggers the imagination to think of the vast majority of elderships – supposedly composed of qualified men – who not only did not convict the gainsayers who turned the churches into mere handmaids (funding sources, in reality) to exalted human institutions, but too often led their flocks headlong into apostasy.[27]

Even today, many can testify to the danger of emphasizing (correctly) the need for Christians to be in subjection to elders – but then appointing to the "office of a bishop" men with marginal biblical knowledge and little ability in other areas of the multiple qualifications. This is a recipe for disaster. As modern Christians, we often talk long and loud about "restoring New Testament Christianity," but in this aspect, brothers and sisters, is it not obvious that we have failed abysmally?[28]

To avoid being misunderstood, let me clear: I have nothing but the highest regard for men who have worked hard to meet the qualifications to serve as elders at the highest level possible, and who expend long hours laboring in word and deed in what is, in many ways, a thankless job. My own father, and his father before him, served for decades each as elders in several different congregations, weathering at least one major apostasy

---

[27] My remarks should not be taken as any endorsement of prevalent views that elders have no "authority" and can lead only by example. In this regard, see the comments of Clinton Hamilton in *Truth Commentaries: 1 Peter*, 282-303 and 423-457.

[28] That these concerns are not mine alone is evident from the number and range of books produced recently addressing eldership/leadership issues. These include, to cite only a few examples, J.J. Turner, *Shepherds, Wake Up! Ancient Training for Modern Shepherds* (Huntsville, AL: Publishing Designs, Inc., 2005); Bobby Duncan, *The Elders Which are Among You: The Qualifications, Selection, and Appointment of Elders* (Huntsville, AL: Publishing Designs, Inc., 1989). These are only more recent works in a long series which stretches back through Lynn Anderson's *They Smell Like Sheep* to H.E. Phillips' *Scriptural Elders and Deacons*, to J.W. McGarvey's *The Eldership* (Murfreesboro, TN: DeHoff Publishing, 1962; reprint of 1876 edition).

and many other challenges over the years. My respect for them, and many others like them, is virtually boundless. I myself have served as an elder for nearly a decade within several different "configurations" with a variety of other men in the eldership. This is not a criticism of the office, biblically defined, or of truly able men who shepherd the flock which is among them. But it is certainly no endorsement of other unscriptural arrangements and unqualified men who tarnish the office and the work by incompetence or base motives. My comments *are* intended to be harshly critical of such pretenders, and to challenge all who hear to reprove, rebuke, and exhort, asking hard questions and teaching the uncomfortable truths on these, as well as other "issues."[29]

"Feed My Sheep" (John 21:17): Qualifications and Abilities/ Effectiveness and Function

The qualifications of elders have been discussed and debated at length both within and outside the "Restoration Movement." In many instances (perhaps too many), the focus has been on the biological qualifications of an elder. What does "believing child" mean? Can a man be qualified with only one child (or one who is "faithful")? Is the word "children" always plural or can it mean only one child? What if a man's children depart the faith after leaving home? What if his wife dies? Such questions too often become the sole focus of discussions regarding elders.

But on what has to be an equally important level, what does it mean to be "apt" (able) to teach? What "degree" of biblical knowledge must one attain to qualify? What are the "minimum standards" of biblical knowledge which one must attain in order to qualify and serve effectively? And should one be considered qualified if only a "minimum standard" is achieved? These and other equally thorny issues are perplexing enough

---

[29] There are obviously other concerns and issues as well in this area. For example, even with a well-qualified and good-intentioned elder, "endless sacrifice and service without training or resources is a toxic mix, and will inevitably result in discouragement, a sense of failure, or burnout" – from the introduction by David Fleer and Charles Siburt, *Like a Shepherd Lead Us: Guidance for the Gentle Art of Pastoring* (Abilene, TX: Leafwood Books, 2006), 10. Like its sequel (Fleer and Siburt, eds., *Good Shepherds: More Guidance for the Gentle Art of Pastoring* (Abilene, TX: Leafwood Books, 2007), these collected essays by various authors are uneven and one could hardly recommend everything in them, as with any book. But they make an attempt to grapple with some thorny issues not often addressed elsewhere in print.

that they have perhaps driven us to ignore them rather than seriously grappling with them.

While the standards of the secular world should not to be substituted for biblical standards, neither does the Bible demand that Christians abandon common sense. Most people understand that simply meeting minimum-standard "qualifications" for a job does not mean that everyone who is technically or minimally qualified for a certain position should be hired. The real standard is: Can that person actually do the job? A useful illustrative analogy might be the difference stated in "want ads" for various positions, identifying first the minimum necessary qualifications or credentials for a given job (say, a high school diploma, college degree, CDL, professional certification, etc.), then providing an actual "job description" (e.g., must have ability to work well with people, willing to travel, able to work with certain computer programs or operate certain equipment, etc.). The first deals with what one has done in the past – minimum qualifications without which one could not even be considered for the job. The second deals much more foundationally with the question: Can this person do the job? We have all perhaps known people who had a degree or license or other paper credential of some sort, but who could not walk and chew gum at the same time. Unfortunately, we have all perhaps also known men who were marginally or technically "qualified" on paper, but who could not organize a three-car parade and are woefully ignorant, not only of the Scripture, but of human nature and behavior as well.

This is not to discount in any way the importance of the list of qualifications revealed in Scripture. One can no more effectively serve as an elder while lacking ability to teach, or not having raised believing children, or being inhospitable, than an illiterate could function as an attorney, or a blind man might be successful as a surgeon. But there are other passages – just as authoritative as the qualification lists, and just as much a portion of God's revelation – which describe for us the actual job functions of an elder, what he must actually be able to DO as a shepherd.

Might it be that we have so focused on the minimum standard qualifications that we have neglected to ask the broader biblical question: Can this man actually do the work of shepherding? Does he even have a vision of what the work is which he undertakes to accomplish? What are we to make of churches which continue to submit to men who have shown by their behavior that they are incapable of (or worse, unfit for) the work of shepherding the flock? If churches habitually install men as "elders" who may have "believing children" but who have little knowledge and ability and conceive of their duties as merely the proverbial "checkbook elders" who see their role as "giving account for the money" (as I have heard elders say) rather than the fundamental work of shepherding, feeding, guiding, and protecting the souls (not dollars) for which they shall give account, and then insist that the congregation give them nearly unlimited authority in decision-making for the congregation, one can hardly think of a broader, smoother road to apostasy – to which we must now turn our attention.

Apostasy: "That Your Faith May Not Fail" (Luke 22:32)

Since elders supposedly function as protectors and providers of the flock, it is particularly sinister when their role is perverted for sordid gain. That elders would, have, and will turn the function of their office to a personal agenda to draw away disciples after themselves (Acts 20:28), cannot be disputed. Scripture plainly predicts that they will, and common experience manifestly demonstrates what the Bible says would happen. More alarming, however, is the unsettling truth that, if such things can befall an elder, it can happen to others. Much of 2 Peter is devoted to sober warnings about the dangers of apostasy – falling away from the living God.[30]

With the exception of the book of Hebrews,[31] or the Lord's stern warn-

---

[30] There is, of course, a massive body of literature on the subject of apostasy. One of the better studies remains Robert Shank's *Life in the Son: A Study of the Doctrine of Perseverance* (Springfield, MO; Westcott Publishers, 1961). Shank was a former Baptist preacher who left that denomination after writing this work and a companion volume on the Calvinistic doctrine of election. The work attracted attention due to its powerful content and the fact that an encouraging and commendatory introduction – just shy of endorsement – was written by William W. Adams, who held the James Buchanan Harrison chair in New Testament Interpretation at the Southern Baptist Theological Seminary.

[31] An intriguing examination of the question of apostasy, based largely on an examination of the Hebrews texts, is found in Section 55 of Dale Moody's systematic theology, *The Word of Truth. A Summary of Christian Doctrine Based on Biblical Revelation* (Grand Rapids, MI: Eerdmans, 1984), 348-365). Moody was one of the most accomplished Baptist theologians of the 20th century (Kent Fellow under Paul Tillich at Union Theological Seminary, who earned an Oxford University DPhil for his dissertation, *Baptism: Foundation for Christian Unity*, later studying with Emil Brunner in Zurich and Karl Barth and Oscar Cullman at Basel; the first Baptist – and only the second Protestant – theologian to lecture at the Gregorian University in Rome; and ultimately a member of the Faith and Order Commission of the World Council of Churches). But it was Moody's insistence on

ings about being cut off, withering and dying and being cast into the fire (John 15:1-7), 2 Peter 2 may contain perhaps the strongest and most extensive warnings in all of the New Testament about the very real danger of Christians falling away from the faith. Peter ties his initial warnings to the history of Israel, which repeatedly rebelled and fell away from the salvation provided for them by Jehovah's grace. The undisputed historical fact that false prophets and teachers arose among God's people in ancient times is all the more sobering to us as we contemplate our circumstances in the modern world. The incorporation of real, actual historical examples belies any attempt to argue that such outcomes for God's chosen people today is merely hypothetical – a theoretical possibility which never actually occurs (as some argue in an attempt to teach the "impossibility of apostasy").[32] The fact that God's people had forsaken the right way causes the discerning reader to wonder, how one can forsake a way which he had never walked previously? How does one stray from a path one was never on to begin with? Any attempt to argue that those who may "appear" to fall away were never truly Christians, never actually a part of The Way, fails at 2 Peter 2:15.

Finally, the graphically disgusting figure at the conclusion of the chapter, by itself, ought to be deterrent enough to any contemplating a lifestyle of rebellion against God. Anyone who has ever slopped hogs can attest to that – to say nothing of the imagery of canine coprophagy or similar behaviors. And yet, like the prodigal, Christians can sometimes fall so far as to ingest spiritual waste products. The very thought is likely to turn the stomach – as it was intended to. Truly, as the text says, it would have been better not

---

dissenting from the traditional Baptist/Calvinist view of apostasy which ultimately led to his leaving Southern Seminary after a 37-year teaching career. Moody later published his views on apostasy, which he insisted had been taught him by A.T. Robertson, in his small monograph, *Apostasy* (Greenville, SC: Smythe and Helwys Publishing, 1991). A sample: "Those who glibly talk about 'once-saved, always-saved,' as if it is a past transaction so that now one cannot lose 'his salvation' miss most of the meaning of salvation" (*Apostasy*, 17), and "A call for salvation is a call to get aboard the ark of salvation. . . . Unless we stay aboard the ship, we will not be saved" (*Apostasy*, 17, commenting on Hebrews 11:7).

[32] An informative wholesale attack on the Calvinistic system is found in Dave Hunt, *What Love is This? Calvinism's Misrepresentation of God* (3rd ed.; Bend, OR: Berean Call, 2006) – though Hunt has some peculiarly wrong ideas of his own.

to have known the way of righteousness and then spurned it for the ugly repulsiveness of a sinful lifestyle.

"New Heavens and New Earth" (2 Pet. 3:13)

Far better is the portrayal of Christians living holy and godly lives, looking forward to the day of God which will bring about the destruction of the ungodly and His gracious salvation of faithful believers. The promise God makes of a new heaven and a new earth, the home of righteousness and righteous ones, is sure – *if* we hold firm to the end. Let us lend every effort to be found spotless, blameless and at peace with God and man, as much as in us lies, remembering that the patience God requires of us in keeping His will leads us to salvation by His grace through the blood of Jesus Christ.

As he did to first-century Christians and pagans, Simon Peter, though long dead, still speaks to us today.

Works Consulted

General Commentaries:

Boring, M. Eugene, Klaus Berger, and Carston Colpe, eds. *Hellenistic Commentary to the New Testament*. Nashville: Abingdon Press, 1995.

Boring, M. Eugene, and Fred B. Craddock. *The People's New Testament Commentary*. Louisville: Westminster/John Knox Press, 2004.

Carson, D. A. *New Bible Commentary: 21st Century Edition*. 4th ed. Leicester, England, and Downers Grove, IL: Inter-Varsity Press, 1994.

Keener, Craig S. *The IVP Bible Background Commentary: New Testament*. Downers Grove, IL, InterVarsity Press, 1993.

Commentaries on the Gospels:

Black, Mark C. *Luke (College Press NIV Commentary)*. Joplin, MO: College Press, 1996.

Bock, Darrell L. *Luke (Baker Exegetical Commentary on the New Testament)*. 2 vols. Grand Rapids, MI: Baker Book House, 1994, 1996.

Craddock, Fred B. *Luke (Interpretation)*. Louisville: John Knox Press, 1988.

Gundry, Robert H. *Mark: A Commentary on His Apology for the Cross*. Grand Rapids, MI: William B. Eerdmans, 1993.

Johnson, Luke Timothy. *The Gospel of Luke (Sacra Pagina 3)*. Collegeville, MN: Michael Glazier/Liturgical Press, 991.

Malina, Bruce J., and Richard L. Rohrbaugh. *Social-Science Commentary on the Synoptic Gospels.* Minneapolis: Fortress Press, 1992.

Marshall, I. Howard. *The Gospel of Luke: A Commentary on the Greek Text (New International Greek Testament Commentary).* Grand Rapids, MI: William B. Eerdmans Publishing Company, 1978.

Robertson, A.T. *Studies in Mark's Gospel.* Nashville: Broadman Press, 1946.

Witherington, Ben III. *The Gospel of Mark: A Socio-Rhetorical Commentary.* Grand Rapids, MI: William B. Eerdmans Publishing, 2001.

Commentaries on Acts of the Apostles:

Ash, Anthony Lee. *The Acts of the Apostles – Part I (1:1-12:25; Living Word Commentary 6A).* Abilene, TX: Abilene Christian University Press, 1984.

Barrett, Charles Kingsley. *A Critical and Exegetical Commentary on Acts of the Apostles (ICC).* 2 vols.: Edinburgh: T&T Clark, 1994, 1998.

Bock, Darrell L. *Acts (Baker Exegetical Commentary on the New Testament).* Grand Rapids, MI: Baker Publishing Group, 2007.

Bruce, Frederick Fyvie. *Acts of the Apostles: the Greeek Text with Introduction and Commentary.* 3rd ed.; Grand Rapids, MI: William B. Eerdmans Publishing Company, 1990.

_____. *The Book of Acts (New International Commentary on the New Testament).* Revised ed.; Grand Rapids, MI: William B. Eerdmans Publishing Company, 1988.

Jackson, Wayne. *The Acts of the Apostles: From Jerusalem to Rome.* Stockton, CA: Christian Courier Publications, 2000; 2nd ed. 2005.

Johnson, Luke Timothy. *The Acts of the Apostles (Sacra Pagina 5).* Collegeville, MN: Michael Glazier/Liturgical Press, 1992.

Larkin, William J. *Acts (InterVarsity Press New Testament Commentary).* Downers Grove, IL: InterVarsity Press, 1995.

Longenecker, Richard N. *Acts of Apostles (Expositor's Bible Commentary 9, John & Acts).* Grand Rapids, MI: Zondervan, 1981.

McGarvey, John William. *(Original) Commentary of Acts of Apostles.* N.p., 1863; reprint, 9th ed.; Bowling Green, KY: Guardian of Truth Foundation, 1990.

Pelikan, Jaroslav. *Acts (Brazos Theological Commentary on the Bible).* Grand Rapids, MI: Brazos Press/Baker Publishing Group, 2005.

Reese, Gareth L. *New Testament History: Acts.* Joplin, MO: College Press, 1966; 2nd ed., Moberly, MO: Scripture Exposition Books, 2002.

Spencer, F. Scott. *Journeying Through Acts: A Literary-Cultural Reading.* Peabody, MA: Hendrickson Publishers, 2004.

Witherington, Ben. *The Acts of the Apostles: A Socio-Rhetorical Commentary.* Grand Rapids, MI: William B. Eerdmans Publishing Company, 1998.

Winter, Bruce D., ed. *The Book of Acts in Its First Century Setting.* Grand Rapids, MI: William B. Eerdmans Publishing Company, 1993-2006. (A series of six volumes sponsored by Tyndale Fellowship in Cambridge, England).

Commentaries on Peter's Letters:

Goppelt, Leonard. *A Commentary on 1 Peter.* Ferdinand Hahn, ed.; John E. Alsup, ed. and trans. Gottingen: Vandenhoecht and Ruprecht, 1978; Grand Rapids, MI: Eerdmans, 1993.

Hamilton, Clinton D. *Truth Commentaries: 1 Peter; 2 Peter and Jude.* Bowling Green, KY: Guardian of Truth, 1995.

Kelcy, Raymond C. *Living Word Commentary: The Letters of Peter and Jude.* Austin, TX: R.B. Sweet Publishing Company, 1972; Abilene Christian University, 1984.

Kistemaker, Simon J. *New Testament Commentary: Exposition of the Epistles of Peter and the Epistle of Jude.* Grand Rapids, MI: Baker Book House, 1987.

Mounce, Robert. *A Living Hope: A Commentary on 1 and 2 Peter.* Grand Rapids, MI: Eerdmans, 1982.

Reese, Gareth L. *New Testament Epistles: A Critical and Exegetical Commentary on 1 & 2 Peter & Jude.* Moberly, MO: Scripture Exposition Books, 2004.

Selwyn, Edward Gordon. *The First Epistle of St. Peter.* London: MacMillan and Company, Ltd., 1946; New York: St.Martin's Press, 1964.

Waltner, Erland, and J. Daryl Charles. *Believers Church Bible Commentary: 1-2 Peter, Jude.* Scottdale, PA; Herald Press, 1999.

Monographs:

Barclay, William. *The Master's Men*. London: SCM Press, Ltd., 1959.

Bauckham, Richard. *Jesus and the Eyewitnesses: The Gospels As Eyewitness Testimony* (Grand Rapids, MI: Eerdmans, 2006).

Colson, Charles, and Richard John Neuhaus, eds., *Evangelicals and Catholics Together: Toward a Common Mission*. Dallas, TX: Word Publishing, 1995.

Corbo, Virgilio. *The House of St. Peter at Capharnaum*. Jerusalem: Franciscan Printing Press, 1969.

Cullmann, Oscar. *Peter—Disciple, Apostle, Martyr: A Historical and Theological Study*. Trans. Floyd V. Filson. London: SCM Press, 1953; 2nd ed., Philadelphia: The Westminster Press, 1962.

Foote, Gaston. *The Transformation of the Twelve*. New York: Abingdon Press, 1958.

Fournier, Keith, with William D. Watkins. *A House United: Evangelicals and Catholics Together*. Colorado Springs: NavPress, 1994.

Goodspeed, Edgar J. *The Twelve*. Philadelphia: John C. Winston, 1967.

Grant, Robert M. *Augustus to Constantine: The Thrust of the Movement Into the Roman World*. London: William Collins & Sons, 1971.

Groome, Thomas H., and Michael J. Daley. *Re-Claiming Catholicism: Treasures Old and New*. Maryknoll, NY: Orbis Books, 2010.

Guthrie, Donald. *New Testament Introduction*. Downers Grove, IL: InterVarsity Press, 1970.

Harrison, Everett F. *Introduction to the New Testament*. Grand Rapids, MI: Eerdmans, 1964; rev. ed., 1971.

Keller, W. Phillip. *A Shepherd Looks at Psalm 23*. Grand Rapids, MI: Zondervan, 1974.

Marshall, I. Howard. *Kept By the Power of God: A Study of Perseverance and Falling Away*. Minneapolis: Bethany Fellowship, 1975.

McBirnie, William Steuart. *The Search for the Twelve Apostles*. Carol Stream, IL: Tyndale House, 1973.

Moody, Dale. *Apostasy*. Greenville, SC: Smythe and Helwys Publishing, 1991.

Nau, Arlo J. *Peter in Matthew: Discipleship, Diplomacy, and Dispraise . . . with an Assessment of Power and Privilege in the Petrine Office*. Collegeville, MN: The Liturgical Press, 1992.

O'Connor, Daniel William. *Peter in Rome: The Literary, Liturgical, and Archaeological Evidence*. New York: Columbia University Press, 1969.

Perkins, Pheme. *Peter: Apostle for the Whole Church*. Columbia: University of South Carolina Press, 1994; Minneapolis: Fortress Press, 2000.

Robertson, Archibald Thomas. *Epochs in the Life of Simon Peter*. Nashville: Broadman Press, 1930; reprint, Baker Book House, 1974.

Shank, Robert. *Life in the Son: A Study of the Doctrine of Perseverance*. Springfield, MO; Westcott Publishers, 1961.

Smith, Asbury. *The Twelve Christ Chose*. New York: Harper and Brothers, 1958.

Strauch, Alexander. *Biblical Eldership: An Urgent Call to Restore Biblical Church Leadership*. Littleton, CO: Lewis and Roth Publishers, 1988.

Taylor, Robert R., Jr. *The Elder and His Work*. Ripley, TN: Taylor Publications, 1989.

Thiede, Carsten Peter. *Simon Peter: From Galilee to Rome*. Exeter, UK: Paternoster Press, 1986.

Walsh, William Thomas. *Peter the Apostle*. London & New York: Scepter Publishers, 1948, 2005.

Wills, Gary. *Papal Sin: Structures of Deceit*. New York: Doubleday, 2000.

Witherington, Ben III. *Troubled Waters: Re-Thinking the Theology of Baptism*. Waco, TX: Baylor University Press, 2007.

Articles:

Filson, Floyd V. "Peter." *Interpreter's Dictionary of the Bible: An Illustrated Encyclopedia*. New York: Abingdon Press, 1962. III:749-757.

Gray, James M. "Peter, Simon." *The International Standard Bible Encyclopedia*. James Orr, et.al., eds. Grand Rapids, MI: William B. Eerdmans Publishing, 1929. IV:2348-2351.

Martin, Ralph P. "Peter," and "Peter, First Epistle of." *The International*

Standard Bible Encyclopedia. Geoffrey W. Bromiley, et. al., eds. Grand Rapids, MI: William B. Eerdmans Publishing Company, 1986. III:802-807, 807-815.

Menen, Aubrey. "St. Peter's," *National Geographic* (December 1971, 140:6), pp. 872-72.

Schoville, Keith N. "Top Ten Archaeological Discoveries of the Twentieth Century Relating to the Biblical World," *Stone-Campbell Journal* (4:1): Spring, 2001.

Shanks, Hershel. "Ten Top Discoveries: Favorite Finds Throughout the Years." *Biblical Archaeology Review* (35:4): July-October 2009.

Strange, James F., and Hershel Shanks, "Has the House Where Jesus Stayed in Capernaum Been Found?," *Biblical Archaeology Review* (8:6): November-December 1982. 26-37.

van Elderen, B. "Peter, Simon." *Zondervan Pictorial encyclopedia of the Bible*. Merrill C. Tenney, ed. Grand Rapids, MI: Zondervan Publishing House, 1975. IV:733-739.

van Unnik, W.C. "Peter, First Letter of." *Interpreter's Dictionary of the Bible: An Illustrated Encyclopedia*. New York: Abingdon Press, 1962. III:758-766.

White, William Jr. "Peter, Second Epistle of." *Zondervan Pictorial Encyclopedia of the Bible*. Merrill C. Tenney, ed. Grand Rapids, MI: Zondervan Publishing House, 1975. IV:726-732.

Webster, William. "Did I Really Leave the Holy Catholic Church? The Journey Into Evangelical Faith and Church Experience." In Alister McGrath, Harold O.J. Brown, et. al., eds., *Roman Catholicism: Evangelical Protestants Analyze What Divides and Unites Us*. Chicago: Moody Bible Institute, 1994, pp. 269-293

Leaders in the Church: Paul
Bruce Key

Can we aspire to be a leader just like Paul? That seems to be a daunting task. After all, we are talking about the most prominent writer in the New Testament—a man who was "of the stock of Israel, of the tribe of Benjamin, a Hebrew of Hebrews" (Phil. 3:5) who, while growing up had received the best theological education available. This was someone who never once violated his conscience, spoke directly with Christ, was "called to be an apostle" (1 Cor. 1:1), and was guided by the Holy Spirit throughout his entire ministry. There is no argument that he was one of the greatest leaders in the Lord's church during the first century. But, can you and I be leaders just like him?

Bruce Key BS, MSE was born in Louisville, Kentucky in December 1961. He developed a love for music at an early age and began to play the piano "by ear" at age five. Bruce loves to sing, contributing his vocal abilities to various choruses, madrigal groups, bands, talent shows, contests, and solo efforts. He once even sang backup vocals with Tammy Wynette, onstage at the Grand Ole Opry House in Nashville. Bruce has always been passionate about teaching and training and is currently the Director of Learning for Morrison Healthcare, a two-billion dollar contract food-service company. In Bruce's previous role as Director of International Services, he was solely responsible for providing training for leaders and colleagues in several countries across six continents. Bruce has been a student of Leadership Development for many years, and has taught audiences in various venues, from a small closet to classrooms and boardrooms, from convention centers to the World Trade Center in Sao Paulo, Brazil. Bruce also has a degree in Education, and worked as a teacher in the Jefferson County Public School system for five years. During this time, he received the Excellence in Education award for his innovative teaching and its impact on the lives of his students. Bruce worships and works with the brethren at Hebron Lane church of Christ in Shepherdsville, KY, where he also serves as a deacon, song leader, and Bible class teacher. He is married to Diane (McGregor) Key. They will celebrate their twenty-fifth anniversary on July 12, 2010. God has blessed them with three boys: Garrett – 23, Grayson – 19, and Gavin – 16.

No. We cannot.

Let me explain. We cannot be a leader "just like" Paul because there *is* no one else just like Paul—or Peter, John, or any other of our first century brethren. When we try to be "just like" any of these brethren (or any other man), we tend to fail miserably, becoming discouraged. Others see us as being less than genuine. Some of us are so intimidated by Paul's "status" as an apostle of Christ and his strong, unwavering faith, that we never quite feel that our efforts to be a leader like him are adequate. Can we even begin to measure up when we compare ourselves to this apostle?

When we use this approach to the study of any individual in the Bible, our thinking is *flawed*. Of course, we cannot be just like Paul, the apostle, because there *are* no apostles today. And we cannot be just like Paul, the individual, because each of us is unique. But, we *can* learn to be a spiritual leader like Paul—the man—by looking at his life, his character, his work, his faith, and his writings. Yes, Paul was given the responsibility as an apostle to give revelation and to confirm it by miraculous signs. Apart from this, everything else seems to be the same for Paul as with any of the rest of us.

When we look at Paul, we need to have the proper perspective. He is not larger than life. Paul is simply an example of a man whose life was changed when he was exposed to the Truth. We can study him closely and come away with a stronger faith in our Lord, a deeper appreciation for God's revealed word, a genuine love for our brethren, and a renewed determination to serve God to the best of our ability.

In other words, we will say, "I want to become a leader just like Paul, *the Christian*."

Today, men can spend a lifetime studying leadership. There must be thousands of books written on the subject, and, in my business life, I have read several of them. We can read about famous leaders in business, politics, the military, the community, and the list goes on . . . but the source of the most valuable lessons in leadership lies within the pages of God's word (Prov. 1:7; Psa. 119:105). It only makes sense that the One who made us has given us "all things that pertain to life and godliness" (2 Pet. 1:3).

Studying the life of Paul can help us to become better spiritual leaders. What do we mean by spiritual leaders? When most of us see this term, we automatically think of elders. But, for the sake of this discussion, a spiritual leader is *any* disciple of Christ. The very influence of the gospel changes our allegiance from this world to Christ and helps us to be an influence on others so that they will do the same. Christianity is influence and, to have influence, you must be a spiritual leader. This does not mean that one has to participate in public service to be a spiritual leader. What about Lois and Eunice? What about Aquila and Priscilla? Lydia? The Philippian jailor? Or Dorcas? Or Gaius (Rom. 16:23)? Spiritual leadership includes all Christians—Jew, Greek, male, female, bond, or free (Gal. 3:27-28).

So, let's take a few minutes to learn some valuable lessons about true spiritual leadership from the life of our beloved brother, Paul.

Spiritual leaders are "made," not "born." Was Saul of Tarsus born a leader? Or was he trained to be a leader? The Scriptures indicate that Saul was brought up at the feet of Gamaliel, given the best education available and trained to be a devout Pharisee. It was this training that helped to mold his conscience to live a life of dedication to God. This very training in the Old Law prompted him to reject Christianity as heresy. Without this training, it would be safe to say that Saul would not have taken such bold steps to stamp out what he thought was a false doctrine.

After Saul had seen Christ on the way to Damascus, his world was shaken and he was ready to obey the Truth. Jesus said that, in the city, he would be "told what to do." Even in his early days at Damascus, Paul was trained by the disciples before he preached Christ in the synagogues (Acts 9:19-20). Later in Jerusalem, Barnabas became Paul's mentor and took him to the apostles. "And he was with them coming in and going out at Jerusalem" (Acts 9:28). It is this exposure to the Gospel that began to make Paul the leader we know.

After he left Jerusalem, Saul went home to Tarsus for an undetermined amount of time. The Scriptures do not reveal what was going on in his life at Tarsus; but later, in Acts 11, Barnabas comes to seek Saul for the work at Antioch. By this time Saul was well equipped to preach at Antioch for a whole year and to "teach much people." Could it be that Saul was being trained while he was in Tarsus? He later states that he received abundant revelation from God (2 Cor. 12:7). Whether or not he received some of this revelation in Tarsus, we know that God prepared him by revealing the mystery of the Gospel to him. Saul took that Truth and shared it with all who would listen.

What about us? If we were not born to be spiritual leaders, what can make us such leaders? The same thing that made Paul a spiritual leader! Have you been exposed to the Gospel? Do you love the Truth like Paul did? If so, do you share it as diligently as Paul did? Today more than ever, we need people to share the Truth with their friends, relatives, and neighbors in an effort to bring a lost and dying world to Christ. Paul teaches us this lesson.

Spiritual leaders do not compromise the Truth—even at great personal cost. If anyone serves as an example in this, it would be Paul. After living a life of devotion as a Pharisee, Paul had achieved prominence in the Jewish community. As difficult as it may have been for Paul to leave this life behind, he did so gladly. This would have been a life of great personal gain for him. He was respected by the entire Jewish leadership and would probably have been groomed for a position of high prestige among the Hebrews. Again, this would have been a life of great personal gain. But Paul had been exposed to the Truth. After that, a life of personal gain meant nothing to him (Phil. 3:7). "But what things were gain to me, those I counted loss for Christ."

Serving Christ meant certain persecution. In Acts 14:8-20, we read that Paul was stoned and left for dead at Lystra. The next day, he left to preach in Derbe. Can we even imagine his physical condition as he preached the Gospel after being stoned nearly to death? Verse 21 says that he even went back to Lystra to preach again! Would we dare to preach to the same audience that had done such physical harm to us?

Paul took a stand against Judaizing teachers (Acts 15; letter to the Galatians). When men began to teach that a Gentile convert must be circumcised and follow the Law of Moses, Paul immediately took a stand for the Truth. He identified the error being taught, exposed those who were teaching it, and confronted them both publicly and privately. For his efforts, Paul's enemies began to undermine his influence with the beloved brethren to whom he devoted his life's work. This attack on his character obviously hurt Paul deeply as he questioned the Galatians, "Am I therefore become your enemy, because I tell you the truth (4:16)?"

Paul was devoted to the Truth at any and all costs, including his very life. He told the Philippians, "For me to live is Christ, and to die is gain." His life was threatened on many occasions, yet he never yielded his allegiance to Christ. We can read about him narrowly escaping death on many occasions. Yet, we never once read about Paul compromising the Truth or even complaining about his circumstances. "I have learned in whatever state I am, therewith to be content" (Phil. 4:11). When the time of his death was near, Paul was able to tell Timothy that he was, indeed, ready to die (2 Tim. 4:6-8).

What about us? In regard to the Truth, we need to be as courageous as Paul—zealous to preach it, ready to defend it, convicted enough to expose error, and strong enough to endure persecution because we take a stand. How can we do that? To start, we need to know the Truth (2 Tim. 2:15). How much time do you spend daily in God's word? We are fooling ourselves if we think that we will not compromise the Truth, yet do not spend time in God's word every day. How much do we love the Truth? Can we identify error? We cannot refute it, if we cannot identify it! Are we convicted enough to become uncomfortable in stating that something is wrong? All of us have abundant opportunities to point out wrongs in the world around us. Have you been ridiculed lately? "Yea, and all that will live godly in Christ Jesus shall suffer persecution" (2 Tim. 3:12).

Spiritual leaders focus on others, not themselves. Jesus said in the great commission, "Go into all the world." In Acts 9, Saul was chosen to bear the name of Christ "before Gentiles and kings, and the children of Israel." From the beginning of his ministry, Paul was focused on others. His purpose was to share the mystery of the gospel to all who would listen (Eph. 3:9). Within the bounds of divine revelation, he was willing to give up his rights and privileges so he could convert others: "To the weak became I as weak, that I might gain the weak: I am made all things to all men, that I might by all means save some" (1 Cor. 9:22). He was willing to make sacrifices so that others would not stumble. "Even as I please all men in all things, not seeking mine own profit, but the profit of many, that they may be saved" (1 Cor. 10:33).

In Acts 17:16, Paul was in Athens, waiting on Silas and Timothy. When he saw that the city was given to idolatry, "his spirit was stirred in him." What does that mean? Was he angry? Was he disgusted? Whatever he felt, he was concerned for the souls of the people of Athens. It could have a meaning similar to Mark 6:34, which says, "And Jesus, when he came out, saw much people, and was moved with compassion toward them, because they were as sheep not having a shepherd: and he began to teach them many things." Paul's concern for the souls of others prompted him to *do something!*

Not only was he concerned about the souls of the lost, Paul was concerned about the safe keeping of the souls of his brethren. As he listed what he

Leaders in the Church: Paul 41

endured in his life of service to Christ, he mentioned many external challenges: beatings, stoning, shipwrecks, and various perils. But, the main concern that plagued his mind constantly was his brethren. "Beside those things that are without, that which cometh upon me daily, the care of all the churches" (2 Cor. 11:28).

We live in a society where there are many rights and privileges. We are free to come and go as we please . . . to live our lives as we want, with very limited restrictions. All of these blessings can cause us to feel self-sufficient. Self-sufficiency is an *enemy* to the cause of Christ. When was the last time we were *stirred* in our spirits by the sin that is all around us? Paul was very serious about spreading the gospel. Are you serious? Or are you selfish? It is not enough to say I have obeyed. It is not enough to say, I worship regularly, I give, I sing, I pray, I take the Lord's Supper (Luke 18:11). One who is truly touched by the gospel reaches out to others! Are you serious or are you selfish?

Spiritual leaders grow other spiritual leaders. One can hardly think about the leadership of Paul without thinking about the encouragement he gave to others. His work with Silas (Acts 15:36-41), Timothy (Acts 16:1-5), Titus, and many others demonstrate his dedication to the spiritual growth of others.

What about us? Do we encourage others to grow in the gospel? When was the last time you had fellow Christians in your home for personal Bible study, or to sing and to pray together? When was the last time you discussed Scriptures around the supper table? Have you offered to take someone to a gospel meeting with your family recently? Or does your family even go to gospel meetings anymore? Our physical families (as well as our spiritual families) need teaching, training, encouragement, and admonition to grow. As spiritual leaders, we need to follow Paul's example in helping others to grow.

When others take a stand for the Truth, do we encourage them? Or do we shrink back at the first sign of resistance? Elders, are you doing everything you can to provide a balanced spiritual diet for the flock that is among you? Or is the congregation, like our society, growing obese from too much "sugar" and not enough "vegetables and protein" (Heb. 5:12)? Are we teaching, training, and building up our young people, or allowing worldliness to choke them out of the Kingdom (Mark 4:19)? "And the things that thou hast heard of me among many witnesses, the same commit thou to faithful men, who shall be able to teach others also" (2 Tim. 2:2).

Spiritual leaders have vision. Paul's vision for the gospel was remarkable. Yes, we have already noted that he was chosen by God to preach to "Gentiles, kings and the children of Israel." But remember that he did have a choice in the matter. In Acts 22, he told King Agrippa that he was "not disobedient to the heavenly vision." Paul wanted to take the gospel as far as he could possibly go: Ephesus, Corinth (1 Cor. 16:5-12), Asia, Bithynia, Macedonia (Acts 16:11-40), Rome (Rom. 1:13-15), and many other places.

Paul's vision, in today's terms, was nothing short of world domination of the Kingdom of God. He took the talents he had, plus the Truth that God gave him, and worked to fulfill the great commission. Paul had the vision to see that the gospel *should* be taken to every creature, including the Gentiles. He knew that it applied to everyone—even the ones who did not want to hear it!

What about us? Do we have the same vision for the gospel? Where are the men who will step out and teach others? Where are the elders who will still put as much emphasis on evangelism as they do on edification and benevolence? In a time where it is becoming so difficult to convert others, where are the spiritual leaders who still can see that the gospel is for *all*? We need men who, while committed to walking within the divine revelation, are looking for ways to reach the lost—thus enabling the Kingdom to grow!

Spiritual leaders never stop being "spiritual followers." Being a leader is not always easy, and Paul shows us that, as he continually relied on Christ to lead him. Things got very difficult for him on many occasions. In Acts 18:9, we see Christ reassuring Paul to give him courage. We can see glimpses of his struggles in passages like 1 Corinthians 2:3—"And I was with you in weakness, and in fear, and in *much trembling*." But his focus was always on following Christ, as in the previous verse, when he said, "For I determined not to know any thing among you, save Jesus Christ, and him crucified."

Barnabas was a mentor to Saul as he began his years of service to Christ (Acts 11:25-30; 13). There were times when Paul drew strength from his brethren, and times when he recognized his need for help: "Praying always with all prayer and supplication in the Spirit, and watching thereunto with all perseverance and supplication for all saints; And for me, that utterance may be given unto me, that I may open my mouth boldly, to make known the mystery of the gospel, for which I am an ambassador in bonds: that therein I may speak boldly, as I ought to speak" (Eph. 6:18-20).

Leaders in the Church: Paul

Paul also examined himself and disciplined himself to make sure that he was following Christ properly: "Know ye not that they which run in a race run all, but one receiveth the prize? So run, that ye may obtain. And every man that striveth for the mastery is temperate in all things. Now they do it to obtain a corruptible crown; but we an incorruptible. I therefore so run, not as uncertainly; so fight I, not as one that beateth the air: But I keep under my body, and bring it into subjection: lest that by any means, when I have preached to others, I myself should be a castaway" (1 Cor. 9:24-27).

So, can we become spiritual leaders like our beloved brother Paul? We can if we determine that we will never stop following the teachings of our Lord and Savior. We can if we look to godly men who will teach us and instruct us in the Way of God. Today, there is a crisis in leadership among the Lord's people. Who among us will become a leader like Paul? Who will study, work, and sacrifice time to become a better spiritual leader? Who will not compromise the Truth—even at great personal cost? Who will encourage others to grow in their spiritual leadership? Who among us still has the vision of the power of the gospel to save? I pray that it is me, and you . . . all of us! If so, we can echo the words of Paul when he said: "Be ye followers of me, even as I also am of Christ" (1 Cor. 11:1).

Leaders in the Church: Barnabas
Steve Niemeier

"And Joses, who was also named Barnabas by the apostles (which is translated Son of Encouragement), a Levite of the country of Cyprus, having land, sold it, and brought the money and laid it at the apostles' feet" (Acts 4:36-37). What an introduction! This is how we meet this man that the apostles nicknamed "son of encouragement." His entrance into our lives through the inspired Scriptures is an appearance that one cannot forget. Many times we meet people who influence our lives one way or another. Some have an effect on us that we had just as soon forget. We can classify others we meet as acquaintances whom we know but really do not know much about or with whom we just develop a cordial relationship. Then there is "Barnabas." You know, the type who, by just being around them, lifts you up, not in the sense of some "putting on the positive attitude air" that is so common today, but in the sense of a genuine, "I care about the Lord and His work and that includes you!"

As Barnabas enters into the events of the early New Testament church,

---

Stephen J. Niemeier was born in Glasgow, KY in 1949. He is the son of Denver and Mildred Niemeier. Denver has preached in and around Indianapolis for about forty years and currently serves as an elder at Jamestown, IN. Steve and his wife Connie (Gary) graduated from Florida College. They have been married forty years and have three children (Rachel Lanius, Tad, and Seth). They have seven grandchildren. Before preaching full-time, Steve served as Vice-President of Indiana Farm Bureau Cooperative (he work for them twenty-five years) and later served as President of Morral Chemical. Since 1972, he has been preaching, sometime by appointed (twelve years). He has preached full-time at Danville, White River, Alexandria, and Greenwood, IN. Steve served as a deacon for two years and as an elder for ten years. He has done foreign work in Moldova and Sierra Leone. Many know Steve because of his fourteen years work as director of the Midwest Summer Camp in Indiana.

we find the world in turmoil. The prophesied Messiah has come, performed many signs and wonders (John 20:30-31), and spoken the words commanded by His Father (John 12:44-50). As a result, this Jesus was rejected by most of His own countrymen. He was betrayed and crucified, fulfilling the old Law. His resurrection brought in a new covenant. Needless to say, the world was turned upside down by these events and has not been the same since. The ones who heard the apostles on the Day of Pentecost, repented, were baptized, and were added to the body of Christ (Acts 2:47), which is His church (Eph. 1:21-22) that He said He would build (Matt. 16:18).

It seems that Barnabas was one of those who believed what was being taught and realized that Jesus was the Messiah. Look at the words of Acts 4:32 as Luke describes the scene of the times of our early brothers and sisters: *"Now the multitude of those who believed were of one heart and one soul; neither did anyone say that any of the things he possessed was his own, but they had all things in common."* This description is followed by another description in Acts 4:34-35: *"Nor was there anyone among them who lacked; for all who were possessors of lands or houses sold them, and brought the proceeds of the things that were sold, and laid them at the apostles' feet; and they distributed to each as anyone had need."* Here is a description that lets us know that many were doing this—and yet it provokes a question, "Why is Barnabas signaled out of this entire group?"

The apostles were very busy after the death, burial, and resurrection of Jesus. Their work load was heavy, their schedules were full, they had newborn babes to watch out for, to feed, and to edify. Yet, they still had a world of people to teach about this Jesus. Government forces were against them, many of their own countrymen were against them, those who believed their reports of who Jesus was and the plan He established for salvation were in for a life of turmoil and, in many cases, persecution both physically and mentally. The needs of these newborn babes were just like any of our needs—food, water, clothing, shelter, and all the other "needs of life" (not the "wants" or the "riches" of this life). These newborn Christians also longed for the food of eternal life that the apostles could give them, as revealed by the Holy Spirit, just as Christ had told them in John 16. How was it that, during this very busy and difficult time, the apostles would know the personality and attitude of this one named Joses (Joseph) well enough that they could "nickname" him "Barnabas"—"son of encouragement"?

While we may never know the answer of that question, we can be assured that he stood out in a crowd of good hearted brothers and sisters, and this the apostles recognized. His attitude was one of a leader, his character was one of encouragement, and his desire was one the apostles saw as a breath of fresh air in a period of stressfulness. We need only to look in Acts 5 to see the story of Ananias and Sapphira and to see just some of the difficulties the apostles faced in trying to do their work for the Lord. What a contrast we see between the one called Barnabas and Ananias and Sapphira.

We next see Barnabas in Acts 9:27. Saul of Tarsus, who had been a major persecutor of the Lord's church, had now become a new convert. (It is amazing what the "Light of the world" can do if we just yield ourselves to Him, isn't it?) Saul is trying to identify himself with the congregation of the Lord's people in Jerusalem. Most probably, none of us would have had our arms open to him; just as the brethren in Jerusalem were scared of him, we would have been also. What Barnabas had been doing between our first meeting him in Acts 4 until now is something we do not know. However, when encouragement was needed, he is back in the picture. It was a time that he was needed. Barnabas takes Saul and brings him to the apostles. You know the rest of this story, don't you? Saul becomes Paul and his ministry continues to turn the world upside down, especially among the Gentiles. Yet in a time of his life when he needed a brother to help him, Barnabas stepped up to the challenge.

The work of Barnabas and Saul, who later became Paul and Barnabas is an example to all of us today. We know what Paul did, but do we really realize the role of Barnabas? Acts 11 through Acts 15:35 shows the attitude of Barnabas that all of us need to reflect upon. In Acts 11:19-24, Barnabas was described as good man, full of the Holy Spirit, and of faith. At that time, a great many people were added to the Lord in Antioch of Syria. Acts 11:23 states that Barnabas encouraged the brethren to continue with the Lord. It seems that he was loved by all and was a great resource for the apostles in the work of the Lord. Remember, Barnabas is the one whom the apostles knew. He is the one who was nicknamed "son of encouragement," and he was the one who seemed to be well known among the apostles. He had their confidence as well as the trust of his brethren. Acts 11:25 tells us that Barnabas went to Tarsus to get Saul and take him to Antioch. Why? Why would he go and get this Saul and bring him to Antioch? He is Barnabas! Doesn't he realize that Saul could hinder his "status" among the brethren? Amazingly, compared to what we might see today among our brethren, Barnabas was more concerned about the Lord's work and what was best for it instead of his own personal "status."

At this time, Barnabas seems to be the "leader" of the team of Barnabas and Saul. In Acts 13:9, something is changing among this dynamic duo for the Lord. Saul, who is also called Paul, becomes the new spokesperson for the team, just as the Lord wanted. We see Barnabas stepping back to assist Paul, not fading away but, as Acts 13:46 states, they were both bold in their teaching of the word of God. They worked at Antioch together, they traveled together, and they taught together. They were trusted by brethren who didn't trust Saul until Barnabas stepped in.

Yet, we find in Acts 15:36 through 41 that they had a difference concerning John Mark. This contention was sharp and they separated ways. We have seen this during our time, haven't we? Brethren who have worked together, traveled together, and even been in danger together have a sharp contention that ends up in a feud that result in trees being chopped down to provide enough paper supply to carry on the dissension for years. However, this is not what happened with Barnabas and Paul. While they could not agree on John Mark, they both went their ways, in different geographical directions teaching the word of God. They did not hinder the work of the Lord trying to justify their respective positions, but they furthered the cause of Christ. Paul mentions Barnabas in 1 Corinthians 9:6, again in Galatians 2:1, in Galatians 2:9, in Galatians 2:13, and again in Colossians 4:10. The comments were not an attack on the character of Barnabas; however, Paul seems very disappointed and surprised in Barnabas being carried away with Peter and the rest of the Jews in the hypocrisy against the Gentiles. Paul was justifiably disturbed about this action.

One interesting factor about the contention between Paul and Barnabas is the reason for this difference—John Mark. You might remember meeting him in Acts 12:12, as it was to his mother's house (Mary) that Peter came after being freed from prison. In Acts 12:25, he accompanied Barnabas and Saul and was at Antioch of Syria with them. However, in Acts 13:13, John Mark left them in Pamphylia and returned to Jerusalem. This is why Paul did not want to take him with them on the journey to revisit the cities they had been to previously (Acts 15:36). Barnabas wanted to take him. As a result Paul took Silas and went through Syria and Cilicia. Barnabas takes John Mark and sailed to Cyprus. In 2 Timothy 4:11, Paul tells Timothy to bring Mark to him as he is *useful* to Paul in the ministry. What changed Paul's mind about John Mark? It would seem that we have seen the "son of encouragement" at work again. Just as Barnabas helped Paul in a time of need, so it seems he did the same for John Mark.

Having the privilege of teaching overseas and experiencing the strain, both mentally and physically, on an individual, one can somewhat understand Paul's frustration with John Mark. Traveling with fellow preachers or elders to a foreign land for intense teaching in a somewhat limited time frame, you rely on each other to carry his portion of the load. If someone leaves in the middle of the trip, then the burden is heavy upon the ones who remain. Paul did not like this it seems and did not want to be put in this position again. Yet, being the type of individual he was, Barnabas made a decision to take John Mark with him to teach him, train him, and help him. Today, we need to see more of this patience and action in the Lord's church. Our young brothers and sisters need to be taught and trained. Yes, it may be frustrating and they may resent it, but it needs to be done. This is another great lesson Barnabas teaches us.

Barnabas was not a perfect man. Yet, he was an example to all of his brethren, including the apostles. The lessons we learn from him are lessons that we should all apply to our lives. The Lord's army needs those like Barnabas today. A quick review of the life of Barnabas shows us that he was:

- Liberal in his giving (Acts 4:34-37)
- An exhorter of others (Acts 4:36; 11:23)
- Not envious but a glad man (Acts 11:23)
- A good man (Acts 11:24)
- A man full of the Holy Ghost and faith (Acts 11:24)
- A man that was "successful" in the Lord's work (Acts 11:24)
- Not afraid to hold his position (Acts 15:37-41)
- One willing to train (Acts 15:39; 2 Tim. 4:11)

What a resume! When we face the perils of this life, the issues that seem to drag us down—the family crisis, the employment crisis, the financial crisis, the health crisis, the "persecuting brother or sister in Christ" crisis, the "lifeless" congregation crisis, or any other crisis in our life—how do we handle them? Confronted with the crisis of selling his property and laying down the money at the apostles' feet, we find Joses doing the Lord's will. Confronted with the crisis of helping a new babe in Christ who had a frightful past, Barnabas stepped up to help. When one needed to step aside to further the work of the Lord, Barnabas yielded to Paul. When a congregation needed to be encouraged, Barnabas was there to do so. Barnabas was sent and he went whenever and wherever he was needed.

Barnabas was a true leader in the church during the New Testament days.

Leaders in the Church: Barnabas 49

We need this kind of attitude and leadership in the church today. We need to consider his good qualities and try to develop these qualities within ourselves whether we are male or female. We must remember that the qualities of Barnabas were real—they were not a "put on," "fakey," or an act. They were genuine as he strived to do the Lord's work and be a true brother in Christ to all of his fellow brothers and sisters. Barnabas was a brother who was a source of encouragement, which was sorely needed then and is sorely needed now! He was one whom the apostles named "son of encouragement" that certainly lived up to this recognition. By the way, have you ever wondered what the apostles might have given you as a nickname?

The Morning Lectures

The Family Qualifications of an Elder
Bobby L. Graham

The Holy Spirit declares that an elder's leadership in his own home is essential to prepare him for leadership in the local church. Of elders, Paul wrote (1 Tim. 3:4, 5): ". . .one who rules his own house well, having his children in subjection with all reverence (for if a man does not know how to rule his own house, how will he take care of the church of God?)." Who can deny that leadership in both realms is the divine objective, with his leadership in the family equipping him with the attitudes and skills needed by him for his work in overseeing the congregation. Thus is established the divinely designated importance of leadership in an elder, both in preparation and in operation, both in his family and in the Lord's church.

In too many instances, however, elders have been chosen and promoted for the eldership because of their business acumen, the number of children they have, or how many of their children "attend church." Occasionally men have even resorted to political means and strategies in their campaigns to become elders, because of their raw, carnal lust to assert their power/

Bobby L. Graham was born August 30, 1946 to Mary and Leon Graham. He spent most of his growing up years under the preaching of Curtis Flatt and Franklin T. Puckett. Bobby graduated from Coffee High School in 1964; attended Florida College and graduated with a B.A. in History from Athens College and finished his Master's Degree in Education at Virginia Commonwealth University. He began preaching in 1962 while still in high school. He married Karen Ruth Hodge in November 1967; they have three children: Richard, Mary Katherine (Darren Winland), and Laura Ruth (Jeremy Paschall). He has two grandchildren. Bobby has preached for several congregations in Alabama, Virginia, and is presently preaching at Old Moulton Road in Decatur, Alabama. He has written for *Gospel Guide* for the last 33 years. He has made many trips to Northeastern and New England states, worked in the Mountains of Virginia and Kentucky, and has made eleven preaching trips to Belize.

control over saints of God. Success in the business or political world, the ability to read a spread sheet and to keep an organization profitable, or the physical prowess to beget children has nothing to do with success as shepherds in the local flock. God informed us that the role of a father leading his family comes much closer to what He desires and the local church needs. Why then do brethren with good intentions keep bringing up the business skills or focusing unduly on the family qualifications of potential elders and forgetting the skills which the head of the church stresses—the positive virtues of his character or those of his leading the family, including his wife and children? Where did Christ ever mention business skills? Spiritual development is all but forgotten in such worldly thinking! The world truly has influenced us too much in this area, just as in other areas. God knew precisely what He desires and the church needs when He had Paul instruct young Timothy concerning the kind of men needed as elders. Who is worthy to serve as His counselor? He needs no one's advice! Let us resolve to learn from Him!

When the inspired men of the New Testament wrote concerning overseers, they employed terms and words under the supernatural guidance of the Spirit of God. Their use of these terms becomes paramount in importance as we seek to learn what elders are, why God desires them, what their qualifications are, and other such relevant matters. Honest readers of the sacred text should satisfy themselves to learn from the writers what they intended to say instead of imposing upon their inspired statements present-day meanings or biases. While it is sinful to disregard what they wrote, it is equally sinful to supplement the inspired text with human opinion, as some have done with supplementary, uninspired qualifications. Qualifications given from the mind of God are necessary if the right kind of men be selected in a local church; otherwise they are irrelevant. On the other hand, human qualifications for elders are as useless as the sinner's prayer is for the alien in conversion. There is no substitute for the Bible itself in gaining an understanding of what the writers meant. Word etymologies and Greek lexicons, while helpful, provide only ranges and possibilities of meaning and limitations for the words which they used. On the other hand, the writer's use of the words in a given context alone determines and assures the meaning which he sought to convey to the reader. Because limited space is available and because the lexicon definitions are generally already known or available, this article will include little of this nature.

The Family Qualifications of an Elder

The Importance of the Family in the Nation and the Local Church

The family is the strength, the spine, and even the bedrock foundation, of the nation and of the church. The virtues encouraged and developed in the family setting become the source of moral and spiritual power in a congregation and in the country. In the ages of history when the family unit was neglected, such neglect became prominently displayed in the weakened condition of both the nation and the church. Parents who are today too busy with efforts other than parenting contribute to such weakness in both realms and are guilty of sin in bringing about the shaky condition of local churches and nations tottering on the brink of death. The family, as designed by God, can be the source of strength and thus the stability of the present and the promise of the future.

It follows that when families weaken, fewer elders are prepared for working in local churches. Parents fail their children and the church in this neglect of duty. When families remain close and the fires of spiritual concern and zeal keep burning, young men see the importance of becoming preachers and elders and young women, of becoming their wives. Churches suffer because parents fail to be parents! How many of us parents and grandparents are guilty of neglect in this area?

The highest source of wisdom says it clearly: "...one who rules his own house well, having his children in submission with all reverence (for if a man does not know how to rule his own house, how will he take care of the church of God?)"! The parenthesis encloses information explanatory, clarifying, or confirmatory to the earlier part of the verse. Let there be no effort to gainsay such wisdom, but a humble submission in life to this wisdom for the good of all concerned. Are we listening?

Elders as Leaders in the Local Church

The assignment of this lesson concerns the leadership of elders, not their authority; thus we shall not much concern ourselves with the latter. The two, however, go hand in hand when the right kind of leadership and the right kind of authority are understood. There should be no doubt that elders are congregational leaders because first they were family leaders. Likewise there should be no doubt that shepherds exercise Christ's delegated authority as those in charge of the souls of His sheep (Heb. 13:17). The family qualifications are crucial in assuring that these men provide proper leadership in the local congregation, and the type of leadership which they exert will become apparent in the following paragraphs.

The scriptural designations used of elders show them to be leaders. Three Greek words depict basically who elders are and what they do; each of them is translated by two notable English nouns, which clarify their leadership. (1) The first Greek word is *episkopos*, which is rendered as overseer or bishop. (2) The second Greek word is *poimēn*, which is translated shepherd or pastor. (3) The third Greek term is *presbuteros*, which means elder or presbyter. The first pair of English words stresses the nature of the man's work among saints as one who, ever alert for forces of error or sin, watches for their souls and sees after their spiritual needs. The second group of English words emphasizes that spiritual care, nurturing, feeding, and tending which he gives to the sheep for their spiritual edification. The final group of English words focuses on the man's spiritual maturity or development, as one who has experience preparing him for his role as a spiritual leader. It becomes clear that elders are spiritual leaders of the flock because of their own spiritual progress in the same areas where they aspire to lead the sheep, according to Christ's direction. Their performance as family leaders greatly contributes to their qualification for these works.

Their qualifications, indicated by the Holy Spirit in 1 Timothy 3 and Titus 1, also show them to be leaders. Without exploring the qualifications specifically, we state that they demonstrate the kind of men elders are by showing their spiritual achievements. Such accomplishments exist because the men have committed themselves to the spiritual pursuit of becoming Christlike. In some areas their qualifications pertain to absolute matters, such as being the husband of one wife (positive) or not being greedy for money (negative). In other areas they show their qualification in relative matters, such as being able to teach (positive) or being hospitable (varying degrees of hospitality). To describe some qualifications as absolute and others as relative simply means that they either exist or do not exist (absolute), or exist in differing degree/amount (relative). They thus position themselves as leaders of the sheep, who are growing in the same areas as their leaders; shepherds are to be clear examples to the flock (1 Pet. 5:3). The sheep are instructed to obey (listen to, be persuaded by) them, while the elders are to be able to teach the people from the vantage point of spiritually mature men truly concerned for them and able to instruct and train them. In character, morality, family leadership, and teaching/ruling the congregation, they have proven themselves capable of leading others in the Lord's way.

Their work shows them to be leaders. They exercise oversight/overseership, work in tending, feeding, shepherding, overseeing, watching for souls, and serving as stewards, caretakers, or guardians of sheep who belong to the Lord. They have long followed the example of the Chief Shepherd, showing they are not self-willed lords, but eager and exemplary men. When they teach, convince, warn, or encourage the flock, they eagerly seek to lead them in the way of Christ. Often their work is a "selling job" of teaching and convincing saints to do right. In seeking to teach the lost or to restore the erring, they set an example of concern that others need to imitate.

The responsibilities of the members of the church to the elders show their role as leaders. Whether they obey them, accept their persuasion, submit to them, esteem them, or refuse to accept an accusation against them, they act in a fashion that honors them for their spiritual maturity and reflects appreciation for them as their leaders (Heb. 13:7, 17). Each congregation needs such leaders and such members who appreciate such spiritual leaders

From all that the New Testament records concerning elders, it is obvious that they are God's leaders in the local church and that the sheep do well in following their spiritual lead. In their esteem for them and their attempts to follow them, they become like their leaders, as they follow Christ.

Why Some Churches Do Not Have Elders

In view of the need for elders in many local churches and God's wise plan of showing the need for them, why do many congregations exist many years without elders? The reasons, of course, are numerous; but they also are often incredible when found among people claiming to believe in the sufficiency of the New Testament pattern! It is time to ask whether it is right to condemn those acts of brethren which go beyond the divine standard, while falling short of that same standard! Is it scripturally correct to criticize the failings of others in this area while not developing ourselves to serve as elders or not working to appoint elders? Is it not the same hypocrisy spoken of by Christ as trying to remove the mote in a brother's eye with a beam protruding from our own (Matt. 7:1-5)?

As we suggest the various reasons for this deficiency in local churches, it will become clear that more teaching and stronger faith will help to remove these reasons and to solve this problem. Each reason found below is rooted in a lack of teaching and faith; brethren have simply not heard enough teaching concerning elders. Preachers, take note! Are you doing your job? Elders already serving, have you attended to this matter? Whether popular or not, convenient or not, easy or not, you have a job to do. Shepherding the sheep and preaching the word include helping a church to understand its need for elders and the men to understand their duty to grow in this matter. Do not we who often decry the wrong of the sponsoring-church eldership commit an equal sin in our failure to have elders or, at least, to teach and encourage to that end? We do if we fail to teach about this matter, and even if we view it as an option!

Some brethren have not seen the need for elders in practice, though many of them have perhaps consented to the theoretical need. Being a Christian and serving the Lord is not a matter of theory, but of practice (Jas. 1:22; John 13:17). The spirit of independence, which sometimes transforms itself into one of rebellion, is too often found in churches among those opposing elders. Such a spirit ill befits one claiming to be a Christian, who should submit to the Lord of heaven and earth. Paul said something was lacking in Crete without elders (Tit. 1:5). While some think they're getting along fine without them, the Lord thinks otherwise. Matters like spiritual growth of Christians, benevolence, and congregational discipline sometimes go lacking without elders.

A second cause of churches not having elders is not understanding the blessing of having shepherds to oversee the flock. More united churches result from strong leadership. Lambs will be nourished and the flock will be better fed. Members will be more dutiful, and the church will be more active. Scattered sheep, a leaderless flock, or a congregation failing to move under the spiritual leadership of godly elders often creates a vacuum in which lovers of preeminence, proponents of error, or carnally minded men take advantage. Why not attend to the Lord's will in this matter?

Some oppose having elders because they fear making a mistake in selecting elders or the trouble the church might then have. They reason that it is better to have no elders than to have bad elders. While it is true that care should be exercised in choosing them, honesty and sincerity should remove any such problems from developing. Even if ungodly members decide to vaunt their own wills, God still wills that local churches have elders. To refuse to have them is to exalt man's will over Christ's. Dangers in any area do not invalidate God's plan. Should first-century churches have refused to have elders because some would later apostatize (Acts 20:28ff)? The principles of truth and righteousness, elsewhere found in the Scriptures, will make the effort successful by divine standards. Humble and mature men will recognize their own flaws, removing themselves from consideration, and subordinate their own opinions, refusing to impose such on others.

The Family Qualifications of an Elder

Some churches have failed to develop men able to serve as elders, and some men have failed to grow toward this end. One failure (sin) does not justify another failure (sin). There must come a time when people and congregations decide to quit their own willful way and repent, so they can please God. It is a necessary conclusion that God desires men and congregations to understand the need to progress along the lines of divine qualifications to have elders. Women have a role in this area of developing themselves and their husbands. What current plans does your congregation have for developing elders, or what are you doing to develop yourself?

Another reason there are not elders in all churches is that many hold an unrealistic view of the qualifications of elders. Some look for perfect men; others have viewed the qualities as an opportunity to disqualify somebody rather than a part of God's plan for men to grow toward the divine ideal; still others have defined the qualifications according to their own selfish ideas. Brethren, we must let God tell us what He means by these qualifications instead of our telling Him what He means! It is not right to demand a meaning contrary to the one demanded by the context in which the qualifications appear. In too many instances, some have chosen meanings appearing in Greek lexicons, when such meanings often appear only as possibilities. Such use of a lexicon is a misuse. Care must be used to make sure that the correct meaning is chosen for the particular reference being cited. A sin committed in early life, if repented of, should not in itself prevent consideration of a man's growth in later years. One man's opinion must not serve as a congregational standard; study and growth should lead to resolution of differences and avoidance of problems.

An additional reason why churches do not have elders is that qualified men sometimes hesitate to accept appointment. Some fear criticism of self or family or their wives' being discouraged by such criticism. Churches need to learn their role in encouraging elders and helping them (Heb. 13:17). Courage is always needed to do what is right. Trust in the Lord is one aspect of faith. Do we fail to pray, to assemble for worship, or to be examples of right because of the same lack of courage? Yes, but we should not do so. Being busy with other involvements sometimes hinders men in this area, as well as fear of inadequacy. Who is adequate for any divinely given task? Is it possible that the lack of desire to serve is sometimes evidence of sin, because the man fails to use his abilities and opportunities in God's service (Matt. 25:14-30)?

Finally, some do not want to surrender their influence or power to elders.

They are like Israel, who did not want God to rule over them when they asked for a king. Carnality is too much alive in too many churches. The rest of the church must not allow such ungodly men to prevail over God's will. There is a godly way to deal with them. Minority rule is not God's way, nor is one-man rule. The Lord instructs us in dealing with such situations.

The Significance of an Elder's Family to His Work: Proving Ground

Notice again what the Holy Spirit said about elders and their families in 1 Timothy 3:4-5: "...one who rules his own house well, having his children in subjection with all reverence (for if a man does not know how to rule his own house, how will he take care of the church of God?)." Is there any doubt about the divine purpose for this qualification on an elder's part, in view of the clearly stated reason given in the parenthetical statement? His family is viewed by the Lord as the proving ground for his work as an overseer.

When the Lord pinpoints the family as the training ground for an elder, it is wise for us to explore that fertile field because of the rich preparation it can provide him. In his faithfulness to his one wife, there is the first training which he needs. He learns endurance in a good thing, even when difficulties arise, as well as loyalty to his wife when others around him are displaying marital disloyalty. His example in this area becomes a strength in leading others in the way of righteousness.

His family is a stewardship like that in the local church. He there learns faithfulness in guarding his family, so that protecting what belongs to another in the church is something for which he has prepared. He has a stewardship in both realms, with one equipping him for the other (1 Tim. 3:4-5).

The family qualifications demonstrate the man's preparation for the care which he gives to the church. He will have successfully demonstrated the following accomplishments, which are part of his family responsibility and are pertinent to his future work as a steward of God's people:

- Faithfulness to his wife
- Benevolent, vigilant rule of his family
- Leadership in encouraging and facilitating his family's spiritual growth
- Management of differences and quarrels
- Experience in developing submission with reverence among his children through his own example and teaching
- Godly attitudes maintained throughout his successes and failures at home

The Family Qualifications of an Elder

- The true test of his character and his understanding of the Scriptures provided in his family dealings

Without this test which he faces in the test tube of family dealings, the other qualifications (knowledge, teaching ability, and the various positive/negative virtues) are academic, leaving real doubt about his ability to maintain them as he functions as an elder. A facade of righteousness is impossible to maintain under the intense heat of family testing, when true character is missing. In summary, the family is the laboratory in which the husband/father shows himself truly qualified to exercise the stewardship of the local church, for which his family stewardship has been making him ready. By his good behavior, he proves that he is a lover of what is good.

He has been preparing himself for his new role in the local church through his fervent love of God, a profound respect for the authority of the Scriptures, prayer to the heavenly Father, careful attention to the spiritual needs of his family, constant vigilance in what the children are learning and doing and the influences to which they are exposed, knowledge of his wife and children, and his courageous and stalwart stand for all that is good and right. He learns from this family experience the importance of giving attention to himself and to the flock which he oversees (Acts 20:28).

Areas of Disagreement in the Family Qualifications

Most of the qualifications of elders provide little room for disagreement, but those pertaining to his family experience are the exception. Most differences in local-church matters pertaining to them have arisen over the man's relationship to his wife and children. Specifically, the following qualifications are the contested areas:

- "husband of one wife" (Tit. 1:6)
- "children" (1 Tim. 3:4; Tit. 1:6)
- "faithful children" (Tit. 1:6)

We shall now give brief consideration to the meaning of each disputed qualification without delving much into technical Greek definitions, which often are found in the writings of brethren on these matters but offer little in the resolution of present difficulties.

"Husband of one wife" (Tit. 1:6): This qualification simply means that the man must have remained the faithful husband of his lawful mate. It requires marriage and prohibits polygamy, as well as the serial adultery so prominent in today's culture. To require more than this (that he never could have been married to another woman, even if she was the unfaithful partner involved in fornication), is to hold the man responsible for the woman's infraction of divine law in certain instances or to say that he becomes tainted by her unfaithfulness. He is disqualified because she sinned, according to some. Who can believe it? From a positive perspective, it is important to remember that his faithfulness in marriage to his wife does two things: (a) it lays the groundwork for his interaction with children and the consequent experience that he gains for use in his work as overseer in the church, and (b) he prepares himself to serve as an example to others in the church (1 Pet. 5:3).

"Children": The contextual demand is that he have enough children for him to rule them. Notice the equivalence between "children" in verse four and "house" in verse five. Yes, Greek lexicons supply *possible* meanings, but only the immediate context determines the *exact* meaning by showing *which meaning fits*. Even the remote context, which shows "children" used in instances where the singular meaning is included in the plural usage, is not the decisive factor in this matter, helping only to a degree. In the final analysis, it is the immediate context which shows what "children" means in the disputed passage. The following paragraph, taken from an article previously written by this writer, helps to express the matter more specifically:

> Must elders have more than one faithful child? 1 Timothy 3:4 says of him: ". . .one who rules his own house well, having his own children in submission with all reverence (for if a man does not know how to rule his own house, how will he take care of the house of God?)." In his letter to Titus, the apostle said it this way: "having faithful children not accused of riot or unruly." In both accounts the plural word "children" appears. It would be easy to say that the plural word settles the matter, but the simple truth is that the Bible elsewhere uses the plural of this very word to include the single child. Two references that should be studied in this connection are Genesis 21:7 and Matthew 22:23-33. In the first passage Sarah is described as nursing children, when she actually had only one child whom she was nursing. In the other passage, reference is to the Old Testament law concerning a man marrying his dead brother's wife to raise up offspring in the name of the departed brother. Verse 24 says, "If a man die, having no children." One child, however, would have fulfilled the requirement of that law so that the remaining brother would not have needed to marry his sister-in-law. In these passages and others, the plural is used, but the singular is obviously included as a possible meaning. For this reason I believe that one child fills the demand of the qualification. Another reason why I believe that one child will qualify a man is that

The Family Qualifications of an Elder 63

Paul used "children" and "house" equivalently in 1 Timothy 3:4. However many children it takes for him to have a household to rule is how many he must have to qualify as an elder. Re-read the verse and see if that is not Paul's point. In verse four Paul's statement of the qualification includes "children"; and in his parenthetical explanatory reason in verse five, he refers to the "house." One child fits the meaning of the qualification. Yes, having more than one child provides more training, but so does having many more children or having both sons and daughters or having children with learning problems or stubborn children. To require more than God said is to impose man's wisdom and will on God's law.

"Faithful children not accused of dissipation or insubordination" (Tit. 1:6) or "having children in submission with all reverence" (1 Tim. 3:4): The positive part of this statement means the children must be faithful to Christ (usual meaning of the words "faithful" and "believe" in NT) during their time under his rule ("his own house," 1 Tim. 3:5). He has no right to rule any house/family besides his own, not even that of his child. The negative part of the statement means that they have not turned from Christ to live a life of abandonment or rebellion against the authority of God, government, or parents. Their later unfaithfulness can, and sometimes does, result from father's failure; but it is not necessarily so (consider God's fatherly relation to rebellious Israel in Isaiah 1). The following question and the accompanying answer frame this matter:

> Must elders and deacons resign when their children living away from home become unfaithful to Christ? In the cases of elders and deacons, the children under consideration are those still at home, as seen in the ruling the father does and the submission shown by the children, in both 1 Timothy and Titus. The qualification does not deal with children in other situations. The submission is not merely to the father, because submission to father does not always mean submission to Christ. If one thinks that this statement covers faithfulness to the Lord, he needs to remember that no child should become a Christian out of submission to his father, nor does he remain faithful out of submission to the father. In the event one thinks that children well trained at home will never depart from the Lord (in view of Prov. 22:6), he needs to remember that children retain free wills and come under other influences later in life. While their later unfaithfulness can reflect on parental upbringing, it does not necessarily do so. If all parental training is shown to be faulty when children stray from the right path, then God was not the kind of father Israel needed. In Isaiah 1, the Lord compared His relationship to Israel to that of a father with his children. He said that He had nurtured and brought up children, but they had rebelled against Him. Are we to think that God failed as Israel's

parent? Certainly not! Does the rebellion of children mean that parents have failed? No. If God was an unfit parent by such faulty reasoning of some, then He also was not qualified to be an elder. It appears that some believe in the impossibility of apostasy, if the parents have taught them properly. The later conduct of grown children does not by itself disqualify their fathers as elders. In a case like this, if the conduct of the children is so flagrant and conspicuous as to make the father's influence void, then he should wisely step aside for the good of the church. However, if his influence is not diminished by rebellious children, then he is not required to resign by the qualifications here studied. The local-church context determines the course of wisdom in this event

Conclusion

Let us remember that God is in charge; we are not! His way is always safe and best. Humble hearts will surrender to God's will. Is our attitude here described?

Local churches need qualified elders. Elders grow out of godly family situations. Men must begin to view their responsibility in this area. What will they do about this need?

Will we adjust our understanding on these matters to conform to what the Bible teaches or seek to impose our judgment on the rest of the congregation? Will we change our practice to reflect God's way?

God will be glorified, saints will be edified, and we will be blessed if we make needed changes.

The Work of Elders
Sherrel A. Mercer
Introduction

Evidence abounds that some churches, like those listed in chapters two and three of the book of Revelation, will ultimately lose their identity as a church belonging to the Lord Jesus Christ. They will "lose their candlesticks." They will have changed so greatly that they are no longer recognizable as churches established in the pattern of the New Testament.

What happened to some of the seven churches of Asia? Ephesus left her first love. Pergamos tolerated error. Thyatira allowed immorality. Sardis was dead. Laodicea was lukewarm and complacent.

Sherrel A. Mercer was born December 22, 1944, the second of five sons of W. H. and Thelma Mercer. He has lived all of his life in Edna, Texas, except for time while in college and later working in the Houston area. He graduated from Rice University with a B.A. in Physics in 1966. He married the former Cecelia Glass of Vinton, Virginia in 1965. To that union were born three children, Elizabeth Thompson of Edna, Richard Mercer (deceased), and Laura Paulsel of Peachtree City, Georgia. There are nine grandchildren, and the oldest seven have been baptized. While working in Houston, he was the preacher for the Cypress-Fairbanks congregation for two years beginning in 1967. The management of two family-owned businesses in Edna, Mercer Construction and Mercer Controls, has occupied him professionally since relocating to his home town in 1971. He was national chairman of the Professional Engineers in Construction division of the National Society of Professional Engineers in 1988-1989. He has served the Lord's church in Edna as deacon and then elder (1984 to present). He, as well as several other men of the congregation, preaches on occasions when the local evangelist is absent. A number of articles have been written by him and published in periodicals printed by brethren. He is a descendant of the Ezzell family, from which many Christians and several gospel preachers have originated since early in the Nineteenth Century in Missouri, Arkansas, Oklahoma, and Texas. A number of articles are planned by him concerning Evidences, since his perspective can be that of a trained scientist/engineer who is a believer of the Bible.

Where was their leadership? What happened to cause the ultimate loss of their identity as churches of Christ? How did error, immorality, and inactivity threaten to destroy these congregations so soon after the death of our Lord? How did they lose their sense of direction? How did they become different from what was intended? How did they cease to be examples of keeping the "unity of the spirit in the bond of peace" (Eph. 4:3)?

As Christians, we need to understand that unity in Christ and faithfulness to His word are achievable and inseparable. They are not just imaginary goals. Jesus prayed for the unity of the believers, noting that unity of the believers is testimony about His divinity (John 17:20-23). Unity will be built upon precept and submission, coupled with a rejection of all that is not authorized. We are reminded to "be faithful until death," thus assuring us that it will be possible for us to be faithful until death (Rev. 2:10).

Properly constituted active leadership is the primary defense in a local congregation against disunity, error, and apostasy. Failure within the leadership at the top of any organization is usually a root cause of failure of the organization to accomplish its stated goals. The attitude and the behavior of the leadership will strongly influence the members.

In the New Testament, elders were appointed in every church. What, then, is the work of elders? And how are they a defense of the Divine Pattern?

The Work of Elders as Defined by the Original Greek Words

There are three words used interchangeably in the New Testament to identify those men occupying the office of elder. Each of the three Greek words translates to a pair of English words. All three of the Greek words appear in some form in the text of 1 Peter 5:1-4:

> The elders who are among you I exhort, I who am a fellow elder and a witness of the sufferings of Christ, and also a partaker of the glory that will be revealed: Shepherd the flock of God which is among you, serving as overseers, not by compulsion but willingly, not for dishonest gain but eagerly; nor as being lords over those entrusted to you, but being examples to the flock; and when the Chief Shepherd appears, you will receive the crown of glory that does not fade away.

The Greek word *presbuteros* is usually translated as "elder" or, in the plural, "presbytery." The term means (a) one who has accomplished greater age, or (b) one who has attained greater rank or responsibility. In either case, there is a level of respect automatically associated with the term "elder."

The Greek noun *poimen* is translated "pastor" or "shepherd," and sometimes a related verb *poimaino* appears, translated as "feed" or "tend." The Greek term *poimen* describes one who tends or feeds a flock of sheep. All of the actions of a shepherd and the word pictures the term draws are appropriately applied to the shepherds of local congregations.

The Greek word *episkopos* is translated as "bishop" or "overseer." The Greek word may be separated into two parts, *epi*, meaning "over" and *skopeo*, meaning "to look" or "to watch." The word *episkopos* is descriptive of one who looks after or watches over persons or activities. The word does not describe casual behavior, but purposeful and responsible watching, intent upon gaining knowledge about the things watched.

The Work of Elders as Divinely Ordained

The apostle Paul defines that the Lord Himself "gave some to be apostles, some prophets, some evangelists, and some pastors and teachers, for the equipping of the saints for the work of ministry, for the edifying of the body of Christ. . . . [that we] may grow up in all things into Him who is the head—Christ. . ." (Eph. 4:11, 15). This divinely ordained work was so important that one of Paul's tasks on his journeys was to appoint elders in every church (Acts 14:23). The appointing of elders was part of Paul's instruction to Titus (Tit. 1:5). The divine purpose for elders cannot be minimized. The scriptural teaching about elders must be granted every consideration of respect and solemnity.

The Work of Elders as Determined by Common Sense

Any organization of men requires established leadership to survive. The absence of leadership results in inactivity, if not anarchy. Even in congregations with no elders qualified and serving, some type of consensus leadership must exist in order for any work to be accomplished as a group.

The Lord totally prepared His church for its survival, because there is a complete pattern granted in the Scripture for all the work and worship of the local congregations. The pattern thus given is the imperative by which all churches must be maintained. Deviation from the revealed pattern is apostasy, as are all actions taken by a congregation in the absence of scriptural authority.

The Work of Elders as Determined from Their Qualifications

The qualifications of elders are found in 1 Timothy 3:1-7 and Titus 1:5-9. The qualifications were given in writing to two evangelists, along with the instruction to see that elders were appointed. Other speakers in this lectureship will surely address the qualifications in some detail. Note simply these few terms among the list of qualifications which reference a continued pattern of behavior or work, first from 1 Timothy 3:

- "Blameless," or of good behavior, conducting oneself above accusation of wrongdoing;
- "Hospitable," giving of oneself and of one's resources to benefit others;
- "Able to teach," not just qualified at a point in time when appointed, but continually;
- "Rules his own house well," a continuous activity;
- "Have a good testimony among those who are outside," again a continuous activity;

And from Titus 1:

- "A steward of God," a manager of the possessions of God;
- "Lover of what is good," living a life in contrast with the lives of those who favor unkindness and evil;
- "Holding fast the faithful word as he has been taught," requiring continuous study and recitation.

Lest any should misunderstand: the qualifications are not a ticket to a position of leadership, but rather they are a proper and divinely authorized matching of capabilities and experience to the eternally beneficial leadership requirements of the church of the Lord Jesus Christ. The behavior and character traits thus listed will be continually exemplified by an elder.

The Work of Elders as Scripturally Defined by Listed Tasks

There are a number of references in the New Testament in which specific tasks are assigned to elders or in which there are examples of work being done by elders. These tasks without exception include a spiritual imperative. In some cases, there is also a physical or personal imperative. Let us examine these tasks in somewhat of a logical sequence:

1. The elders *represent* a local congregation (Acts 11:27-30). When famine relief was sent to the brethren dwelling in Judea, it was sent "to the elders" by the hands of Barnabas and Saul. Every organization is legitimately represented by its leadership, and the local church is no exception.

2. The elders *rule* over the local congregation (1 Tim. 5:17-18). The word from which "rule" is translated means literally "to stand before," in effect signifying leadership, tending to a group with care and diligence. They do

The Work of Elders

not serve as lords or masters, but rather they lead by example (1 Pet 5:3) The level of service incorporated in the rule of elders and the respect given to them are such that compensation or salary may be scripturally provided an elder by the congregation (1 Tim. 5:18).

3. The elders *take heed* over the local flock (Acts 20:28). The word literally means "to pay attention." The activities of elders are misplaced if they make no effort to know the members, to recognize their spiritual condition, and to regard the brethren with honor.

4. The elders *shepherd, tend, and feed* the local flock (Acts 20:28; 1 Pet. 5:2). The diet of spiritual food for the congregation is the responsibility of the elders, not the evangelist. The evangelist properly responds to the wishes and imperatives of the elders, and serves the spiritual food from time to time from the pulpit. The elders do not limit the preaching of the Gospel. They encourage the evangelist to preach the "whole counsel of God." The evangelist is then properly subject to the elders, as are all of the members of the congregation. We are reminded often of the word pictures about a shepherd feeding and tending his flock of sheep. The safety and well-being of the flock are the responsibility of the shepherd. He takes care of their every need. The spiritual responsibilities of elders are similar.

5. The elders *equip the saints spiritually* (Eph. 4:11-15). The responsibility to equip the saints defines the spiritual purpose of tending and feeding the flock. The action of equipping the saints properly is to prepare the members for the work of ministry, to edify the body of Christ, to further unity, to cause the members to develop in knowledge, to help the members to mature, and to help the members be able to resist Satan and his deceits. These things are done so that all may grow up in all things into Christ. No task of the elders is more important.

6. The elders *watch for the souls of the members* (Heb. 13:17; Acts 20:31). The word used in the Greek text in Acts 20:31 suggests vigilance, such as in keeping awake, especially spiritually. The word used in Hebrews 13:17 implies that the watchfulness requires going without sleep while watching those who may be intent upon doing something. The watchfulness may require preventing someone from falling while exposed to danger. As a result of watching so intently, it is obvious that the elder will be required to point out and draw lines of behavioral limits where the weak or erring member cannot or will not draw those lines. Too often elders yield to the temptation to do or say nothing or to look the other way while errant

behavior becomes obvious. While counseling about behavioral questions, some tend to erase lines of distinction, instead of reinforcing those lines. Elders must draw lines and define standards of behavior. They should use more chalk and less eraser!

7. The elders *admonish and warn the unruly* (1 Thess. 5:12-14). The same Greek word, *nouthesia,* is translated both "admonish" and "warn" in this passage. It means "to put in mind" as in training by word, whether in encouragement or in reproof and correction. A different Greek word is used when admonition involves encouraging the level of personal self-discipline wherein someone properly or repetitively performs some action. Since the word in the passage noted is "to put in mind," there is no question about the requirement for a deep love and understanding of the Scriptures on the part of the elder.

8. The elders must *rebuke those who are unruly or insubordinate* (Tit. 1:9-13). There are those who reject the idea of being in subjection to divinely-constituted leadership. The elder must be able to handle the Scriptures in such a way as to teach against the practices of the unruly. He must also possess some amount of skill to be able to "stop the mouths" of those who subvert. The scripture is not teaching physical restraint of the gainsayers. Rather, the proper application of the scripture and the arming of the brethren with truth will cause the unruly to have no audience. Their mouths are effectively stopped.

9. The elders must *support the weak* (Acts 20:35). There is by implication a necessity for the elders to judge the spiritual maturity of the members. That is part of taking heed to the flock. Support of the weak requires strengthening where strength is wanting. It requires edification where and when knowledge is lacking. Churches will always have among their members some who are weak. Those weak ones are not to be overlooked, rather they are to be encouraged as a work in progress.

10. The elders must *take heed to themselves* (Acts 20:28). No one in a position of leadership should ever be so bold as to believe that he is above being tempted or above falling. We read in 1 Timothy 5:19-20 the procedure given for receiving an accusation against an elder on the strength of two or three witnesses. Elders are encouraged to evaluate themselves continually in light of the Scriptures, addressing both their spirituality and their qualifications for service as an elder. Take continual heed to study, to purity of heart, and to absence of pride. Take heed to prevent lording it over the

The Work of Elders

members (1 Pet. 5:3). Take heed to the authority of the Scriptures. And take heed to the diet being provided to the members.

Other Work of Elders That May Be Necessarily Inferred

1. The elder is administering for an absolute monarch, Jehovah God, whom he serves as a steward (Tit. 1:7). Therefore, the elder does not legislate. The pattern for the church has once for all time been set, and the Word is complete (Jude 3).

2. The elder must make hard decisions, as part of the task of leading, tending, feeding, and shepherding. Some decisions will not be received well by some of the members.

3. The elder must act out of conviction, without indecision, holding fast the faithful word (Tit. 1:9). There is no room for action based on what sounds good, or wherein someone says, "I think it is all right." The imperative is "Thus saith the Lord!" Adherence to this simple precept would have prevented much of the division that has troubled churches in every age and in every place. More recently, the incorporation of entertainment and the social gospel into the work of the church, the use of the "fellowship hall," the support of human institutions, and all other departures from the divine pattern, are examples in which the leadership has failed to abide by the scriptural instruction to hold fast the faithful word. Failing to abide within the doctrine of Christ places one outside of the doctrine of Christ (2 John 9).

4. The elder must realize that, by being "apt to teach," he will be in demand by members who wish to increase their own knowledge about biblical subjects and difficult matters. He may even be in demand by other congregations, if there is the perception that he may be especially well informed on a specific biblical subject.

5. The elder must exhibit a posture of even-handedness, showing that he has a fixed sense of direction. He must not show a posture of being a men-pleaser. Serving in the eldership is *not* the result of a popularity contest. The elder is not competing for a temporal reward.

6. The elder will be an exemplary student of the Bible, as well as an example of the best personal behavior (1 Pet. 5:3). The office of elder is the highest spiritual office on earth. There is a high standard of conduct to be expected of someone who serves as an elder.

7. The elder must respond speedily to heresy, error, and gainsaying (Tit.

1:11-13). To fail to respond speedily is to fail to stop the mouths of the unruly. In order to respond speedily one must be available to the work at hand. A pattern of personal obligations which severely limits time available for spiritual endeavors is counterproductive.

8. The elder will be required to skillfully show the ultimate consequences of a member taking a path of error. He will often need to extend false arguments to their conclusion. This kind of activity is included in watching for the souls of the members (Heb. 13:17). It is a required manifestation of wisdom.

9. The elder must be available to the members (James 5:14). The passage specifically refers to one who is sick and asks for the presence and/or assistance of the elders.

10. The elder must realize, as part of the leadership, that he is ultimately responsible for the financial affairs of the congregation as well as the spiritual affairs. Business experience is valuable in that regard. Transparency is required. Note that the local church is not a business, and must not be "in business," but it operates much like a business, with a specific leadership structure and a recognized chain of authority.

11. The elder must motivate the members by teaching and by example, while equipping all for the ministry (Eph. 4:11). He must always be searching for ways to encourage the members to further self-improvement.

12. The elders as a group must properly direct the deacons. The level of service of the deacons requires that a sense of direction and instruction be given to them. We may necessarily infer that in the absence of elders to direct the deacons, there can be no deacons in office. There is a tendency among small institutional churches to empower men with the title of deacon while no elders are in office.

13. The elder must be an example of sacrifice (Acts 20:35). Paul used himself as an example of sacrifice, and then said that it is "more blessed to give than to receive."

14. An elder must admit his mistakes. He must know how to repent, apologize, and make amends for his mis-steps.

15. An elder must be an example of patience, but not to the extent that his patience is judged as a softness on correcting error.

16. The elders are responsible for the worship services being conducted

decently and in order (I Cor 14:40). Elders should always be prepared to prevent anything that causes a loss of decorum in the worship, such as uncontrolled emotional outbursts, irreverent activities, disruptions, improper public accusations given by the disgruntled or the heretic, or public teaching of error. Terminating a worship service may be necessary. In addition to being a forum for teaching and serving, the worship services are the repetitive, obvious testimony to the community about our reverence for God and our honor for His Son. Leadership over a congregation requires establishing order and maintaining a level of control over the content and spirit of the worship services. The control of the worship can be appropriately delegated, but never relinquished. All things are to be done for edification (1 Cor 14:26).

Failures of Leadership by Elders Concerning Preachers

A very grave challenge will be present in local congregations where elders place themselves subservient to the evangelist. Doing so is contrary to the scriptural pattern which places the elders in charge of feeding the flock. Some evangelists, unfortunately, will not accept the task of preaching for a congregation where the elders truly discharge their responsibilities to tend and feed the flock. Those evangelists wish instead to be in total charge of the preaching program. By thus subverting the divine order, churches create what one departed preacher once called the "preacher-pastor system." Such a system displays a denominational bent, and it overturns the pattern of the New Testament.

In some congregations, the elders create an improper work relationship with the local evangelist. He is not to be considered a hireling, an employee whose every activity is defined, monitored, and metered. He is instead to be considered a professional who performs his functions to the best of his ability, within comfortable guidelines, always realizing that he will himself be judged by how he discharges his responsibilities as the evangelist. In addition, the elders should refrain from enforcing a vow of poverty on gospel preachers. The object of the church is to save souls. The method the Holy Spirit chose to save souls is by preaching. Elders must in every way steadfastly encourage the preaching of the gospel. Proper and generous salary consideration goes a long way toward encouraging the preaching of the Gospel.

In supporting preaching, the elders must know the preacher well. Sometimes there are scoundrels, masquerading as preachers, who receive regular or temporary support from churches. They exist not only in foreign lands.

Good stewardship demands that the elders know where and how the funds of the Lord are being used. There may be a need to send messengers—or to go personally—to inquire as to the nature of the work being performed by a preacher who is being financially supported in another place. Sometimes it is necessary to refuse to advertise the presence of a known false teacher conducting a gospel meeting nearby. The elders must give account!

Failures of Leadership by Elders Concerning Other Members

In addition to those things already enumerated, we note a few additional examples:

- Elders fail to lead when they fail to delegate. Two reasons are apparent: First, the Scripture gives example as to how the elders are to handle the spiritual matters, while others, specifically the deacons, are to "serve tables." Second, the opportunity for others to grow into a higher level of service is limited if there is no delegation of responsibilities.

- Elders also fail when they try to micromanage. Elders should not attempt to determine or dictate every purchase down to the brand of paper clips or the kind of paper towels. Delegate the lesser matters.

- Elders fail their members when they "say but do not do." Good leaders in any organization never ask of the members that which the leaders would not do themselves. The elders must be the examples.

- Elders fail their members when they do not maintain a familiarity with the diet of spiritual food given to the members in the Bible classes. Leadership in the local congregation requires looking at the whole picture, to see that the saints are properly equipped. Planning is required.

- Elders fail their members if they change their standards for making decisions when a hard decision must be made about members of their own families. The reliance upon a plurality of elders is one protection against that failure. Truth must rule: blood is not thicker than spirit.

- Elders fail their members when they become parochial. When someone fails to recognize that there are other avenues of scriptural service beyond what is familiar, or that there are other names by which scriptural things may be called, or that there are other ways of doing things acceptably and with authority, that person is considered parochial in his outlook. Elders should be widely read, willing to listen to other points of view, and always reconciling their own personal ideas and thoughts to the truth of the Scripture. The Scripture is not to be twisted to match a personal point of view or a personal, limited level of understanding.

- Elders fail their members when they tolerate error, rather than handle it promptly. "A little leaven leavens the whole lump" (Gal. 5:9). Error that is tolerated will fester and destroy.

- Elders fail their members when they are not open about the activities of the congregation. Certainly there are some items of personal counseling and discipline done by the elders which should remain private. But when the congregation is not made aware of actions taken, purchases made, preachers supported, or needs that appear, the perception of being less than transparent is easily generated.

Conclusion

God's plan for man and for the local church includes leadership vested in men called elders. The elders are restricted to leading the saints "among which the Holy Spirit has made you overseers" (Acts 20:28).

All Christian men should engage in a lifelong preparation to serve in this most noble and necessary endeavor. All Christian women should strongly encourage their husbands in a way that the husbands will be prepared to eagerly and willingly accept those reins of leadership when appropriate.

There is no doubt that serving as an elder brings pain and distress at times. There are also rewards now and in the life to come that result from service as an elder.

Properly constituted leadership, faithfully discharging its scriptural obligations, is a great comfort to the souls of the brethren. Such leadership gives spiritual direction to the local church and maintains its identity. The unity of the believers is preserved and souls will be saved.

References Cited

Bible. All references are from the NKJV.

West, Earle H. "A Talk to New Elders," *Preceptor,* 58:10 (October 2009): 7-8.

Training Men to Serve

Gary Watt

(Note: all Scripture references herein are from the New King James translation.)

For a qualified Christian man who so desires, serving as an elder (bishop) in a local church of our Lord is a good work (1 Tim. 3:1). The instruction to Titus in 1:5 of Paul's letter confirms that our Lord wants elders appointed in every church and it should, therefore, be the goal of every congregation to create and sustain such an eldership. All congregations, with or without an eldership, should create a nurturing environment that both encourages qualified men to serve as elders, as well as prepares young men to become future elders.

With that basis, the scriptural qualifications of an elder imply that

---

Gary Watt was born in Austin, TX in 1947 and remained there through graduation in 1970 from the University of Texas at Austin with a degree in mechanical engineering. Early in his college years, he met Joan Willis, a Christian from Houston, TX, and they married in 1970. Due mainly to the example and influence of his wife, Gary obeyed the gospel at the Norhill church of Christ in Houston in 1974. Gary's father-in-law, the late Dan Willis, served as his elder role model during his many years of service to the Norhill congregation. As a result of numerous military and career transfers over the years, Gary and Joan have worshipped with churches in Aurora, CO; Bristol, England; Houston, TX; and the Chicago, IL area. Gary served as a deacon at the Kleinwood congregation in the Houston area until 1998 and, since 2001, serves as one of five elders at the Downers Grove church of Christ in Downers Grove, IL. Both Gary and Joan continue to teach Bible classes of various age groups. They are the parents of two sons: Dan Watt, his wife, Summer Fleener Watt, and son, Silas, live in Columbia, MO; Jason Watt and his wife, Katy Brewer Watt, live in Spokane, WA. Their sons and daughters-in-law are active Christians in their local congregations. Gary is a sales and marketing executive in Oak Brook, IL and Joan is a former high school mathematics teacher and current math tutor.

training, either formal, informal, or both, will assist men in meeting those qualifications (1 Tim. 3:2-7; Tit. 1:6-9). I submit that the wisdom of God is shown in Paul's inspired word to Timothy that a man should first desire the position of an elder (1 Tim. 3:1), for it's that desire that helps create a "trainable" heart.

Consider the following opportunities for training men to serve:

1. A student of God's Word. An elder must be able to "hold fast the faithful word as he has been taught" (Tit. 1:9). How is that possible without training?

Preferably it begins at an early age. I suggest that it begins in the home as I'm reminded of Timothy's early exposure to God's Word from his mother Eunice and grandmother Lois (2 Tim. 1:5). Christian parents and grandparents providing homes where the Bible is taught regularly is a solid foundation from which to encourage and prepare young men to obey the gospel, as well as become future elders. Supplementing, rather than replacing, this home teaching of the Bible, congregations must have a thorough and enriching Bible class program that progressively exposes students to greater understanding and application of Scripture in their lives. Christian youth devotionals and summer camps are other opportunities for students to grow in their knowledge and understanding of the Bible. Without this early, consistent, repetitive foundation from his youth, I suggest that it will be more challenging for a man to achieve the "behavioral" qualifications of an elder – i.e., blameless, husband of one wife, holy, etc.

However, some men who eventually serve as elders, like myself, become Christians as adults. Compared to those who grew up in Christian homes and obeyed the gospel at an earlier age, these adult men may have some catching up to do. Although not a necessity, the living example and spiritual encouragement of a Christian wife, perhaps also the very person who converted him, is a tremendous asset to a potential elder starting his preparation later in life. Not only did I benefit early on from such a blessed spouse, but I also learned much from the example, instruction, and mentoring of her father, a long serving elder of the local congregation where I was baptized. I recognize that all potential elders do not have spouses who were Christians from a young age or other relatives who served as elders, but all have a Bible and the opportunity to study.

As I referred to earlier, the thorough and enriching Bible class program of a local congregation is also critically important in preparing adult men to become elders. Classes should challenge adults personally to study God's Word and share their thoughts and questions with fellow Christians under the guidance of experienced teachers. The goal of the classes should always be to increase the knowledge and understanding of the Bible for all students while also making it relevant to the world in which Christians live. Evangelists and elders should be watchful for men capable of becoming future elders and afford them additional opportunities for Bible study – including one-on-one. While beneficial to all Christians, potential elders should particularly be encouraged to supplement their home and class study of God's Word by participating in gospel meetings, Scripture-based lectureships, Bible studies with non-Christians, and similar opportunities.

As a student of God's Word, an elder never stops training.

2. The heart of a servant. Peter describes elders as *"serving* as overseers" (1 Pet. 5:2). As "a fellow elder" (1 Pet. 5:1), Peter further indicates how elders (overseers) serve. He describes them doing so "willingly" (v. 2), "eagerly" (v. 2), and as "examples to the flock" (v. 3). Though not as an elder, Paul referred to himself as a servant to Titus (1:1) and to the church in Corinth (1 Cor. 9:19). He implied the same to Timothy (2 Tim. 2:24) by describing a servant of the Lord as "gentle" (v. 24), "patient" (v. 24), and showing "humility" (v. 25). I believe these apply to all servants of the Lord, including elders.

Although the first century definition of a servant was more aligned to a slave or bondservant, the modern definition is not dissimilar – one who serves another. In the context of the church, a servant of the Lord has always been one who does His will by putting the needs of others ahead of his own. It is this very "heart of a servant" that needs to be developed as early as possible in those who may become elders. In my opinion, it is a significant part of what leads one to desire the position of an elder.

Developing the "heart of a servant" should be an outgrowth of Bible study and practical application, both at home and at church. The numerous Bible examples of people, from slaves to kings, who were faithful servants of the Lord form the basis of instilling the concept of personal service to our Lord as well as to fellow men. For young children, Christian parents should exemplify this in their daily actions, explaining why they're doing so and allowing the children to participate as well. Similarly, the church should create age appropriate and scriptural opportunities for youth to provide service.

Training Men to Serve

Churches should encourage Christians of all ages to be active in service to the Lord. Bible classes and sermons should periodically emphasize the importance of such service. Existing elderships should personally encourage members to use their talents in service to the congregation and in seeking the lost. All Christian men should be encouraged to participate in the worship roles of the church. Training should be provided as needed to develop the skills helpful for those roles. Men's training classes are one proven method of developing the worship leadership skills of Christian men.

As potential elders are identified, they should particularly be given a variety of service opportunities, under the guidance of existing elders, deacons or more experienced servants. Such opportunities offer the congregation time to observe a potential elder, his emotional and spiritual maturity, and how he handles responsibility while displaying leadership, decisiveness, and interpersonal skills. Elders are admonished not to abuse their authority by being "lords over those entrusted to you" (1 Pet. 5:3). Such roles could include chairing a group of members tasked with a specific project by the elders, or, if scripturally qualified, serving as a deacon for a specific need of the congregation. In the absence of an eldership, this could include chairing men's business meetings.

Existing elders, the evangelist, and members should give personal encouragement and support to these men. On a personal basis, I can recall several occasions over the years when an evangelist or elder took me aside to encourage me to greater service to the Lord. When this is done correctly, it is very uplifting.

A concurrent training program of consistent Bible study coupled with practical "on the job" applications of increasing responsibility often results in potential elders becoming more evident to the congregation. I believe the ultimate success of such training is not simply their performance of assigned responsibilities but rather their simultaneous demonstration of the attributes noted by Peter and Paul – thus confirming their "heart of a servant."

3. *Able to teach.* An elder must be "able to teach" (1 Tim. 3:2). To me, this is a natural combination of the knowledge of God's Word and the "heart of a servant." It implies not only an ability, but also a willingness to teach God's Word. While secular training is available to develop and improve general teaching skills as well as effectively utilize various teaching aids, I believe that the most beneficial teacher training for a potential elder is the "on the job" variety.

Again, if a congregation has that nurturing environment referred to earlier, teaching opportunities will be available for potential elders to learn and develop their skills. Congregations always need Bible class teachers and should therefore have a plan for training and developing new teachers. Co-teaching a Bible class with an evangelist or experienced teacher is often an excellent way for a new teacher to refine presentation skills and gain self-confidence.

The same is true in assisting an evangelist, elder, or other experienced Christian in Bible studies with non-Christians. The more intimate environment of a personal Bible study can require additional skills beyond the classroom setting. Thorough lesson preparation, pre-class role playing with the more experienced teacher, a clear division of teaching responsibilities, and a full understanding of the student's religious background provide a useful learning experience for the developing teacher.

Whether in a classroom setting or a personal Bible study, the new teacher's experienced partner should mentor him by providing adequate teaching time as well as constructive and encouraging comments regarding his performance. And, as with most things in life, practice makes perfect. Congregations should, therefore, provide developing teachers with plenty of opportunities to use their skills. Especially for the potential elder, teaching opportunities should be offered frequently enough that his skills are honed rather than allowed to lapse.

4. Hospitable. An elder must be "hospitable" (1 Tim. 3:2). Some might not think this is a trainable qualification, but I disagree.

In this context, it is generally agreed that the word means "fond of guests or given to hospitality." This, too, can be introduced early in the life of a potential elder if he grows up in a home where guests are welcome and he observes the hospitality offered by his family. Even more so if he interacts with the guests on those occasions and grows comfortable with extending the friendship of the home.

As a potential elder, he will depend upon the support and cooperation of his wife in his achieving this qualification. It is beneficial if she had a similar home experience in her youth. Even if that's not the case for one or both, they will need to adopt and practice this attribute, if he's to be qualified to serve. A joint study of God's Word regarding hospitality and examples thereof will establish a basis from which to grow together. "On the job" training can begin as simply as jointly hosting guests with more experienced Christians. That can progress to the potential elder and his wife hosting guests to hospitality outside their home. Once they become more comfortable with the process, hospitality can be offered in the more relaxed and welcoming environment of the home.

I believe the key to success is practice and avoiding the excuses commonly given as reasons for not offering hospitality – too busy, house too small, can't afford it, uncomfortable with strangers, etc. Hospitality is the act of offering kindness to guests, not how much money is spent or the lavishness of the surroundings. I believe the reluctance to offer hospitality is a growing problem among Christians today, as some apparently believe it is solely the responsibility of the elders, evangelist, or fellow members, as opposed to all Christians.

I think we again see the wisdom of God's Word in this qualification when combined with the admonition for elders to be "examples to the flock" (1 Pet. 5:3).

5. *Shepherding the flock.* An elder's first priority is identifying and meeting the spiritual needs of his congregation.

This spiritual relationship follows the example our Lord made of Himself to His followers when He said, "I am the good shepherd. The good shepherd gives His life for the sheep" (John 10:11). Near the end of his work, the Hebrew writer refers to our Lord as "that great Shepherd of the sheep" (Heb. 13:20).

Peter's clear exhortation to his fellow elders was to "shepherd the flock of God which is among you" (1 Pet. 5:2). In his meeting at Miletus with the elders of the Ephesian church, Paul said, "Therefore take heed to yourselves and to all the flock, among which the Holy Spirit has made you overseers, to shepherd the church of God which He purchased with His own blood" (Acts 20:28). Following our Lord's example, Peter and Paul are clearly drawing the analogy of an elder's relationship to his congregation to a shepherd's relationship to his flock. It was a practical analogy to which the people of the first century could clearly relate.

Although today we do not see in our country as many secular shepherds working their flocks of sheep in the fields, we know from history the primary duties of a shepherd to his flock – guide, protect, feed, nurture, and sacrifice. Such is the spiritual work of an elder with his congregation. If an elder has been well trained as a student of God's Word and is able to teach, then he is better prepared to guide his congregation while being ever vigilant and protecting them from false teachers, spiritual error, and apostasy. In addition, if he has developed the heart of a servant and is hospitable, he is better prepared to "feed" his congregation God's Word, nurture their ongoing spiritual development as fellow brethren in Christ, and be willing to sacrifice his personal time and goods for the greater needs of his congregation.

A very important part of a future elder's preparation is the emphasis to not lose sight of this highest of priorities. Unfortunately and on too many occasions, elders are distracted with the fiscal needs of the congregation and time is robbed from their all-important role of shepherds. Often, I fear, congregations are unable or unwilling to appoint more than the minimum two elders needed to satisfy the scriptural requirement. As well, there may not be enough men qualified or willing to serve as deacons. Or, worse still, deacons fail to perform their assigned tasks. When these situations occur, the fiscal burden often reverts to the elders to perform. And the result is an opportunity for an "unequal yoke" between spiritual and fiscal responsibilities. This is a dangerous situation as distraction can allow error to creep into the congregation without prevention or early detection.

To me, the Hebrew writer underscored the sobering importance of the elders' role as shepherds when he said, "they watch out for your souls, as those who must give account" (Heb. 13:17).

In summary, I suggest that effective elders are rarely created by sheer luck of circumstance. Rather, they are trained over a period of years, formally and informally. Congregations should always strive to fulfill the requirement of an eldership and, therefore, be continually training men to serve. Fulfillment of this goal will do much to avoid "A Crisis in Leadership" in our Lord's church.

The Non-Family Qualifications of Elders

Bobby Schrimsher

For most of my years of preaching I have labored with congregations without elders. Recently, I moved to work with a congregation that has elders. This has caused me to appreciate more deeply God's plan for the church to be organized with elders and deacons. God saw fit that qualified men should "shepherd the flock of God among them" (Acts 20:7). God gave us the pattern for a scripturally organized church: *"Paul and Timothy, bondservants of Jesus Christ, To all the saints in Christ Jesus who are in Philippi, with the bishops and deacons"* (Phil. 1:1). This leads us to the topic of this lecture. My task is to discuss the "non-family" qualifications of the men who are appointed to serve as elders. After examining these qualifications, we will be better able to appreciate the kind of men who should be occupying this very special office in the Lord's church. It is our hope and prayer as well that this understanding will cause men to prepare themselves for the eldership. It is our hope that men will step to the front

---

Bobby W. Schrimsher, Jr. was born in Lakeland, FL on April 3, 1960. He and his wife Dianna have two children: Wayne and Ashley (FC and WKU). Bobby received his formal education at Florida College (A.A. 1995; Certificate of Achievement in Bible 1997; B.A. in Biblical Studies 1997) and Johnson Bible College (Graduate work 1995-1997). He began preaching the gospel in Jacksonville, FL where he worked with the Orange Park church (1988-90). He has also worked with the church in Ft. Meade, FL (1990-2000); the Westview church in Austintown, OH (2000-2008); and the Edgewood church in Lakeland, FL (2008-present). He spent six week in South Africa in 2007 doing evangelistic work and hopes to return again this summer. For the past eight years he has worked with Camp N.O.A.H in Toledo, OH. Bobby has written several articles for various brotherhood papers and spoke on the Florida College Lectures in 2009.

when called upon to fill the office. This is not something that can wait. Men must be preparing themselves now. Now let us look at the qualifications with a view toward preparation for service.

The "Non-Family" Qualifications

1. A man (1 Tim. 3:1; Tit. 1:6). While some would debate whether this is a qualification to be listed, it is important to deal with this issue. This is especially true in light of the growing movement toward women occupying pulpits and offices in denominational organizations. We might think that is something with reference to which we don't need to concern ourselves. After all, the Lord's church would never digress into such error! Or, would it? Those of us who are old enough to remember have seen many things happening in the Lord's church that we never would have dreamed possible. We have watched those who are of the Restoration Heritage go further and further into apostasy. God's people are not that far behind in embracing worldliness and error.

The Greek phrase used here is *ei tis*. The first part of the phrase *ei* is a conjunction while the second part *tis* means "some one, a certain one" (Vine, 389). Vine goes on to say that it is rendered "a man" or "a certain man." While Paul does not use the Greek word for man, it is apparent that a man is intended. If we look at the family qualifications (covered in another lecture), we see the requirement that the elder be the husband of one wife. This rules out women because women do not marry other women according to God's plan.

2. Desire the office (1 Tim. 3:1). Once again, some would not list this as a qualification. It is inconceivable to think that a man could be forced into taking this office in light of the meaning of the word used by Paul. The word *oregetai* is from the word *orego* which Thayer says means "to stretch one's self out in order to touch or grasp something, to reach after or desire something" (452). Vine says that it "is used only in the middle voice, signifying the mental effort of stretching oneself out for a thing, or longing after it, with stress upon the object desired" (162).

Let us think a little more about the idea of desiring the office of bishop. Suppose that a man is somehow coerced into serving as an elder. Many have probably known men who had no desire to serve but felt compelled because of the need of the congregation. What attitude would he have in the performing of his duties? Would he resent every time he was called upon to perform some duty of shepherding?

And yet, we must also teach men to develop an attitude of service that will be ready when called upon. Men must be trained to think in terms of readiness to serve when asked or called upon. Young Christian men need to have impressed upon them the need for being prepared to serve. They need to be taught to prepare themselves and to choose a mate who will help them be ready when God needs them.

Perhaps the shortage of qualified men to serve as elders would not exist if attitudes were different.

3. Blameless (1 Tim. 3:2; Tit. 1:6). This qualification is found in both 1 Timothy and Titus. Although they come from different Greek words, their meaning is almost the same and is often translated "blameless" in both texts. Another translation is "above reproach" (NIV, ESV, *et al*).

The Greek word *anepileptos* is found in 1 Timothy 3:2 and means "not apprehended, that cannot be laid hold of; hence that cannot be reprehended, not open to censure, irreproachable" (Thayer, 44).

The other Greek word is *anegkletos* is found in Titus 1:6 (and also in 1 Timothy 3:10 of deacons) which means "that cannot be called into account, unreproachable, unaccused, blameless" (Thayer, 44).

Notice what Phillips says about these two words: "In Timothy the word appears to mean that the person has lived so that men *will not* accuse him of evil, while in Titus the word appears to mean that the person has so lived that men *can not* accuse him of evil" (94).

It must be understood that, while these men are to be blameless, it does not mean that they can attain absolute perfection. No one can meet a qualification of perfection. The meaning of this qualification then seems best summed up in Thayer's definition for *anegkletos:* "there is nothing that can be called into account." There is nothing on the balance sheet that is owed by this man. He is irreproachable. The same is required of all Christians. We are to "become blameless" (Phil. 2:15).

4. Temperate (1 Tim. 3:2; Tit. 1:8) {Vigilant (1 Tim. 3:2)} {not self willed, not quick tempered, self-controlled (Titus)}. Thayer tells us that this word can mean "sober, temperate, abstaining from wine, either entirely or at least from its immoderate sense" (425).

As seen above, the word *nephaleon* can be translated by three words (temperate, vigilant, sober) and all would be correct. It can also include some of the requirements that we see in Titus. However, there seems to be a different nuance of meaning for these words. Since the Holy Spirit saw fit to use *sophron* next in order in the requirements, it seems that He intended a different shade of meaning between these words.

Consider the definitions given by Webster:

> **Temperate** – moderate in the indulgence of the appetites; moderate in one's actions, speech, etc.; characterized by moderation (Webster does include moderation in the use of alcohol here, 1877).
>
> **Vigilant** – watchful; characterized by vigilance; especially, alert to danger (2038).
>
> **Sober** – temperate in the use of alcoholic liquor (1722).

From the examination of these definitions it would seem that the quality suggested here by the word *nephaleon* is that of moderation in all things. One who has this qualification is not going to go off in a fit of rage and let his speech be improper. And, he will be one who models this behavior before the congregation over which he is a shepherd.

As noted above, this requirement encompasses some of the requirements found in Titus. Let us look briefly at those requirements now.

a. Not self-willed. This is the word *me authade*. Vine tells us that this is "one who, dominated by self-interest, and inconsiderate of others, arrogantly asserts his own will" (559). It is not difficult to see how this dovetails with the idea of being temperate. A man who would be a bishop in the Lord's church cannot place his own interests above that of the congregation. In matters of doctrine, there is no room for compromise. But in matters of opinion, he may have to put his feelings aside. Thus the bishop takes into consideration the sheep in his flock.

Consider the following scenario: A congregation, overseen by elders is seeking a new minister. One elder favors a certain candidate for the position. Among the flock are those who have some problem with the man. The other elders do not think this man to be the best candidate. If the elder who favors the man runs rough-shod over the flock and the other elders, imposing his will, he is self-willed and not fit to serve as an elder.

b. Not quick tempered. The word here is *me orgilon*. Thayer says it is one "prone to anger" (452). The word is sometimes translated "not passionate." Certainly there will be times when shepherds are taxed to the fullest measure of endurance while keeping watch over the flock. Sheep are going to do things that will cause elders to need a lot of patience. A man who is prone to anger, or quick tempered, may not be temperate in his speech or actions toward that member of the church.

Again, consider a scenario. One of the sheep has a complaint at every service. Something is always wrong. They repeatedly berate one elder in particular about this issue until that elder cannot bear up any more. The elder snaps back in anger at the member. We might say we understand that everyone reaches a boiling point and not even elders can endure forever these kinds of things. But what does that say of his character? Now suppose that the same situation occurs, except that the elder snaps the head off of the member every time he makes a complaint. Is not the elder "quick tempered"? The elders must be able to deal patiently with the flock and endure many a trying moment as they do the work of shepherding.

c. Self-control. The final phrase in Titus that is included in the requirement to be temperate is **self-controlled.** Vine tells us that *enkrates* is akin to *enkrateia,* which is from *kratos* which means "strength" (620). This word is translated as "temperance" or "self-control."

If we think in terms of the elder being temperate and include within that the idea of self-control, we see a picture of a man who does not give in to his passions, his own self will or his anger. He has the strength of character to be in control of all these things. This makes him temperate. And again, as with many of the requirements for elders, temperance is also required of all Christians (1 Pet. 5:8; 2 Pet. 1:6).

5. Sober-minded (1 Tim. 3:2; Tit. 1:8). To be sober-minded is included in the idea of being temperate as seen above. But the word used here is *sophron* not *nephaleon.* As stated in the previous section, it seems that the Holy Spirit intends us to understand the slight difference in the two words.

The word *sophron* as defined by Vine means "to be of sound mind" (*sozo,* "to save," *phren,* "the mind"); hence, "self-controlled, soberminded" (583). The word can also be translated as "discreet" which may help us to better understand the meaning of *sophron.* Thayer tells us this is one who is "of sound mind, sane, in one's senses" (613).

This tells us that there is more involved than just being free of the influence of alcohol. The man who serves as a bishop must not be influenced by his own instability. He must have a good mind and be faithful in executing the duties charged to all elders. This, in part, comes through experience. Whereas a younger man, a more immature man, a novice might be swayed into false doctrine, the man who is sober-minded can be counted on to make good decisions. Interestingly, all Christians are charged with "living soberly" (Tit. 2:12).

6. Good behavior (*kosmion*, 1 Tim. 3:2). The idea conveyed in this requirement is of a man who leads a well ordered life. The same word is used in1 Timothy 2:9 where Paul instructs the women to adorn themselves properly (orderly). The implication for the elder is that his life is to be orderly as well. Thayer tells us that this word means "well arranged, seemly, modest: of a man living with decorum, a well ordered life" (356). The bishop's life must be an example, not only in spiritual matters, but in all phases of his life. His behavior must be good in his place of employment, in his recreation—in fact, in all areas of his life. He must also dress and talk in such a way as to be an example to the flock. Elders should set the example for others to follow in these areas. Another matter for the elder to lead in is his speech. It must fall into line with what is considered good behavior. His speech must not be coarse or of such a nature that people are offended. If he is dealing with people in the world, they must be able to see his conduct as being good. If dealing with the sheep, he must avoid causing harm with his speech. There is no more powerful example and influence for the Lord's church than elders and Christians who are behaving well.

7. Lover of what is good (Tit. 1:8). The word used here is *philagathon*. Vine says it means "loving that which is good" (383). This word is a compound of *phileo*, "to love" and *agathos*, "good." This depicts an elder who loves what is good. The opposite of this word is found in 2 Timothy 3:3 where Paul speaks of men as "despisers of good."

The King James Version and Young's Literal Translation render this as "lovers of good men." This conveys to us that the overseer must love, not only "good things," but "good people" as well. He should be instrumental in cultivating young men to develop their talents in the Lord so that they will be ready to serve at some future time. The elders must also love good people outside of the church. All of us have to deal with irascible people from time to time, but we should make good people our choice of friends in the world.

Christians in general are encouraged to meditate on things "of good

The Non-Family Qualifications of Elders

report" (Phil. 4:8). Far too often, we are guilty of embracing that which is not "of good report." We are not lovers of good things or people. We tend to be lured away by that which is not exactly fitting for children of God. Consider how easy it is to be taken in by coarse speech. We hear an off color joke and we secretly enjoy it and laugh inside. We tend to idolize those in the entertainment industry who are held up by society as good role models. Yet they are engaging in behavior that is not pleasing to the Lord. We should seek out those who are good and good things. These will influence us for good instead of compromising our values.

8. Hospitable (1 Tim. 3:2; Tit. 1:8). This requirement is found in both 1 Timothy and Titus. The Christian is enjoined to "be hospitable without grumbling" (1 Pet. 4:9). *Philoxenos* is a compound word. Once again we see *phileo,* "love," and we also have *xenos,* "hospitality shown to others." Thayer adds the idea of "generous to guests" (654) while Vine tells us it involves strangers (312). Taken together then, we would understand that the elder must be hospitable to those members in his flock and also to strangers.

As we seek to make application of this requirement for elders consider what Stahlin writes: "One of the most prominent features in the picture of early Christianity, which is so rich in good works, is undoubtedly its hospitality" (Kittel, V: 23). Add to that the admonitions given to us in Scripture about hospitality or entertaining: Romans 12:13 tells us to be "given to hospitality"; Hebrews 13:2 says that "some have unwittingly entertained angels"; and let us not forget Paul's instruction from Galatians 6:10 to "do good to all."

What does this mean for the elder? It means that he must be hospitable to strangers and friends as well. It also means that he must have the means and ability to do so. A most valuable asset to an elder in doing this will be his wife. While not trying to encroach on another lecture, let me just say that it will certainly be a challenge for a man serving as an elder to continue to be hospitable if he has been widowed. It is understandable that his character has already been proven and he has demonstrated that he possesses the requirements to be a shepherd. However, his ability in this and other areas is going to be greatly diminished and may perhaps disqualify him for the office.

9. Apt to teach (1 Tim. 3:2; Tit. 1:9). The word *didaktikos* is used in 1 Timothy 3:2 and also in 2 Timothy 2:24. Its basic meaning is "skillful in teaching" (Vine, 619). Rengstorf suggests that false (*pseudo*) teachers were creating difficulties that threatened the church. Thus it was necessary that a bishop be able to teach (Kittel, II:165). What a shame it is when the elders of a congregation have no more Bible knowledge than the average person in the pew. In fact, I have known some members who could put their elders to shame with their Bible knowledge. This ought not to be so.

I was taught that, to be good at preaching, one had to wear out the seat of his pants in studying. That advice has served me well through the years. My greatest fear has been not being prepared well enough for a Bible class or getting something wrong in a sermon. This need for being "apt to teach" is also especially important for elders. Sadly, congregations exist with elders who don't meet this qualification. Sometimes, the elders never do any public teaching. How does/did the congregation know of the man's abilities in the area? It has been espoused by some that an elder doesn't have to do any teaching; he just has to be able. This seems a bit ludicrous to this author. Why wouldn't he teach? Why wouldn't he use his God-given talents? Some have also argued that private teaching will suffice. This is certainly better than nothing, but again I wonder how the congregation will ever know of his ability to teach, if it is never demonstrated.

Phillips has this to say about elders and teaching, "The term 'shepherd' or 'pastor' indicates that the nature of an elder's work is to 'feed' or teach the gospel" (167). Brother Phillips goes on to suggest that the teaching may be either public or private, that an evangelist may be hired to assist with the teaching, and that the elders should be involved in the training of all teachers. This writer's opinion is that the teaching should be public. Brother Phillips does state, "There are times when only the eldership can be effective in admonishing and teaching some members who need correction" (168).

The requirement is stated this way in Titus 1:9, *"holding fast the faithful word as he has been taught, that he may be able, by sound doctrine, both to exhort and convict those who contradict."* Part of the teaching that an elder will have to do is to "exhort and convict those who contradict." The elder must be knowledgeable in "sound doctrine" so that he can be on guard for false teaching. This has been left to the preacher far too often and has had disastrous consequences in some cases. The beauty of God's plan for a plurality of elders is that the congregation is not relying on just one person to guard against error. Paul warned that the apostasy would come from within the eldership (Acts 20:29). A plurality of elders will not be as easily swayed into error as one man.

The Non-Family Qualifications of Elders 91

As young men prepare themselves to be elders one day, this is a requirement that needs much attention. Not just the young men but all Christians are to be able to teach and defend the truth (see 1 Pet. 3:15; 2 Tim. 2:2, 24).

10. Not given to wine (1 Tim. 3:3; Tit. 1:7). Ephesians 5:18 says, *"And do not be drunk with wine, in which is dissipation; but be filled with the Spirit."* As we consider this admonition to all Christians, we need to remember that an elder is to be an example to the flock. Phillips says, "We are aware that the Bible does not literally forbid the drinking of any intoxicating drink, but the principles of Christianity do forbid it" (262).

It would be a mistake to think that deacons might indulge a little in the drinking of intoxicating drink while elders are completely forbidden. What kind of example would they be to the flock? How will they "obtain for themselves a good standing?" (1 Tim. 3:13). Perhaps the strongest influence a Christian can have is his example. If elders (or Christians) conduct themselves in a way that is not setting a good example, how will they answer in the judgment? The abuse of alcohol can certainly lead one to be a stumbling block to other Christians, not to mention leading to bad behavior (brawling).

Notice now the meaning of the word *me paroinos*. This is an adjective composed of *para*, "beside," and *oinos*, "wine," describing one who stays near wine. If we consult Vine we learn that the word *paroinos* literally means "tarrying at wine" (77). When used with *me* it is negated. This word is also translated "brawler." Thayer tells us that its use in these two passages "give it the secondary sense, 'quarrelsome over wine'; hence, *brawling, abusive*" (490). Brawling or being abusive is a side effect of staying long beside the wine. This is certainly not an admirable quality for any Christian much less an elder.

11. Not violent (1 Tim. 3:3; Tit. 1:7). Thayer tells us that *plektes* means a, "bruiser, ready with a blow; a pugnacious, contentious, quarrelsome person" (516). As noted above, this is a reaction often seen in those who drink.

The apostle Paul says we are to "live peaceably with all men" (Rom. 12:18). If we, as Christians and elders, are going to be lights to this dark world, we must not be violent. If one serving as an elder is prone to resort to violence with those who disagree with him, he is not fit to serve. There will no doubt be times when elders disagree amongst themselves and with the members of the congregation. This can take the form of either physical or verbal abuse. Elders must be able to resolve differences with the same spirit manifested by Christ.

12. Not greedy for money (1 Tim. 3:3; Tit. 1:7; 1 Pet. 5:2), This quality is desired for elders and deacons (see 1 Tim. 3:8). Talking about this requirement for deacons, Kenyon says, "Money hungry individuals are not fit to be special servants in the Church of Christ" (468-469). The same is true of elders. Those who are possessed with a desire to make money will spend most, if not all, of their time trying to gain it. This leaves no time for the work of the elder. While honest work and earning an honest living are to be commended, this obsession with money can take a man away from his responsibilities in the church. Far too many men serve as elders or deacons who don't have the proper time for doing the work. They are so busy with the cares of this world and making money that they neglect the job in the Lord's church to which they have been appointed.

The Greek word here is *aischrokerdes*. It simply means "greedy of base gains" (Thayer 384). We would all do well to remember Paul's warning: *"For the love of money is a root of all kinds of evil, for which some have strayed from the faith in their greediness, and pierced themselves through with many sorrows"* (1 Tim. 6:10).

13. Gentle (patient) (1 Tim. 3:3). Once again we should be aware that this is a requirement for all Christians. Many of the requirements for elders are also given for Christians. Paul admonishes "gentleness" for all Christians (Phil. 4:5) and that servants must be "gentle to all" (2 Tim. 2:24). Some versions use "patient" to translate this word.

Preisker reminds us that a form of the same word *epieikes*, is used "In 2 C. 10:1 *epieikeias tou christou* refers to the meekness of Christ as a model for Paul and the community" (Kittel, II:589). Thayer defines it as, "from *epi*, 'unto,' and *eikos*, 'likely,' denotes 'seemly, fitting'; hence, 'equitable, fair, moderate, forbearing, not insisting on the letter of the law . . . it is rendered 'gentle' in1 Tim. 3:3, RV (KJV, "patient"), in contrast to contentiousness; in Titus 3:2, 'gentle,' in association with meekness" (263).

The quality of meekness must be employed by elders. They cannot lose their temper easily or talk harshly to a member of the flock. They must be authoritative yet meek. Perhaps Peter's thought sums this us best:

> *Shepherd the flock of God which is among you, serving as overseers, not by compulsion but willingly, not for dishonest gain but eagerly;* ***nor as being lords over those entrusted to you****, but being examples to the flock* (1 Pet. 5:2, 3).

14. Not quarrelsome (1 Tim. 3:3). Thayer lists the definition for *amachos* under "brawler" and "contentious." It has been translated in English versions both ways. The definition Thayer gives us is: "lit. 'not fighting' (*a* negative, *mache*, 'a fight, combat, quarrelsome'), primarily signifying 'invincible,' came to mean 'not contentious,' 1 Tim. 3:3, RV; Titus 3:2 (KJV, 'not a brawler,' 'no brawlers')" (126). This gives us the picture of a man who will not sink to the level of brawling to settle disputes. Not only will he not stoop to brawling, but he will not be quarrelsome over matters. This is not to say that he won't "fight" for what is doctrinally right. He will seek a peaceful solution to matters other than doctrinal. In fact, the definition given by Bauer, Arndt, and Gingrich is "peaceable" (44).

It should be noted that this is also required of all Christians (Tit. 3:2).

15. Not covetous (1 Tim. 3:3). *Aphilarguros* is a double compound word comprised of (*a*, negative, *philos*, love and *arguros*, money. Paul says the bishop must not be greedy for money. In other words, he must be free from the love of money. This is in keeping with the command to all disciples to be "without covetousness" (Heb. 13:5) and Paul says that no covetous man will have any inheritance in the kingdom (Eph. 5:5).

Vine tells us that Trench points out the distinction between *pleonexia* (covetousness) and *aphilarguros* is the difference between "covetousness" and "avarice." He says, "The 'covetous' man is often cruel as well as grasping, while the avaricious man is simply miserly and stinting" (136). This certainly gives us a fresh lens through which to consider this requirement.

Elders are going to be in charge of dispersing the money collected on the first day of the week. They must be free from the love of money. The temptation may not be so much to steal the money, but rather to hoard it up. We must always keep in mind the basic meaning of the word, which is to desire what another has. However, the definition before us suggests something else. Elders who are covetous with the Lord's money may stockpile it against a "rainy day." The thought process is that they need to keep a reserve on hand. This thinking seems logical on the surface, but is it really sound? This suggests that the Lord's people are going to quit giving altogether and that the elders will have to manage for years with that reserve only. Really? If this flaw is pointed out by someone, such as the preacher, they are quick to tell him that it is for his own good. They are trying to make sure that they have a big enough balance to support him for a while. Most preachers would probably say that they have enough faith in the Lord to provide and that the money should be used for evangelism and benevolence. Perhaps it could be in the form of a well deserved raise for the preacher, foreign evangelism, or other deserving evangelistic work here at home. I wonder what these men will tell the Lord when He comes back and they are sitting on a big balance in the church treasury, while the lost are dying without anyone to preach the gospel to them because no one supported the work.

The other side of this equation is "avarice." This is seen in the elders who are stingy with the Lord's money. They only pay the preacher enough for him to just scrape by. Or they refuse to spend money on much needed classroom material or equipping the teachers with what they need to teach. Are these men not charged with shepherding the flock? Does that not include feeding them?

16. Not a novice (1 Tim. 3:6). The word *neophutos* literally means "newly planted." It "denotes a new convert, neophyte, novice" (Vine, 436). The word "neophyte" is a transliteration of the Greek word. *Neo* means "new" and *phuo* means "to bring forth, produce" (Vine, 436). This obviously gives us the idea that the elder cannot be a new convert. He needs time to grow and mature before taking on the responsibility of watching over the flock.

How long does it take for a man to be qualified in this regard? That depends on the person. Some mature faster than others. One thing that helps determine when a man is qualified for the eldership is having believing children. If a man has been a Christian before his marriage and having children, he will have a number of years to grow. This time should be spent in study. If a man comes to obedience later in life, he may not have believing children and he may not have enough time to grow in his knowledge.

While this requirement is for the elders only, the Hebrew writer tells us that all Christians are expected to grow (Heb. 5:12).

17. Good testimony among those outside (1 Tim. 3:7). One might ponder the necessity of this requirement. Why would the overseer need to have a good report from outside the church? Doesn't his role as an elder mean that he is to shepherd the flock of God "among them"? Yes, that is true. His work will be with the sheep of his congregation. However, think about his effectiveness and his example for Christ. These men who serve as elders are going to have a profound impact upon the community in which they live. Thus, the reason for this qualification is obvious.

The phrase in the Greek is: *kalos,* "good," *marturia,* "report" or "testimony," *apo,* "off" or "away," *exothen,* "away" or "external." The idea conveyed by this phrase is the "reputation" of the man. Is he of good reputation with those in the community? Can he use that influence for good in the kingdom?

We must also understand that the bishop may sometimes be hated by his neighbors without good cause (Matt. 10:22; 2 Tim. 3:12). The pastor may also be the object of derision by those whom he has disciplined. This does not cause his reputation to be tarnished nor does it mean he has a bad report. If the elder is honest, hard working, compassionate, and concerned for the souls of men (especially those in his flock), then he will have this "good testimony."

Let us be reminded of the words of our Lord, "Let your light so shine before men, that they may see your good works . . ." (Matt. 5:16). Also, let us be reminded of the example of Demetrius' good testimony (3 John 12). Let us all seek to have a good reputation among our fellow man. It will be necessary to start early in life to establish this good testimony.

18. Just (Tit. 1:8). The general definition given by Thayer for *dikaios* is: "righteous, observing divine and human laws" (148). This gives the sense that the elder will be one who is morally upright, one who values justice (justice is from the same root word), one who is fair and impartial.

The more specific definition is: "In a narrower sense, *rendering to each his due;* and that in a judicial sense, *passing just judgment on others,* whether expressed in words or shown by the manner of dealing with them" (Thayer, 149).

There is no doubt that the elder will have to render decisions. In matters of doctrine, his decision must be in keeping with God's word. In other matters, he must render decisions that are fair, non-partial, upright, and equitable. In fact, isn't this what all Christian are to do (Phil. 4:8)?

19. Holy (Tit. 1:8). 1 Peter 1:6 says, *"Be holy, for I am holy."* The last requirement listed in Titus is that the elder must be "holy" (*hosios*). Arndt and Gingrich define the word as "of men *devout, pious, pleasing to God, holy"* (589). The Greek word is translated as "holily" (KJV) and "devout" in the NKJV. The latter seems to get us to the heart of this requirement.

None of us can attain the perfect holiness of God. However, we can be pleasing to Him. This comes by being devoted (devout) to Him. Phillips says it means "undefiled by sin, free from wickedness and wrong" (187). All of us sin (Rom. 3:23). But the elder is one who is not stained with sin. He does not allow sin to dominate his life so that he becomes defiled. Of course, this is desirable for all of God's children but the man who would serve as an elder will be mature in his faith and will not be overcome by the evil one and his temptations.

Notice now the larger context of the passage we cited to begin this section,

> . . . *as obedient children, not conforming yourselves to the former lusts, as in your ignorance; but as He who called you is holy,* **you also be holy in all your conduct***, because it is written, "Be holy, for I am holy"* (1 Pet. 1:14-16).

Conclusion

The picture painted of elders by the Apostle Paul is complex. Yet, at the same time, it is rather simple. We look at this list of qualifications and realize that the man who would occupy this office is one who will stand head and shoulders above the rest of the congregation. There are many things that go into meeting God's standard. Their spirituality and maturity in the faith should be evident to all. It is rather simple in the fact that these men begin by simply being what God wants all of us to be.

Under the section about "desiring the office," we raised the idea of an elder shortage. The suggested reason for this was stated as an attitude problem. Misunderstanding or lack of understanding the office of the bishop has probably contributed to this problem. It is my belief that several generations of men have seen the problems faced by elders, beginning with the division over institutionalism in the 1950s and 1960s and continuing until present times, and want no part of being shepherds. Elders have also had to deal with localized problems and a lack of respect from their congregations. Make no mistake; the battle had to be engaged. But, the viciousness of that battle no doubt soured some on being an elder. Perhaps a lack of training young men has contributed to the shortage since then. Whatever the cause, we must correct that in future generations. Young men must be counseled to prepare themselves. Young ladies need to be taught to be wives who will support their husbands in the work of this office. God's plan is for the church to be organized ". . . *with the bishops and deacons* (Phil. 1:1). Let's get to work!

More battles will come. The Lord's church will no doubt be further divided. The only hope of preserving a remnant is to have good, qualified men filling the office of elder as God intended.

Works Cited

Arndt, William F. and F. Wilbur Gingrich. *A Greek-English Lexicon of the New Testament.* Chicago: University of Chicago, 1957.

Cox, James D. *". . . With the Bishops and Deacons."* Delight (AR): Gospel Light, 1976.

Kenyon, Bryan R. "The Qualifications and Work of Deacons: A Word Study." *Do You Understand Leadership?* Florida School of Preaching Lectureship, 2001. Ed. Bryan R. Kenyon. Pulaski (TN): Sain Publications, 2001: 465-480.

Kittel, Gerhard and Gerhard Friedrich. *Theological Dictionary of the Greek New Testament.* Grand Rapids: Eerdmans, 1971.

Phillips, H. E. *Scriptural Elders and Deacons.* Bowling Green (KY): Guardian of Truth, 1959.

Thayer, Joseph Henry. *The New Thayer's Greek-English Lexicon of the New Testament.* Peabody (MA): Hendrickson, 1981.

Vine, W. E. *Vine's Expository Dictionary of Biblical Words.* Nashville: Thomas Nelson Publishers, 1985.

Webster, Noah. *Webster's Deluxe Unabridged Dictionary.* 2nd Ed. New York: Simon and Schuster, 1983.

The Elders' Relationship to the Church

Jesse Flowers

"I am the good shepherd; and I know My sheep, and am known by My own" (John 10:14).

I believe the words spoken by Jesus in John 10:14 is a fitting way to introduce our subject concerning the elders' relationship to the church. Here we find one of those great "I Am" statements of John's Gospel. In this passage of Scripture, Jesus speaks of the close relationship that exists between Himself and His sheep.

Those in the Lord's audience could readily relate to the imagery employed of the shepherd and his sheep. The bond formed between a shepherd and his sheep was very special and unique.

> A good shepherd does not envision his responsibility as just a job. Sheep, at the time of Jesus, were very valuable animals. They provided food and wool for clothing. The care and protection of the flock was the shepherd's life. The shepherd would lead his flock to pasture and water; tend to their wounds; guide them; calm them; keep them together; and, rescue them from pitfalls and briar patches. He was the sole provider of all that the flock needed.

Jesse A. Flowers was born in Louisville, Kentucky on June 21, 1974 to Jesse E. and Charlotte Flowers. At the age of two, his family moved to Bowling Green, Kentucky where his father preached the gospel until the day of his death in August of 1992. Jesse has worked with churches in Kentucky, Indiana, Canada, Missouri, Florida, and Texas. Jesse met his wife April while working with the Trilacoochee Church of Christ in Dade City Florida (2003-2008). Jesse and April have been blessed with two sons: Jesse Stephen (age 2) and Josiah Edward (five months). Jesse is currently serving as the evangelist for the Church of Christ at Pruett and Lobit in Baytown, Texas (2000-2003, 2008-present).

Sheep are single minded, skittish, near-sighted, critters. They are one of the few creatures who, if let on their own, will totally destroy their pasture. They are easily terrified and prone to wandering off from the flock. They require constant attention. They will continually repeat wandering and getting into dangerous situations without ever learning to avoid them.

The relationship between a shepherd and his flock is very unique. Jesus outlines part of this relationship in John 10. It was common, at various times, for shepherds to bring their flocks into community pens at night. Several flocks would be housed together. Yet, when it came time to separate the flocks all that was necessary was for the shepherd to call out to his sheep to lead them out of the pen. "To him the doorkeeper opens, and the sheep hear his voice; and he calls his own sheep by name and leads them out. And when he brings out his own sheep, he goes before them; and the sheep follow him, for they know his voice" (John 10:3-4).

The shepherd kept the flock together by calling wandering individuals back to the fold and, when necessary, brought hard-headed sheep back by gentle application of his staff. Should one of the sheep manage to get separated, and lost, the shepherd would actively seek that lost sheep until it was found. If necessary, he would risk his own life to save that sheep from any dangerous situation that it got itself into. Should a predator attack the flock the shepherd would willingly give his life to protect his sheep. The bond between the shepherd and the flock is very similar to that of a father and his family.[1]

The elders appointed in a local church are described as shepherds (Acts 20:28; 1 Pet. 5:2), and the members under their care are described as a flock, or sheep (Acts 20:28-29; 1 Pet. 5:2-3). There should naturally be a close, loving relationship between the elders and members. Just as an actual shepherd *knows* his sheep and the sheep *know* him, so should it be with the elders and the church. To know one another unmistakably infers a relationship shared.

The Importance of This Relationship

The relationship between the elders and the church is by far the most important of spiritual relationships that exists within a local church. I believe Hebrews 13:17 speaks directly to this truth. "Obey those who rule over you, and be submissive, *for they watch out for your souls*, as those who must give account. Let them do so with joy and not with grief, for that would be unprofitable for you." A healthy and close relationship does not automati-

---

[1] Charlie Martin, *The Good Shepherd and His Sheep. http://acharlie.tripod.com/shepherd.htm*

cally form between the elders and the members. It takes times to create it and to grow it. It requires diligent work. It demands constant attention. And that relationship must not be one-sided. If it is, then it will fail. However, if the elders develop the kind of relationship with the church that the Lord desires, then great things will take place. And if the members positively cooperate in that relationship, then much good will be accomplished in that local work.

The Current State of This Relationship

This is impossible for me to know of course, but I wonder in how many churches of God's people today exists a loving and healthy relationship between the elders and the church they shepherd? I am confident that, in some locations, the relationship that the elders share with the members is flourishing, that the pastors and their flock work harmoniously together in the work of our Lord. I fear, however, from personal experience and reliable testimony through the years, that too many congregations are greatly ineffective within and without because of an unhealthy relationship, or simply, the lack of a relationship existing between the elders and the saints.

So what should be the relationship between the elders and the church they oversee? How can elders form and develop the kind of relationship that God desires to exist between a shepherd and his sheep? And what responsibility do the members have in all of this?

Ways for Elders to Form and Grow Their Relationship with the Church

1. Be friendly. "A man who has friends must himself be friendly" (Prov. 18:24). Every elder must be friendly and kind if he is to form any sort of meaningful and beneficial relationship with the members. Elders must not be standoffish to the saints they oversee. Can you imagine an actual shepherd ignoring, or acting aloof around, his sheep? The results would be disastrous! Elders must be personable; they must possess people skills. If they do not, then they need to develop such. If kindness (1 Cor. 13:4; Gal. 5:22; Eph. 4:32; Col. 3:12; 2 Pet. 1:7) is missing in their attitudes and actions toward the flock, the sheep will not feel very comfortable around them. Friendliness is a relationship builder!

2. Spend time with the members. One key reason why little to no relationship exists between some elderships and the congregations they oversee is because the elders are not spending any time with the members. The elders need to spend both quality and quantity time with their flock. Remember, the actual shepherd is with his sheep constantly! So a few hours a week at services will not cut it. A few words or sentences spoken each week do not build the unique relationships that must exist between a shepherd and his sheep. No doubt, this is one reason for the necessity of the qualification of hospitality (1 Tim. 3:2; Tit. 1:8). All Christians are to be "given to hospitality" (Rom. 12:13); elders even more so. Demonstrating hospitality affords the elders' opportunities to grow closer to the members and vice versa.

3. Be tactful. This point cannot be overemphasized. I have witnessed and heard of too many occasions where an elder has lacked tact in speaking to the members. If not resolved, the damage done can possibly be irreparable. It is crucial for elders to use tact when meeting with members to discuss various concerns or problems that arise. It is not helpful when elders are abrasive in their speech. The wise proverb reads: "A soft answer turns away wrath, but a harsh word stirs up anger" (Prov. 15:1). Another proverb reads: "There is one who speaks like the piercings of a sword, but the tongue of the wise promotes health" (12:18; cf. 25:15; 29:11). If an elder is truly gentle, not quarrelsome, not quick-tempered, and self-controlled (1 Tim. 3:3; Tit. 1:7, 8), then he will most certainly exercise tact in his speech.

4. Communicate often and effectively. Something that is vital to any good relationship is communication. Herein lies one of the most important aspects of the elders' relationship to the church. The eldership is not to be some secretive organization within the church, where all outsiders have no clue about anything that transpires. Of course, that is not to suggest that there are not many private matters that must be kept confidential among the elders themselves. On occasion, some loose-lipped elders (or wives) have caused unnecessary problems by sharing information that should not be disclosed. On the other hand, some elderships function in such a way that the congregation is rarely informed of anything! After a while, if members are kept in the dark about practically every decision the elders make, then a disconnect will result. If this continues, then distrust and even animosity can form. Each eldership must, of course, use good judgment and wisdom about what to make public and what to keep private. Yet, they must learn to strike a good balance. When announcements are delivered and, at the occasional congregational meeting, it is a good time for the elders to inform the members of helpful and needed information. Communicating often and effectively will foster goodwill and trust between the eldership and the congregation. The members will feel both at ease and confident to follow their lead.

Almost twenty years ago, brother Ron Halbrook wrote an excellent series of articles entitled "Elders and Communication." I wanted to include a few excerpts for us to ponder:

> If he is to pastor and oversee the church, he must be a leader of men with the ability to communicate clearly and effectively in setting goals, in expressing mature judgment on a wide range of matters, and in generally giving direction, encouragement, and counsel. That lesson can be learned from the terms which define the essence of the office: elder, pastor (or shepherd), and bishop (or overseer). This is essential if elders are to "take care of the church of God," "rule well," and "watch for . . . souls" (1 Tim. 3:4-5; 5:17; Heb, 13:17). . . .Sometimes men who are fully and truly qualified are appointed as elders, but they do not fully utilize their opportunities or do not fully develop their potential for leading the church. They may even do an excellent job in teaching the word. Their failure to provide strong leadership may be in the area of communicating with the church in matters of direction, judgment, and counsel. Neglect in this area can lead to stagnation in the church's program of work—evangelism, edification, or benevolence. Another result may be that some person or persons in the church with strong opinions and dominant personalities will in effect steal away the reins of leadership from the elders. When elders conduct all of their work "behind closed doors" and neglect avenues of open communication with the church, they cut themselves off from the help of good brethren and stunt their growth while also giving some Diotrephes plausible grounds upon which to lead a rebellion. Elders everywhere need to be convinced of the importance of good communication with the church.[2]

5. Be a good listener. James said, "Let every man be swift to hear, slow to speak, slow to wrath" (James 1:19). All Christians are called upon to obey these inspired instructions. But for those who are responsible to shepherd and oversee the flock, it is a must! When some members come to confide in the elders, to discuss various problems, or to simply voice a concern some elders tend to be slow to hear, swift to speak, and at times quick to wrath. All elders must learn to be good listeners. Instead of interrupting or just waiting to get your point across, please listen to what a member is trying to express. "He who answers a matter before he hears it, it is folly and shame to him" (Prov. 18:13). When elders really listen they will: (a) be more respected, (b) mutual trust will form, (c) be able to more effectively respond and address the needs of their flock, and (d) will find strong support as the leaders.

---

[2] Ron Halbrook, *Guardian of Truth* XXXIV: 17 (September 6, 1990), 522-523.

6. Be trustworthy. "A talebearer reveals secrets, but he who is of a faithful spirit conceals a matter" (Prov. 11:13). The man who serves as an elder in the church will be responsible to conceal many church-related matters. Brethren will periodically meet with the elders to confide in them about: (a) marital issues, (b) personal sin, (c) rebellious children, (d) doctrinal questions, etc. The overseers must be very careful not to betray the trust of the members who meet with them in confidentiality. One way that these men prove themselves to be blameless (1 Tim. 3:2) and self-controlled (Titus 1:8) is by being trustworthy. If an elder "reveals secrets," that trust will be destroyed. Once that trust is lost, it may be very difficult to restore.

7. Judge righteously. Jesus warned, "Do not judge according to appearance, but judge with righteous judgment" (John 7:24). Much of an elder's work relates to making decisions and rendering judgments. All of their decisions will not be perfect, but they must ever strive to judge righteously. In the decision-making process, elders must ever be guided by the perfect standard of God's Word (Psa. 19:7-9; 2 Tim. 3:16-17). If they are truly "just" (Tit. 1:8), then they will judge righteously. The shepherds must be careful to hear both sides of a story before rendering a decision. "The first one to plead his cause seems right, until his neighbor comes and examines him" (Prov. 18:17). They must not show partiality when it comes to family members or certain prominent members in the church. Like God, they must be no respecter of persons (1 Tim. 5:21; James 3:17). Praying continually for God's provision of wisdom will prove most helpful (James 1:5).

8. Be decisive. One way elders can strengthen their relationship with the church is by being decisive. One sure way to weaken that relationship is through indecisiveness. Being decisive in the right ways (truth and attitude) is a mark of strong leadership. At times, elders can drag out their decisions (and the announcements of those decisions) over an extended period of time. An elder must not be "a double-minded man" who is "unstable in all his ways" (James 1:8). After a matter has been thoroughly discussed, a unified decision rooted in Scripture needs to be reached (2 Cor. 1:17-20), and then, if not private, made known to keep the congregation well informed. In matters of church discipline, elders must be decisive. In matters of doctrinal purity, the elders must be decisive. In regards to the teaching program, the elders need to be decisive. When it comes to congregational goals, the elders need to be decisive. When members are able to consistently witness their elders being decisive, trust and confidence in their leadership will be the result.

9. Lead by example. Peter, an elder, instructed his fellow elders not to be *"lords over those entrusted to you, but being examples to the flock"* (1 Pet. 5:3). What faithful Christian does not admire an elder who leads by example? Righteous shepherds setting righteous examples inspires the flock to follow. If elders desire the members to be faithful in their attendance (Heb. 10:25), then they too must put first things first (Matt. 6:33). If an elder expects the members to arrive punctually, then so must they. The elders can set the proper example to be followed by beginning the services on time, greeting the visitors, staying afterwards to visit, practicing hospitality, ruling their own houses well (1 Tim. 3:4-5), and maintaining moral and doctrinal purity in their lives. Of course, by continuing to meet all the specified qualifications (1 Tim. 3:1-7; Tit. 1:5-9), elders will indeed lead by their godly example.

10. Love the flock. The "good shepherd" does not have to be told or reminded to love the fock. For him, it comes naturally. He loves his sheep so much that he is willing to lay down his life for them (John 10:11). In fact, the mutual love of every saint is to be so strong and deep that we are willing "to lay down our lives for the brethren" (1 John 3:16). If that is so, and it is, then surely the shepherds of the flock are to love the sheep among them to such an extent that they are willing to die for them. An elder's love is proven time and time again by faithfully watching out for our souls (Heb. 13:17). There will be occasions when that love has to be firm and unwavering, but it is always based with the members' best spiritual interests at heart. An elder must love his sheep "in deed and in truth" (1 John 3:18). First and foremost, the elders' relationship to the church is strong and unique because of the genuine love that flows from the shepherd to his sheep (1 Pet. 1:22).

Ways the Church Can and Should Strengthen This Relationship

1. Show them honor. It must always be remembered that the work that elders do is a God-appointed office (1 Tim. 3:1, KJV). Thus, it must be an office that is honored. Elders deserve the respect of the members (1 Tim. 5:17). Honor is due them (Rom. 13:7). The way we speak to them and answer them ought to demonstrate this respect. At times members do not show elders the honor they deserve. Yelling at an elder is not respectful. A raised, agitated, or demeaning voice is not showing them honor either. Berating them behind their backs is not showing these men the respect God requires. The relationship shared between elders and members will be strengthened when saints show them honor.

2. Obey them. "Obey those who rule over you. . ." (Heb. 13:17). *Over-*

The Elders' Relationship to the Church

seers, or elders, rule over us (Acts 20:28; 1 Pet. 5:2), and saints are to obey them. It is not an option that is left up to each member. Rather it's a clear command of the law of Christ. There will always be some in the church who do not want elders. Such a mindset is not only foolish, but in rebellion to the very will of God (Acts 14:23; Tit. 1:5; Phil. 1:1). There will always be some who will be unhappy with practically all decisions the elders make, and are convinced they could do a much better job. Well, if they desire the office of an elder and meet all the qualifications required (1 Tim. 3:1-8; Tit. 1:5-9), then step up and stand in the gap! Otherwise, be quiet and obey them! Again, the elders will not always be perfect in all the decisions they make. But conscientious men of God will strive to do their best to lead the flock faithfully in the ways of God. I know of only one exception to the command to obey elders, and that is when obeying them causes one to sin. "Do not receive an accusation against an elder except from two or three witnesses. Those who are sinning rebuke in the presence of all, that the rest also may fear" (1 Tim. 5:19-20). Saints who truly obey the elders will do much in strengthening this relationship.

3. Submit to them. The sacred text also instructs Christians to "be submissive" to "those who rule over you" (Heb. 13:17). Every saint is called upon to submit "to one another in the fear of God" (Eph.5:21). Therefore, it should not be difficult for a member of the Lord's body to submit to "those who *rule* over" the local church. For the Christian to be "submissive" to an elder (or any Christian for that matter), he must possess a certain mindset— one of humility (1 Pet. 5:5), service (Gal. 5:13), and willingness to render honor or preference (Rom. 12:10; Phil. 2:3-4). Each member must be willing to surrender himself to the direction and guidance of the eldership. Some brethren refuse to submit themselves to the elders. They seemingly go against them at every turn, and even justify such behavior. Please understand that, when any saint refuses to submit to an elder, he is refusing to submit to God, "who will render to each one according to his deeds" (Rom. 2:6). However, when saints gladly submit themselves to the elders, the work in that local church will be both prosperous and harmonious.

4. Love the elders. I suppose this should go without saying, but I believe it is a point worth stressing. Just as the shepherd loves the sheep, the sheep should respond in kind. How can we not possibly love those who watch out for our souls (Heb. 13:17)? Nothing is more valuable than the soul (Matt. 16:26), and they are the appointed ones who keep constant guard over them. Paul wrote to the church in Thessalonica: "And we urge you, brethren, to recognize those who labor among you, and are over you in the Lord and admonish you, and to *esteem them very highly in love* for their work's sake" (1 Thess. 5:12-13). When faithful elders protect the flock from false teachers (Acts 20:28-31), love them for it. When faithful elders carefully plan out a teaching program for the Bible classes, love them for edifying the saints (Eph. 4:12). When faithful elders schedule faithful preachers (2 Tim. 4:1-2) for gospel meetings, love them. When faithful elders actively support local and foreign evangelism (Mark 16:15; 1 Thess. 1:8), love them for it. When faithful elders lead the congregation in assisting needy saints (Acts 11:27-30), love them for doing so. When faithful elders "withdraw from every brother who walks disorderly" (2 Thess. 3:6), love them for their work's sake. When faithful elders are willing to drop what they're doing to come meet with you, love them for their time and concern. Genuine love for the elders will naturally lead one to honor them, obey them, and submit to their rule. When saints love the elders, the relationship they share will grow stronger and closer with each passing day.

5. Help their work to be pleasant. "Let them do so with joy and not with grief, for that would be unprofitable for you" (Heb. 13:17). What an awesome and sobering responsibility elders have been given in the local church. There are often many challenges and stresses to the work they do. The many problems and needs that have to be addressed can be quite taxing on them and their families. The New Testament instructs saints to do their part in helping make their job easier and more enjoyable. If we don't cooperate as they strive to watch out for our souls, it will most certainly be unprofitable for us. Follow their leadership and support their leadership, so long as they hold fast to the word of life (Phil. 2:16). If there are areas where the elders seem to be weak (personal evangelism, church discipline), then encourage them to step up and lead the flock in those necessary and beneficial matters. If there are areas of compromise (moral or doctrinal), rebuke them (1 Tim. 5:19-20). Otherwise, give them your full and unwavering support. Thank them often. Let them know how much you appreciate the work they do. Thank them for the long hours they spend in leading and overseeing the flock. Elders need encouragement also, if not more so. When the members allow the elders to lead with joy, their relationship will only flourish in the Lord.

6. Pray for them. If we are to pray for our civil leaders (1 Tim. 2:1-2), then how much more should we offer up prayers to God on behalf of our spiritual leaders (Heb. 13:17)? Pray that God would grant the elders wisdom to lead the congregation in what is best (James 1:5). Pray that the elders will hold "fast the faithful word as he has been taught, that he may be able, by sound doctrine, both to exhort and convict those who contradict" (Tit. 1:9). Pray that they might prosper in health so as to continue to serve (3 John 2). The elders and the work they do should be on our minds to such a degree that we pray for them without ceasing (1 Thess. 5:17). Continually offering up petitions on their behalf will most certainly profit the relationship that exists between the shepherd and his sheep.

The Problems of a Weak Relationship Between the Elders and the Church

When there exists a weak relationship between the elders and the church, the elders will be quite ineffective in leading the flock that is among them. Try as they will, if the relationship is poor or even non-existent, the sheep will not follow. That local congregation will lack "the unity of the Spirit in the bond of peace" (Eph. 4:3), that God desires and demands. The saints may be present for every service, but the work of the Lord will suffer and become stagnant in that locale. In some churches, there seems to be an awkwardness between the elders and the members. They more or less tolerate one another. They don't seem to be on the same page. They seem to be thinking and going in different directions. All of this speaks to the weakness in their relationship. Perhaps there is fault on both sides. If this is the case, things must change immediately. Things must change in order to please God, and in the hopes of avoiding disaster. How many more churches would be growing in faith and in number if elders and saints functioned in the body of Christ as the Lord intended? There is nothing good that can come out of a weak relationship between the elders and the church. Satan wins, we lose!

The Benefits of a Strong Relationship Between the Elders and the Church

God desires very strongly for a close relationship to exist between the shepherd and the sheep. Since He desires this, so must we. A close relationship between elders and the members will make for a strong, united church (Eph. 4:3; 6:10). Such a church will be active in the Lord's work (1 Cor. 15:58). The saints will "grow in the grace and knowledge of our Lord and Savior Jesus Christ" (2 Pet. 3:18). Sowing and watering of God's Word will occur, and precious souls will be saved (1 Cor. 3:6-7). Truth will be upheld and error will not be tolerated (Jude 3; 2 John 9-11). The local church will be kept pure (1 Cor. 5). Such a church, will be a beacon of light "in the midst of a crooked and perverse generation" (Phil. 2:15). Souls will be kept safe from the attacks of the devil (Heb. 13:17; 1 Pet. 5:8). Peace, joy, and love will be the fruits of such a close relationship (Rom. 14:17; 1 Cor. 16:14). Indeed, much hinges upon a strong relationship between the elders and the church! When you have the shepherds in a church meeting all of their responsibilities to the flock and the sheep fulfilling all of their duties, much spiritual good will result.

Conclusion

The inspired writer penned the following words in regard to the elders and the work they do: "as those who must give an account" (Heb. 13:17). It matters greatly how an elder serves and oversees the flock (Acts 20:28). It matters a great deal the kind of example they set to be followed (1 Pet. 5:3). It matters tremendously that they effectively watch out for souls (Heb. 13:17). It matters significantly the kind of relationship that exists between themselves and the flock they shepherd. All of this deeply matters, because elders must give an account before Almighty God for the work that they do. "When the Chief Shepherd appears," elders who shepherd the flock of God faithfully, "will receive the crown of glory that does not fade away" (1 Pet. 5:4). What a great reward it will be for the shepherds and the sheep (2 Tim. 4:8; Rev. 2:10)!

The Terms Used to Describe Elders
Michael L. Vierheller

As a young boy growing up, I looked up to my grandparents. I loved to spend time with the older generation. They were full of knowledge and wisdom and experience. The values I hold dear in life came from my grandparents and parents. They were role models and I learned much from them. "I said, 'Age should speak, and multitude of years should teach wisdom'" (Job. 32:7). The older generation has much to teach the younger. Life would be better and easier for the young, if they would learn from those older and wiser. This same thing is true of an eldership ordained by God. "Remember those who rule over you, who have spoken the word of God to you, whose faith follow, considering the outcome of their conduct" (Heb. 13:7).

Paul told Titus to "ordain elders in every city" (Tit. 1:5). Men who possessed certain qualification were selected to lead, guide, direct, oversee, or superintend the work of the church. "Juniors" do not lead the church. It is led by men who possess the qualifications laid down in God's Word.

In this study of elders it is interesting to see that those appointed to the eldership were appointed in a short period of time. I think this tells us something about the qualifications necessary to become elders. The Bible

Michael Vierheller was born January 5, 1948. He married Cynthia Jane Gibson in 1969 and to that union three daughters were born. He attended Florida College (1969-1973) and began preaching the gospel in Cameron, Ohio (1973-1978). He has been preaching in Cambridge, Ohio since 1978. He also serves as one of the elders of the church at East Cambridge. Michael and Cynthia are blessed that their three daughters and their husbands are faithful Christians. Two of his sons-in-law are deacons in the church and all three of them do some preaching. They have ten grandchildren and three of them are also Christians. Michael recently published his work on the Holy Spirit entitled, *Let's Study the Holy Spirit*.

does not require elders to have supernatural powers. This seems to present a problem in many places when it comes to appointing elders. Members make the qualifications higher than God does. In reality, God's qualifications are qualifications that men in the New Testament time already met in their daily lives. Yet, at the same time, we should not set the qualifications lower than God's standards just because some men do not meet all the qualifications that God requires of an elder.

It would seem that we have failed in our homes and in the church to give proper emphasis to the eldership. The work of appointing elders begins when our children are young. Waiting until they become men could be waiting too long. God has shown us the pattern to make men qualified to be elders. "Therefore you shall lay up these words of mine in your heart and in your soul, and bind them as a sign on your hand, and they shall be as frontlets between your eyes. You shall teach them to your children, speaking of them when you sit in your house, when you walk by the way, when you lie down, and when you rise up. And you shall write them on the doorposts of your house and on your gates" (Deut. 11:18-20). Children learn from what they see in the home. Usually it is in the home where they learn to love and respect God. The opposite is also true, children learn not to love and respect God by what they see at home.

Let us look at some Greek studies to see how the words used for elders are defined:

Elder: *Presbuteros*: KJV — elder 64, old man 1, eldest 1, elder woman 1;
  1) elder, of age,
     1a) the elder of two people
     1b) advanced in life, an elder, a senior
        1b1) forefathers
  2) a term of rank or office
     2a) among the Jews
        2a1) members of the great council or Sanhedrin (because in early times the rulers of the people, judges, etc., were selected from elderly men)
        2a2) of those who in separate cities managed public affairs and administered justice
     2b) among the Christians, those who presided over the assemblies (or churches). The NT uses the term bishop, elders, and presbyters interchangeably

The Terms Used to Describe Elders 111

2c) the twenty-four members of the heavenly Sanhedrin or court seated on thrones around the throne of God (Thayer's, *Online Bible Electronic addition*).

Presbuteros: comparative of *presbus* (elderly); older; as noun, a senior; specifically, an Israelite Sanhedrist (also figuratively, member of the celestial council) or Christian "presbyter": elder (-est), old; (Strong's, *Online Bible Electronic addition*).

Presbuteros: a cptv. of presbus *(an old man); elder:—*

NAS – elder (3), elders (57), men of old (1), old men (1), older (1), older man (1), older ones(1), older women (1), women (1) (N.A.S.V., 1995, *Online Bible Electronic addition*).

Presbuteros: an adjective, the comparative degree of *presbus*, "an old man, an elder," is used (a) of age, whether of the "elder" of two persons, Luke 15:25, or more, John 8:9, "the eldest"; or of a person advanced in life, a senior, Acts 2:17; in Heb. 11:2, the "elders" are the forefathers in Israel; so in Matt. 15:2; Mark 7:3,5; the feminine of the adjective is used of "elder" women in the churches, 1 Tim. 5:2, not in respect of position but in seniority of age; (b) of rank or positions of responsibility, (1) among Gentiles, as in the Sept. of Gen. 50:7; Num. 22:7; (2) in the Jewish nation, firstly, those who were the heads or leaders of the tribes and families, as of the seventy who assisted Moses, Num. 11:16; Deut. 27:1, and those assembled by Solomon; secondly, members of the Sanhedrin, consisting of the chief priests, "elders" and scribes, learned in Jewish law, e.g., Matt. 16:21; 26:47; thirdly, those who managed public affairs in the various cities, Luke 7:3; (3) in the Christian churches, those who, being raised up and qualified by the work of the Holy Spirit, were appointed to have the spiritual care of, and to exercise oversight over, the churches. To these the term "bishops," *episkopoi*, or "overseers," is applied (see Acts 20, ver. 17 with ver. 28, and Tit. 1:5,7), the latter term indicating the nature of their work, *presbuteroi* their maturity of spirtual experience. The Divine arrangement seen throughout the NT was for a plurality of these to be appointed in each church, Acts 14:23; 20:17; Phil. 1:1; 1 Tim. 5:17; Tit. 1:5. The duty of "elders" is described by the verb *episkopeo*. They were appointed according as they had given evidence of fulfilling the Divine qualifications, Tit. 1:6-9; cp. 1 Tim. 3:1-7; 1 Pet. 5:2; (4) the twenty-four "elders" enthroned in heaven around the throne of God, Rev. 4:4,10; 5:5-14; 7:11,13; 11:16; 14:3; 19:4. The number twenty-four is representative of earthly conditions. The word "elder" is nowhere applied to angels (*Vine's Expository Dictionary of New Testament Words*).

In the Christian Church: Acts 11:29, 30; 14:23; 15:1-35; 16:4, 5; 20:17, 28-32; 21:18; 1 Tim. 4:14; 5:17-19; Tit 1:5-9; Heb 11:2; Jas 5:14, 15; 1 Pet. 5:1-5; 2 John 1:1; 3 John 1:1.

Apocalyptic Vision Of: Rev. 4:4, 10; 5:5, 6, 8, 11, 14; 7:11, 13; 11:16; 14:3; 19:4.

Bishop: *Episkope:* KJV - visitation 2, bishoprick 1, office of a bishop 1; 4
1) investigation, inspection, visitation
   1a) that act by which God looks into and searches out the ways, deeds character, of men, in order to adjudge them their lot accordingly, whether joyous or sad
   1b) oversight
      1b1) overseership, office, charge, the office of an elder
      1b2) the overseer or presiding officers of a Christian church (Thayer's, *Online Bible Electronic addition*).

Episkope: inspection (for relief); by implication, superintendence; specially, the Christian "episcopate":— the office of a "bishop," bishoprick, visitation (Strong's, *Online Bible Electronic addition*).

Episkope: a visiting, an overseeing: – NAS – office (1), office of overseer (1), visitation (2); (N.A.S.V., 1995, *Online Bible Electronic addition*).

Bishop (*episkopos*): lit., "an overseer" (*epi*, "over," *skopeo*, "to look or watch"), whence Eng. "bishop," which has precisely the same meaning, is found in Acts 20:28; Phil. 1:1; 1 Tim. 3:2; Tit. 1:7; 1 Pet. 2:25. See OVERSEER.

Note: *Presbuteros*, "an elder," is another term for the same person as bishop or overseer. See Acts 20:17 with verse Acts 20:28. The term "elder" indicates the mature spiritual experience and understanding of those so described; the term "bishop," or "overseer," indicates the character of the work undertaken. According to the Divine will and appointment, as in the NT, there were to be "bishops" in every local church, Acts 14:23; 20:17; Phil. 1:1; Tit. 1:5; Jas. 5:14. Where the singular is used, the passage is describing what a "bishop" should be, 1 Tim. 3:2; Tit. 1:7. Christ Himself is spoken of as "the . . . Bishop of our souls," 1 Pet. 2:25 (*Vine's Expository Dictionary of New Testament Words*).

Pastor: *Poimen*: of uncertain affinity (TDNT, VI:485, 901); n. m.; KJV—shepherd 15, Shepherd 2, pastor 1; 18
1) a herdsman, esp. a shepherd
   1a) in the parable, he to whose care and control others have committed themselves, and whose precepts they follow
2) metaph.
   2a) the presiding officer, manager, director, of any assembly: so of Christ the Head of the church
      2a1) of the overseers of the Christian assemblies
      2a2) of kings and princes

The tasks of a Near Eastern shepherd were:
- to watch for enemies trying to attack the sheep
- to defend the sheep from attackers
- to heal the wounded and sick sheep
- to find and save lost or trapped sheep
- to love them, sharing their lives and so earning their trust (Thayer's, *Online Bible Electronic Addition*).

Poimen: of uncertain affinity; a shepherd (literally or figuratively):—shepherd, pastor (Strong's, *Online Bible Electronic Addition*).

"Things That Are Lacking"

"For this reason I left you in Crete, that you should set in order the things that are lacking, and appoint elders in every city as I commanded you" (Tit. 1:5).

Paul's statement about elders in the book of Titus was needed then and is still needed now. The one thing lacking among churches today is men qualified to become elders. It has been said that the only thing worse than not having elders in the church is having unqualified elders. God instructed by inspiration the necessity of elders ("… appoint elders in every city as I commanded you"), and for anyone to argue against elders is misguided. God also gave us the qualifications for elders in Timothy and Titus. There is undisputed evidence in the Scriptures for the need of "elders in every church."

One reason for a lack of elders in churches is the failing of brethren to have the foresight to start preparing young men to be elders. We need to be teaching and encouraging young men to prepare themselves to become elders, just as we prepare them in school to get an education to have good careers. It would be good for churches to have classes for young men giving them the training (over several years) they need to be qualified to become elders. Some churches have training classes for young men to prepare them to become preachers. This is a needed work. We also need to have such training classes in the church to teach young men the things necessary to become elders. It would be good for elders to be involved so they can be the inspiration to encourage young men to become elders.

Young women need to be prepared to be the kind of women who can be elders' wives. "Do not let your adornment be merely outward—arranging the hair, wearing gold, or putting on fine apparel—rather let it be the hidden person of the heart, with the incorruptible beauty of a gentle and quiet spirit, which is very precious in the sight of God. For in this manner, in former times, the holy women who trusted in God also adorned themselves, being submissive to their own husbands" (1 Pet. 3:3-5). It seems that the feminist movement has had its impact on the church. It is necessary today for women to be educated and even have a job to help their families because of our economy. However, it is not necessary for our young ladies to think that they are co-heads of the house with their husbands. Young women need to be taught the commandment of God that they must be in subjection to their husbands. Being in subjection to your husband is not just a good idea to make the family life run smoothly, it is a commandment to be obeyed. Those who do not obey this command will be lost just the same as committing any other kind of sin.

Godly women have a great influence on the home and the kind of children that are raised. Women who are in subjection to their husbands are good examples to girls who may become elders' wives someday. The can also have also a good influence on their boys to teach them to marry the kind of girl who would make a good elder's wife. Mothers are with the children more than the fathers and they have a great influence on the children. The things godly women teach their children through their examples will have a great influence on the church in the future. God said, ". . . the older women likewise, that they be reverent in behavior, not slanderers, not given to much wine, teachers of good things—that they admonish the young women to love their husbands, to love their children, to be discreet, chaste, homemakers, good, obedient to their own husbands, that the word of God may not be blasphemed" (Tit. 2:3-5).

There is a great need in the church for the influence of godly women. Some women may not feel that they have an important part in the church of our Lord, so they want to have a leadership role. This is the influence of the feminist movement. Women have not been given a public role in

The Terms Used to Describe Elders

the church, but believe me, no one plays a greater role in the work of the Lord than women. Older women have much to give to the younger women in wisdom and the instruction of godly things. Women can help to make our homes a better environment not only in the church but the world also. Divorce is getting to be a real hindrance in having full and unified families. Children are torn between two families, not belonging to either. Such an environment cannot produce good leadership in the church.

Elders must have good wives, but all members, including preachers, need godly women to help them in the service of the Lord. So, in reality, women do have a part in the leadership of the church. They are the ones helping to raise good children who will be the backbone of the church and they are the mothers of future leaders in the church. Godly women provide a special quality of love and compassion that young men need to learn so they can have the capability to be good, merciful leaders in the church.

The names used for elders in the New Testament define for us something of the work or duties of men who are elders:

The Word "Elder"

The word "elder" includes in it the idea of an older person. "Elder" carries the idea of age as it applies to one's spiritual maturity. "However, we speak wisdom among those who are mature, yet not the wisdom of this age, nor of the rulers of this age, who are coming to nothing" (1 Cor. 2:6). The wisdom that elders are to have is not of a worldly nature. An elder's wisdom is to come from the Word of God. Wisdom is needed for a man to rule the house of God the way God wants it to be ruled. "Him we preach, warning every man and teaching every man in all wisdom, that we may present every man perfect in Christ Jesus" (Col. 1:28). The wisdom that elders are to have is for the purpose of instructing every member in God's Word so they are able to save their souls. ". . . receiving the end of your faith—the salvation of your souls" (1 Pet. 1:9). We can see God's wisdom in wanting spiritually mature men (elders), full of wisdom, to rule the church. Those who are full of spiritual wisdom see the real goal in life, the salvation of the soul, not the possessions of this life. It is so easy to get wrapped up in the affairs of this life without realizing it. A wiser and older man can see these things and have the wisdom needed to approach a member without offense.

We normally identify wisdom with those who are old in age (elders) because of their experiences in life. "Wisdom is with aged men, And with length of days, understanding. With Him are wisdom and strength, He has counsel and understanding" (Job 12:12-13). Understanding gives us the very basis of wisdom. Before one can have wisdom he must apply himself to studying the Word of God. One must have a good knowledge of the Word of God before one is able to put together the teachings of the Scriptures to obtain the wisdom God's Word gives to us. "My son, if you receive my words, And treasure my commands within you, So that you incline your ear to wisdom, And apply your heart to understanding; Yes, if you cry out for discernment, And lift up your voice for understanding, If you seek her as silver, And search for her as for hidden treasures; Then you will understand the fear of the Lord, And find the knowledge of God" (Prov. 2:1-5). Wisdom, understanding, and knowledge are the three necessary ingredients to be a mature Christian. To get wisdom, understanding, and knowledge, one must have a strong desire to achieve these in his life. "Incline your ear," "apply your heart," "cry out for discernment," "lift up your voice," "seek as silver," and "search for her," teaches us how much work it is to become a mature Christian. A Christian cannot become mature spiritually by occasionally studying the Word of God. It takes years of study with a strong desire to achieve spiritual maturity.

The Word "Bishop"

The word "bishop" carries with it the idea of the work undertaken. The work is that of oversight of the work of the local church. The oversight is to be taken by one who is freely willing to have the oversight. Overseeing the work of the church is taking the responsibility of seeing that the local church fulfills the work God intended. Overseeing does not necessarily mean doing the work, but seeing that it is done as God commanded. One must oversee the work of the church where he is an elder, not that of another church. "Shepherd the flock of God which is among you, serving as overseers, not by compulsion but willingly, not for dishonest gain but eagerly" (1 Pet. 5:2). No elder has the authority to tend a flock of which he is not the bishop or elder.

Overseeing the work of the church is serious business. Those who exercise oversight also have the responsibility of the souls they are overseeing. "Obey those who rule over you, and be submissive, for they watch out for your souls, as those who must give account. Let them do so with joy and not with grief, for that would be unprofitable for you" (Heb 13:17). The elders not only carry the burden for their own souls but also for those they oversee. We can see from this the wisdom of selecting older, mature men to take on this responsibility.

The Word "Pastor"

The word "shepherd" describes for us the kind of overseeing that is necessary for one to be a pastor. Sheep need to have water, food, and protection from wolves. Souls need to drink from the fountain of eternal life, partake of the milk and meat of the word and be able to identify the evil one. ". . . newborn babes, desire the pure milk of the word, that you may grow thereby" (1 Pet. 2:2). "For though by this time you ought to be teachers, you need someone to teach you again the first principles of the oracles of God; and you have come to need milk and not solid food. For everyone who partakes only of milk is unskilled in the word of righteousness, for he is a babe. But solid food belongs to those who are of full age, that is, those who by reason of use have their senses exercised to discern both good and evil" (Heb. 5:12-14). It is the Word of God that makes the sheep strong enough to be able to overcome the evil one. Overseers have a grave responsibility to see that the sheep know what the Word of God says. ". . . lest Satan should take advantage of us; for we are not ignorant of his devices" (2 Cor. 2:11). Ignorance is not bliss when it comes to the devices of the devil.

Some Observations on Elders

Duties to God:

Elders are to take heed, "Therefore take heed to yourselves and to all the flock, among which the Holy Spirit has made you overseers, to shepherd the church of God which He purchased with His own blood" (Acts 20:28). The idea of "taking heed" is to realize the importance of this office. This commandment is written to the character of an elder. Elders must be men who are always willing to examine themselves (2 Cor. 13:5), according to the Bible to see if they are following the faith. One should test himself to see if he is doing what is commanded or he will become disqualified. The measurement is always the Word of God (2 Cor. 10:12). Elders must be willing to discipline their bodies and bring them into subjection daily (1 Cor. 9:27).

Elders are to be guided by the Word. "So now, brethren, I commend you to God and to the word of His grace, which is able to build you up and give you an inheritance among all those who are sanctified" (Acts 20:32). It is the Word of God that builds up the elder and gives him the assurance of the inheritance. When being guided by God one must be willing to hold fast to the Word to have the knowledge to exhort and convict with sound doctrine (Tit. 1:9). It must always be the elder's desire that the Lord's will is the deciding factor, in making decisions (Luke 22:42). When it comes to matters of judgment, it must always be a matter of faith (Rom. 14:23). An elder cannot be dogmatic on matters of judgment. No one has the right to make "matters of faith" an issue of fellowship, not even elders. "And I will give you the keys of the kingdom of heaven, and whatever you bind on earth will be bound in heaven, and whatever you loose on earth will be loosed in heaven"(Matt. 16:19).

Examples:

1. Elders must be examples to the flock of God, of which they are overseers. ". . . nor as being lords over those entrusted to you, but being examples to the flock" (1 Pet. 5:3). Even when dealing with truth, an elder must not be someone who intimidates others into subjection. Being an example makes an elder a leader, not a tyrant. The words used to describe the work of elders that have been previously defined, have at their central point that of leadership. Leaders lead by example, so others are willing to follow. Being an example is the opposite of lording. "But he who enters by the door is the shepherd of the sheep. To him the doorkeeper opens, and the sheep hear his voice; and he calls his own sheep by name and leads them out. And when he brings out his own sheep, he goes before them; and the sheep follow him, for they know his voice" (John 10:2-4). Notice, the "shepherd" goes before the sheep. He is leading the sheep where they need to go. Elders must be leaders, not followers. Leaders will always give proper consideration to decisions that need to be made for the flock. Making the best decisions for the local church will make for a sound church.

2. Elders are examples of what fatherhood is. "Not because we do not have authority, but to make ourselves an example of how you should follow us" (2 Thess. 3:9). Elders have authority over the local church to which they are appointed. They need to set the example to the flock as to the kind of earthly father God wants all fathers to be. Fathers are not to provoke their children to wrath (Col. 3:21). This is another reason elders are not to lord over the flock. Members of the church are discouraged when elders are stubborn men unwilling to listen to scriptural reasoning from the Word of God. The apostle Paul told Timothy to rebuke an elder that sinned. "Do not receive an accusation against an elder except from two or three witnesses. Those who are sinning rebuke in the presence of all, that the rest also may fear" (1 Tim. 5:19-20). As a father figure, an elder needs to be able to correct those who need correction with love and mercy. Earthly fathers find no pleasure in correcting their children but do so because they know that it

The Terms Used to Describe Elders 119

is best for the one receiving the correction. Correction teaches us to "be in subjection to the Father of spirits and live" (Heb. 12:9).

3. Elders are to be good examples of a husband. "Husbands, love your wives, just as Christ also loved the church and gave Himself for her" (Eph. 5:25). Elders who love their wives also love the church as Jesus loved it—enough to die for it. This directly deals with an elder's ability to be a leader of the church. Just as the wife will love a husband who loves, respects, and honors her, elders who love the church will be loved and respected by the flock. Elders are to love their own wives (Eph. 5:28). Elders who love their wives should "rejoice with the wife of your youth" (Prov. 5:18). An elder's work for God should be one of rejoicing. Part of being a good husband is also being the head of the wife (1 Cor. 11:3). A wife should be happy to be in subjection to a husband who is kind and thoughtful toward her. The church will be willing to be in subjection to elders who love them and work toward what is good for the flock.

4. Elders must be able to teach to be effective (1 Tim. 3:2). An elder is to be an older man and through his experience he should be able to teach and defend the gospel of Jesus Christ. "Holding fast the faithful word as he has been taught, that he may be able, by sound doctrine, both to exhort and convict those who contradict" (Tit. 1:9). The devil does all he can to hinder the teaching of the gospel. An elder who is not able to effectively teach would cause a local church to be weak and subjected to the devil's influence. Elders need the ability to be able to teach so that others can become effective teachers (2 Tim. 2:2). Elders must be able to know how to give a reason for their faith with grace and not offense (Col. 4:6). Once again we see God's wisdom in selecting older men to become elders because their answers come with experience. Youth does not always give one the ability to have his speech seasoned with grace and salt. "The glory of young men is their strength, and the splendor of old men is their gray head" (Prov. 20:29).

5. The duty of an eldership is to be found as a good example of faithfulness. How could an elder lead if he is not faithful in all his duties and service to the Lord? It is a requirement of the Lord for His servant to be found as an example of faithfulness. It is through faithfulness that a man's example is to be found as a testimony of the hope that he has (Heb. 3:5-6). To be effective in his work an elder is to be found as a faithful and wise servant. It is through such faithfulness that the Lord will be able to say "well done" (Luke 12:42-43). How could an elder be effective in getting the flock to follow him, if he is not going before the flock and setting the example of faithfulness that they need to have to be pleasing to the Lord? Faith is not able to develop as it should without a commitment in doing service for the Lord. An elder's service is a reflection of the value he places upon his work for the Lord. If an elder's work were not important to him, it would be nearly impossible to inspire service from the flock.

6. When members see the elders being good workers in the Lord's church they are willing to work too. "I must work the works of Him who sent Me while it is day; the night is coming when no one can work" (John 9:4). Elders set the example in the importance of the work. It is important for the members to see that the work we are to do is to be done together. We need to work together for the furtherance of the gospel. Elders set the example that we are not to fall short in the Lord's work (Heb. 12:15). They set the importance of showing the flock that we are to be "good stewards" of the work necessary to save souls. We have such a limited time on this earth and the work that is set before us is great. "Do you not say, 'There are still four months and then comes the harvest'? Behold, I say to you, lift up your eyes and look at the fields, for they are already white for harvest!" (John 4:35). Elders are to set the example for the flock so that they may know how important the work of the Lord is.

7. Another important example that elders need to set for the church is the example of being peacemakers. "Blessed are the peacemakers, For they shall be called sons of God" (Matt. 5:9). In too many churches there are problems that are never dealt with. These problems are just festering under the surface. These problems always seem to impede the work and unity of the church. Elders are to be men who can deal with problems and be peacemakers, instead of dictators. To be a peacemaker one needs to "be swift to hear, slow to speak, slow to wrath" (Jas. 1:19). To stop trouble, elders need to listen and hear someone out and really give his idea some thought. It never hurts to be slow and deliberate in studying something out. Elders need to pray, study, and give serious thought to things before they speak. This too comes with maturity. Peacemakers will be called God's sons because they are developing the character of God (Matt. 5:9).

Wrath should always be a very slow process. It is right to be angry about sin but we are never to hate the sinner. "'Be angry, and do not sin': do not let the sun go down on your wrath" (Eph. 4:26). Uncontrolled anger never produces peace, but war. Mature godly men have control over such thoughts. "Let all bitterness, wrath, anger, clamor, and evil speaking be put away

The Terms Used to Describe Elders

from you, with all malice" (Eph. 4:31). If they have studied the Scriptures as they should, elders know that God wants them to live peaceably (Rom. 12:16-18). To have peace in the church, elders need to set the example for the flock. Peace is important in the church, but there needs to be peace in the elder's home, too. Homes that are peaceful tend to produce peace in the church. Peace in the church tends to be able to attract others to want to become members of the body of Christ. Peace in the church also produces unity in the body of Christ. "For God is not the author of confusion but of peace, as in all the churches of the saints" (1 Cor. 14:33). "Till we all come to the unity of the faith and of the knowledge of the Son of God, to a perfect man, to the measure of the stature of the fullness of Christ" (Eph. 4:13). The work that elders are to do is produce the "unity of the faith" and the "perfect man" (a mature Christian). This is the gift given to the church by God (Eph. 4:11-16).

Summary

Being an elder is a high calling for a Christian man and one that should be received with all joy. The church clearly needs good leadership. The church cannot grow spiritually as it should without good leadership. God saw the necessity for the church to have qualified leadership. God, through the Holy Spirit, inspired the apostles to give the qualifications for those who are to serve the church as elders. Not having elders to serve in the church is to be not scripturally organized. There are decisions that need to be made about the work of the church which need to be decided by men of experience and wisdom. Unqualified men and younger men do not have the wisdom and experience to make these decisions about the work of the church. The work of the church is the most important work in the world. All material things will be destroyed with the earth, but souls are eternal. How we live here on earth will determine where we will live in the next life. We only have one chance to get it right on this earth.

It is an honor to be chosen to be an elder. Every male child needs to set this as his true goal in life, to serve with honor in the most important office which a man could ever be called to serve. Serving as an elder is very demanding, but it is also very exciting. Elders have the joy of seeing people grow in their Christian faith to be a full grown and dedicated servant to the Lord. Those who once were young and weak in their faith grow to the point that they are able to teach and follow the truth. Seeing Christians overcome great adversity and become stronger and more committed to God is the greatest of all joys in this life.

Our Bibles tell us that those who serve as elders will receive double honor, "Let the elders who rule well be counted worthy of double honor, especially those who labor in the word and doctrine" (1 Tim. 5:17). They are to be esteemed, "And we urge you, brethren, to recognize those who labor among you, and are over you in the Lord and admonish you, and to esteem them very highly in love for their work's sake. Be at peace among yourselves" (1 Thess. 5:12-13). Elders will receive a crown from the Chief Shepherd, "and when the Chief Shepherd appears, you will receive the crown of glory that does not fade away" (1 Pet. 5:4). May we all strive to understand and respect this high calling from the Lord!

Bibliography

Accordance. Oak Tree software Inc.

Bible Explorer Macintosh. Word Search Media.

Bible. *New King James*. Nashville: Broadman and Holman Publishers, 1996.

Dehofff, George. *Dehoff's Commentary*, VI. Murfreesboro, TN: Dehoff Publications, 1982.

MacArthur. *The MacArthur Topical Bible*. Nashville: Thomas Nelson Publisher, 1999.

Online Bible Macintosh. Cross Country Software

Phillips, H.E. *Scriptural Elders And Deacons*. Bowling Green, KY: Guardian of Truth, 1959.

Quick Verse Macintosh Gold. Find Ex. Company Inc.

The Qualifications as They Relate to the Work of Elders

Randy Blackaby

Virtually any study or discussion of church elders immediately focuses on the qualifications for this office. Does the person have "believing children," what does that entail, and must all his children be faithful? Is the person "apt," or able, "to teach" and is he a good leader in the home? But when was the last time you heard a significant discussion of the "work" of elders?

What is the role or work of elders in the Lord's church? Ask 100 members of the Lord's church and you're liable to get that many varied views. Many answers will be correct, though very generic. Others will be misguided, viewing pastors as everything from business managers, to near monarchs, to absolutely perfect models of faith.

Those ordained to be elders must meet the divine qualifications enumer-

---

Randy Blackaby lives in Medway, OH and preaches at the nearby New Carlisle Church of Christ, not far from where he grew up in Xenia. He serves as one of three elders in New Carlisle. He has preached for nearly forty years, about twenty-two in a full-time capacity.

He and his wife, Karen, have four sons (Joshua, Josiah, Ezra, and Amos) and now enjoy five grandchildren.

From 1971 to 1988, he was a reporter and later managing editor of the *Xenia Daily Gazette* in Ohio, while also preaching for congregations in Ohio, Indiana, and Kentucky. He has used his writing experience in producing op-ed columns on moral issues in the news, as well as Bible Q&A columns in a variety of local newspapers since leaving the newspaper business.

In 1988, he began full-time work at the Courtland Ave. Church of Christ in Kokomo, IN. He left there in 2002 to preach in New Carlisle.

Randy is a staff writer for *Truth Magazine* and also contributes to several other publications. He has authored workbooks on *Galatians* and the life and work of *Moses* for the Guardian of Truth Foundation.

ated in Scripture. Yet, it is not unusual for a congregation to study these qualifications for years, spend months selecting and ordaining men, only to discover the new elders have little idea what it is they are supposed to do.

Many preachers may err in judgment, spending weeks on lessons focused on the "qualifications" listed in 1 Timothy 3:1-7 and Titus 1:5-9 and then doing, perhaps, only one lesson on the "work" of these men.

And thus, when the preaching is accomplished and the men appointed, it still is not uncommon to find preachers doing the elders' work, elders doing the deacons' work, and the deacons doing little or nothing. This is both unscriptural and impractical, and any congregation in such a situation suffers.

The Common Approach

Much of the explanation of elder function has centered on the terminology used in Scripture to describe the office, words like "elders" (*presbuterion*), "shepherd" or "pastor" (*poimen*), "overseer" or "bishop" (*episcopos*), and "steward" (*oikonomos*). There is absolutely nothing wrong with this approach, for it does give us our fundamental concept of what the Lord has in mind for those who lead and feed the local flock.

But often there is no clear linkage made between the qualifications set forth by the Apostle Paul and the nature and methodology of a pastor's work. Common sense dictates that God has not arbitrarily mandated standards for those who undertake this service. Each standard, condition, or experience demanded directly relates to accomplishing the work expected.

Further, many questions about "how" elders are to accomplish their commissions can be answered by understanding the need and purpose for each qualification.

Let's now observe how the standards set forth by the apostle relate to the nature and execution of the job of overseeing a local body of saints. First, we'll look at the standards in a general fashion, later more specifically.

Elders Need to Be Mature Christian Men

To develop a more comprehensive view of an elder's work, it is critical to see in the job qualifications more than mere hurdles to be cleared. That said, it quickly is observable that only a handful of the criteria are unique to elders. Not every Christian must be a man, husband, father, or non-novice. But all the other qualifications are character traits and behaviors to which every Christian is directed to grow.

Thus, what an overview of 1 Timothy 3 and Titus 1 demonstrates is that local congregations should be looking for "mature" Christian men with experience in leading a smaller group (their families), so they can lead a larger group (local church). They must be men who not only are growing toward these standards but who have, to a discernible and significant degree, achieved those goals.

Does this mean bishop candidates must be sinless and thus perfect in that sense? Obviously not, or no congregation would have elders.

We observe that a few of the qualifications are what might be called "absolute." A person either is a man, a father, a husband or not. There is little or no room for human judgment here. On the other hand, the remaining requirements are somewhat "relative."

Calling them "relative" does not suggest they are unimportant or that they can be ignored. It merely acknowledges that men will have achieved these goals in varying degrees and that what is sought in an elder is a man who has achieved them to an appreciable degree. Each congregation will have to use some judgment here.

None of the inspired qualifications can be ignored. All are "musts" (1 Tim. 3:2, 7). No one qualification is more important than the others. That said, it often is the case that one elder may have achieved a higher degree of accomplishment in one area than another elder. There may be degrees of attainment, yet all must be significantly achieved *before* appointment.

There are degrees of ability to teach. Such is likewise true with hospitality and success in guiding one's own house. Being human, the qualifications of temperance, sober-mindedness, and loving good can't be measured in absolute perfection.

Yet, each congregation needs mature men able to do the work of elders, able to set an example of the behaviors and character traits, which every Christian is commanded to develop.

Still looking at the criteria for serving as an elder in a general sense, we observe both positive and negative qualifications. Again, this is instructive as we observe that elders are to be models or examples to less mature Christians (1 Pet. 5:3). They are to be men who have added to their lives certain positive characteristics and, conversely, are successful in having removed certain negative behaviors.

So, again, while all Christians are under obligation as they mature in the faith to "put on" the positive traits and "take off" the negative ones (Eph. 4:22-24), not every Christian is yet fully mature in such matters. Yet the man to be considered for the office of an elder must be mature. If he is less than mature, or worse, a novice, he will be unable to carry out the task.

This maturity requires some experience. How do you get experience before you undertake the office of the eldership? We see in the qualifications that it is by having been successful as a husband and father, leading and guiding a wife and family. Such success won't be observable for a number of years, thus young men are not qualified to be pastors of the church.

The Home: Microcosm of the Church

In many ways, the home is a microcosm of the church. If a man learns to exercise God-given authority in the home, in the manner that God directs, then he has the necessary ability to exercise a very similar form of authority in the larger venue of the church. The apostle declares this point in this manner: "one who rules his own house well, having his children in submission with all reverence (for if a man does not know how to rule his own house, how will he take care of the church of God?)" (1 Tim. 3:4-5).

This is a critical part of an elder's training. It is crucial experience. God has given men leadership and authority over their wives and children in the home (1 Cor. 11:3; Eph. 5:22-23; 6:4). Yet, a man can't exercise that authority through brute force or by merely demanding they obey his orders. He must lovingly lead and guide his family, putting their needs before his own, teaching them that following his lead is God's will, not merely his own.

The parallel should be clear. The authority of elders isn't like that of a corporate chief or military officer. He must lovingly lead the flock of God over which he has oversight, teach members that obedience isn't merely to his opinions or desires, but to God's declared and codified will.

More often than not, the obstacle to Christian men serving as elders is past failure at home. This is sad. It isn't something that a man can go back and repair, in most cases. It also suggests the need to teach young men and women more earnestly about the need to live faithful to God's standards from the very beginning of their married lives. And it suggests that waiting to preach on the eldership until the need arises is shortsighted.

When we look at the qualifications for elders as a whole, we see they involve the totality of a man's experience, reputation, domestic relations, character, habits, knowledge, and capacity to teach others.

These domestic qualifications never have been of greater importance than in the present generation. Our culture knows nearly nothing about the godly exercise of authority. In fact, authority itself is largely disdained. Such disdain, combined with the impact of radical feminism, has resulted in a vacuum of home leadership or a perversion of God's plan for such.

The popular mythology of home leadership today is "joint" or "shared" leadership involving husband and wife. Such is oxymoronic, if one has any sense of true leadership. So, it is not surprising that many brethren, under such influence, seek to direct both the home and church by "committee" or some amorphous method of "collective agreement."

God has authority, which He exercises. His earthly shepherds also have authority, and must know how to exercise it correctly.

A Closer Look: What Each Qualification Shows Us About the Work

An elder should be a man, because the office involves the exercise of authority. Perhaps the most important concept to be derived from the requirement that an elder be a man is that the job of pastor involves the exercise of authority. God has given men, not women, authority in both the home and church. Just before beginning his recitation of elder qualifications in 1 Timothy, Paul clearly declared, "And I do not permit a woman to teach or have authority over a man, but to be in silence" (2:12).

Nothing in Scripture suggests women are spiritually inferior or inept in judgment. But it does declare their role is not to involve authority over men.

While the Greek word for "man" in Timothy and "if any" in Titus are not definitive as to gender, the requirement to be "the husband of one wife" (1 Tim. 3:2; Tit. 1:6) clarifies the Divine will, as does the qualification that such a person "rule his own house well" (1 Tim. 3:4).

A man who is a godly husband and head of a family understands the nature of the authority granted him. Ephesians 5:22-24 is instructive. "Wives, submit to your own husbands, as to the Lord. For the husband is head of the wife, as also Christ is head of the church; and He is the Savior of the body. Therefore, just as the church is subject to Christ, so let the wives be to their own husbands in everything."

Understanding a man's authority in the home reveals much about the nature of an elder's authority in the church. We learn from the Apostle Paul that "the head of every man is Christ, the head of woman is man, and the head of Christ is God" (1 Cor. 11:3). Thus, such delegated authority is subject to a higher authority, and is not absolute or undefined.

Yet, as in the home, the role of church bishop definitely involves the proper exercise of authority. In Hebrews 13:17 we are exhorted to "obey those who rule over you, and be submissive, for they watch out for your souls. . . ." The words "obey," "rule," and "be submissive" demonstrate that authority adheres to the job.

It is not the style of authority exercised in the world (Gentile-style) and elders aren't "lords" over the flock, but it certainly involves the congregation voluntarily deferring to, submitting to, and obeying the leadership of its overseers (Matt. 20:25-28; 1 Pet. 5:1-3).

Exercising authority in a godly manner is much more difficult than merely giving commands, and thus part of the reason for the extensive qualifications.

Desiring the "work" demonstrates that the eldership is not a mere honorary position. If we had only the English words "office" or "position" before us, we might reach erroneous conclusions about the role of shepherds. It is not uncommon in politics for men and women to be elected to an office and really do no work. Some offices are created as honorary positions. But the apostle closes the door on that concept when he declares that a man must desire the "work" (1 Tim. 3:1).

As we continue to explore the requirements of this office, we further see the nature of the work to be done. And while the work is multi-faceted, the qualifications show it to be less an administrative or mere decision-making role and more a matter of comprehensive leadership, not unlike that exercised in the direction and oversight of a home. And the prerequisites of holding the job show clearly its main objective is the spiritual welfare of God's flock, not merely making decisions about mundane matters.

Thus, a shepherd's work can't be done in a board room or in executive session. His primary responsibility is to "watch out for your souls" (Heb. 13:17), not watching the church checkbook.

Blamelessness shows the need for leadership in obedience. The church's pastors are to be obeyed, as already noted. But the fact that God requires a man to be blameless before assuming this authority demonstrates that he also must be a man known for his own obedience—to the will of God.

This is doubly important to his work. He must first set an example of obedience to those under his direction. Secondly, no sound congregation should want a man directing them who has not demonstrated a habit of living and making decisions in accord with the declared word of God. His leadership is worthless if it doesn't accord with Scripture.

The requirement, set forth in 1 Timothy 3:2 and Titus 1:6, does not imply that a man must be sinless. Common sense and the declaration of Romans 3:23 that "all have sinned and fall short of the glory of God" eliminate false views that a man must never have sinned or never makes a mistake.

The idea, in actuality, is that he is a man against whom charges of wrongdoing can't be sustained, a man "not open to accusation" or, similarly, "above reproach."

If a man's life as a Christian is marked by a high degree of obedience to God and a willingness to repent anytime he finds sin or error in his life, then he will meet the standard of "blameless." When sin is repented of and forgiven, it can't be held to a man's account.

The idea here is very similar to that depicted in 1 John 1:5-10 in reference to "walking in the light." It is absolutely necessary that a man walk in the light, but John also declares that, if any man says he never sins, he's a liar. However, if we confess our sins, God is faithful to forgive us.

The Apostle Peter served as an elder (1 Pet. 5:1) and thus was subject to the requirement of blamelessness. Remember that he was earlier impulsive, even denied the Lord three times at a most critical hour, and once had to be rebuked by the Apostle Paul. But these were exceptions, not the character or pattern of his life.

What brethren should look for is a man whose habit of life is to live godly. He will be a good example and likely to lead you in the right direction. You don't want a man who claims to be sinless. What a terrible and damning example that would be to follow.

A successful husband is a man who is capable of loving leadership. There are no bachelor bishops in the Lord's church. We are told that shepherds must be "the husband of one wife" (1 Tim. 3:2; Tit. 1:6). While marriage teaches many ancillary lessons and produces a myriad of useful experiences, the fundamental thing a man obtains in this relationship that prepares him for the role of an elder is leadership ability.

There are many styles of leadership, from military, to executive, to dictatorial. But God has not selected any of those as the model for shepherd-style leadership. Rather, he has chosen the model of a loving, nurturing husband.

A righteous, Christian husband can't "make" his wife obey him by threat of bodily harm or other intimidations. He is commanded to love his wife as his own body and as Christ loved the church and died to bring it to salvation. He is to nourish and cherish her in the process of leading her (Eph. 5:25-29). Though a few elders seem to think otherwise, they can't "force" their wills on a congregation, either. The congregation must be led in a very similar manner as a husband is to lead his wife.

Both the roles of husband and pastor require that a man understand his responsibility and his accountability for being "out front" in guiding, teaching, correcting, and exemplifying God's will among those he leads.

No man is qualified to lead a local congregation who has left the spiritual leadership of his home to his wife. Yet, sadly, male spiritual leadership in the home has been more the exception than the rule in the last half century among God's people. And, thus, many congregations continue, decade after decade, unable to find men qualified to lead the church, too.

Godly spiritual leadership is never easy work. Those who want to just sit in a meeting, make a decision, and go out and announce it to the congregation will be sorely disappointed and discouraged. And so, when you can't just order righteous behavior and thinking, a great deal of time must be spent teaching and explaining, exhorting and admonishing, and living the message to be conveyed.

When you find a man who has learned to lovingly and actively lead his wife by proper example and consistent appeal to God's word as their guide, you have found a man with the requisite experience and talent to lead a congregation.

On the other hand, when you have a man who sees his role in the home as merely "giving orders" and "bringing home the bacon," you have a man who, when appointed a bishop, thinks he is empowered to arbitrarily enforce his personal opinions on the lives of those in his charge. Many a church has been devastated by such men.

The Qualifications as They Relate to the Work of Elders 131

When a church is under assault by errors being taught or brethren being tempted or succumbing to sin, you don't so much need an "executive committee" as "shepherds." And a man learns the art of shepherding as he leads the woman who is as dear to him as the church is to Christ.

Being a father offers further evidence of leadership ability. Leading a wife, in the role of a husband, entails an experience, generally, with someone of similar maturity or at least age. But being a father expands this leadership experience by learning how to train, guide, gently discipline, and encourage those with little or no knowledge or experience.

The Bible teaches that fathers are to be nurturers or trainers of their children (1 Tim. 6:4). Again, the world assigns this task to mothers primarily and when Christian men abdicate this role, not only do their children suffer but the men are left without the requisite experience needed to nurture and train God's people in a local assembly.

The Bible declares that a bishop must be a man who "rules his own house well, having his children in submission with all reverence" (1 Tim. 3:4) and having children "not accused of dissipation or insubordination" (Tit. 1:6).

The importance of having mature men exercising authority in both the home and the church is so that those under their guidance are led to live holy lives in submission to God's precepts. If a man can be successful in guiding those closest to him on this earth, then he likely can lead the church of the living God.

It is worth pointing out again that the role of a father is not an easy one. It is not enough for a father to live righteously himself, though this is critical. It isn't enough that he be a Christian and worship God. Much more is entailed. He must exercise his leadership as a father in such a way that he does not discourage his children but teaches them God's will and enforces obedience in a godly way so that righteousness and obedience to the divine will become the habit of his children's lives, their character.

He will be daily involved in teaching, encouraging, warning, and illustrating in his own behavior what he (and God) wills for these precious souls. The work of an elder is virtually the same.

That is why the apostle declares that a man who would serve as a church overseer must "rule his own house well, having his children in submission with all reverence (for if a man does not know how to rule his own house, how will he take care of the church of God?)" (1 Tim. 3:4-5).

Faithful children are evidence of successful leadership ability. There are many issues surrounding the demand that an elder have "faithful children" (Tit. 1:6) that will be left to others to address. But as we explore how the qualifications help us understand the work of elders, let it be seen that success in shepherding one's own children in the faith is *prima facie* evidence of an ability to lead God's children (in the context of the church) in the faith.

Among the great tasks of elders is to keep brethren in their charge faithful to the Lord and to draw the unsaved to Christ. Having done so in his family provides confidence in his ability in a larger venue.

So, it is clear why the domestic prerequisites for an elder are divinely ordained. And whether one looks at these in the broadest or narrowest interpretations, their critical importance to success in guiding the spiritual lives of the saints is beyond any reasonable question.

Shepherd's Work Requires Proper Mental State

A vigilant, temperate man is needed to guard the flock of God. Elders or bishops are called "shepherds" for a number of reasons, not least among them the fact that they must protect God's "sheep" against "wolves" (Acts 20:29; Matt. 7:15) and the "roaring lion" who is Satan (1 Pet. 5:8), each seeking to destroy faith and souls.

Sleepy shepherds are abominations. They are as useless in this aspect of their work as a slumbering sentry at the battlefront (Ezek. 34:8).

The word Paul uses in writing to Timothy, which is translated "vigilance" or "temperance," is the Greek word *nephaleon*. It is defined as "to be sober, to be circumspect, temperate, abstaining from wine." So, looking at the concept in its aggregate, perhaps it is fair to say the idea is that of being spiritually and morally alert and observant.

Elders must be self-controlled, both as an example of mature faith to others and so as to have a demeanor to properly handle the myriad issues, crises, and conflicts that will arise as they work in a local church.

While all Christians need this character trait, it generally isn't fully developed in the average saint. Yet the church's leaders must possess the watchful attitude, the observant character, and the not easily frightened or flustered attitude needed to deal with dangers of all sorts.

All need to be made aware that the "Day of the Lord" is coming at an undeclared and unexpected time (1 Thess. 5:1-8). Brethren must be encouraged to live in constant expectation of the glories of God's kingdom yet to be realized.

An elder must have the ability to discover what may not be noticeable to the less observant. Small changes in attitudes, attendance, demeanors, and behaviors should have the vigilant shepherd at attention, not waiting for someone to come tell him they have a problem.

Pastors who aren't observant, either because they aren't vigilant or because they refuse to look, won't see problems developing in the lives of those in their charge. They will answer to the Almighty as did Israel's failed leaders.

The need for alert-minded men as shepherds is further illustrated by the writer of Hebrews, who said, "Obey those who rule over you, and be submissive, for they watch out for your souls, as those who must give account" (13:17).

The work of an elder often involves confrontation and conflict and thus requires the character also described by the word "temperate." Such situations require a man who is self-controlled, moderate, with a cool and calm disposition. He will face people making rash charges, people who themselves are extremely upset and not looking at things very rationally or spiritually. He will be hearing opposite and conflicting stories and must not jump too quickly to conclusions, but be "swift to hear, slow to speak, slow to wrath" (James 1:19). In all this he also must be "gentle" (1 Tim. 3:3).

Further, he must be sober-minded or serious. He can't have his judgment clouded by alcohol, drugs, or sinful passion. He can't be a jokester who takes nothing seriously, for his duty as an elder involves superintending the very souls of God's beloved. Neither can he be ego-driven because a man only thinking self-centeredly hardly can be observant of others.

Some of the negative qualifications support this idea of being self-controlled. He can't be "given to wine" or "greedy for money" or "covetous" (1 Tim. 3:3). Each of those things would become ungodly controlling factors in his life.

Positively, he must be "gentle" or "patient" (1 Tim. 3:3), suggesting a forbearing attitude toward those in temptation or sin, but without compromising with error. This isn't easily accomplished. It takes control not to lash out verbally at some of the absurdities of sinful people. It takes all one's senses not to become "quarrelsome" (3:3) in heated discussions. He must at all times keep the well-being of the "sheep," not just himself, in view.

This qualification seldom is given the attention that the domestic criteria get, but it should be clear how critical it is to success in an eldership.

Self-control or discipline is needed to exemplify right walk. While some translations use the same English word—temperate—the Greek word Paul used in writing to Titus about elder requirements is different from the one he used in writing to Timothy (alluded to above). In Titus, the apostle uses the word *egkrata* to describe another quality necessary to the proper execution of an elder's work.

The word Paul used in writing to Titus means "having the mastery over, having possession of, having control over oneself, self-disciplined, curbing, restraining."

Self-control is a "fruit of the Spirit" mentioned in Galatians 5:23. It is part of the gospel message itself, for Paul preached of such to Felix (Acts 24:25). And it is one of the Christian graces each saint must add to his or her faith (2 Pet. 1:6).

A bishop must first be an example to those who are following him. Self-control is absolutely necessary in a person's disposition, thinking, and character to avoid sins of passion like murder, brawling, fornication, and a host of verbal sins. Thus, negatively, the apostle says an elder can't be "self-willed," "quick-tempered," or "violent" (Tit. 1:7). Neither can he be "quarrelsome" (1 Tim. 3:3).

A disciplined life is necessary to win the ultimate crown of life. Paul wrote, "Do you not know that those who run in a race all run, but one receives the prize? Run in such a way that you may obtain it. And everyone who competes for the prize is temperate in all things. Now they do it to obtain a perishable crown, but we for an imperishable crown. Therefore I run thus: not with uncertainty. Thus I fight: not as one who beats the air. But I discipline my body and bring it into subjection, lest, when I have preached to others, I myself should become disqualified" (1 Cor. 9:24-27).

One of the key duties of a church shepherd is to lead God's flock safely around or through the temptations of life. Most, if not all, sin is the result of losing self-control or personal discipline. Thus, the self-disciplined or God-disciplined life is necessary for living faithfully unto death and receiving the promised crown of life.

Newer Christians must be taught this principle. What an elder teaches verbally he needs to practice in his own life, demonstrating he truly believes such and demonstrating that it is possible to accomplish.

It is not unlike in the home. Parents who want behaved, self-controlled children must themselves be such. Jesus, the "chief shepherd," illustrated this supremely, keeping every false emotion, erroneous impulse, and physical desire under control. He did so up to and including the point of death. Elders need to lead others to live as Christ.

And in dealing with brethren of all levels of maturity, and in times of conflict and confusion, God's leaders must not let their judgment, exhortations, or admonitions be clouded by uncontrolled passions or emotions. They must calmly and rationally explain what God's word demands.

The ability to keep one's senses is critical to a shepherd's work. While it may be simply another variation of the previous qualifications to be vigilant, temperate, and self-controlled, the Scriptures declare a bishop's work demands a man who is "sober" (KJV), "sober-minded" (NKJV, ASA) or "sensible" (RSV, NRSV). The Greek word originally used was *sophrona* and means "discreet, moderate, temperate, chaste, sober, of sound mind, sane, in one's senses, curbing one's desires or impulses."

Some additional shades of meaning can be seen. Sober-mindedness, it is arguable, underlies the vigilance or temperance previously examined. The word speaks to the nature of a person's mind, which in turn effects how the person acts.

God's word is the Christian's greatest tool, and thus, a church overseer's most important. It is a communication from God. It is at once law, guidance, and encouragement and reproof.

Its value is intrinsic, but its impact and power in individual lives is proportional to the nature of the mind receiving it. This, in part, was Jesus' point in the parable of the sower (Matt. 13:1-8, 18-23).

In religion in general, and thus sometimes in the Lord's church, many people are swept to various conclusions and actions by excitements and emotions. But truth is established by a sensible, rational examination of what God's word (the Bible) declares. Elders must be men able to lead people in such a sensible exploration of the divine message.

When Paul was before Festus, he was accused of being out of his mind, beside himself and "mad." But the apostle denied that and declared that he spoke "words of truth and reason" (Acts 26:24-25). He used reason with Festus and sought to get him to use the mental capabilities God had given him to see the truth. Such is the work of elders.

Sobriety certainly demands the mind not be clouded by alcohol or other drugs. But it also demands that a man not think too highly of himself or his own judgment (Rom. 12:3-8).

A bishop who presumes his office makes him of greater importance or value than the Christians in his care is an abject failure. He has failed miserably to understand his role. He must realize he is doing a job for the Lord, while realizing that all other members have important roles in the kingdom as well (Rom. 12:3-8; 1 Cor. 12:12-31).

Such soberness or clear thinking also prevents fear from paralyzing or provoking the child of God. Fear is a very powerful motivator. Much sin is committed out of fear. Elders demonstrating clear-headedness and trust in God go far in leading others to do the same.

Not a few elders have failed in their duties because they feared disciplining members would result in a decline in membership, loss of friendships, prestige, or honor. Or, they simply may fear making the wrong decisions. Such men are not sensible enough for the job.

The role of elder requires a clear-minded ability to search the Scriptures for the truth, a sober trust in God that allays fear, and a serious approach to the work that keeps him able to teach and ready to reprove. Men who must "feel the pulse" and "test the winds" of the congregation aren't using the senses God gave them.

Teaching Role of Elder Requires Total Life Effort

Leadership and example are critical roles for the Lord's shepherds, but he also must be a teacher. To a degree, this already has been observed in the domestic qualifications, where he is to have shown a level of success in, not only leading, but teaching his family, particularly his children.

But teaching is a comprehensive role, not limited to the home, pulpit, or classroom. It is accomplished by both verbal instruction and exemplified in a consistent pattern of living. Thus, the bishop is to be "able to teach" (1 Tim. 3:2) and observant to "hold fast the faithful word as he has been taught, that he may be able, by sound doctrine, both to exhort and convict those who contradict" (Tit. 1:9).

It is sad when brethren assume that a man is qualified to shepherd the flock of God when the most "teaching" he has accomplished is to stand in a Bible class and read the questions someone else has written and nod knowingly at every answer given.

This is not to say an elder must be a scholar, pulpit preacher, or even that his main venue for instruction must be a public assembly. But the ability to teach is absolutely critical, because "feeding" in the shepherd model is the spiritual equivalent of "teaching."

The shepherd can't "protect" the flock either, if he can't adequately demonstrate the error of certain practices and beliefs and the righteousness of others. Brethren who are sinning, struggling, or seeking will need instruction, rebuke, and exhortation. All that takes an ability to present what God's word declares.

If false teaching presents itself, the elder must know God's word well enough to be able to use "sound doctrine" and the "faithful word" to effectively "exhort," "convict," and "convince" those in error. He must be able to shut the mouths of false teachers (Tit. 1:9-11). Thus, both knowledge and teaching ability must be effectively combined.

That said, each congregation will have to make a judgment about each potential shepherd's teaching ability. Just remember, a man can't teach what he doesn't know.

Teaching is also done through an elder's example. Many a preacher and many an elder have preached the right words but seen them ignored because they didn't practice what they preached. Thus, God has ordained that his servant-leaders not only enunciate truth, but be habitual practitioners of it. He is to be "of good behavior" (1 Tim. 3:2) and "a lover of what is good" (Tit. 1:8).

Unlike some of the other requirements, these are very general, suggesting that all aspects of an elder's life and character must be habituated in goodness. Living a good life is what he is to teach others to do, and so he must lead by example.

The phrase "of good behavior" comes from the Greek word *kosmion* and describes a person who is moderate, regular, orderly, well-behaved, modest, well arranged. It is used of a person living a well-ordered life. Interestingly, the word also is used in regard to a righteous woman's adornment (1 Tim. 2:9).

Being a comprehensive concept, good behavior must be seen in every aspect of life, from business dealings to language to dress, just to mention a few things.

Hospitality is a teaching tool good elders utilize. The Apostle Paul declared an overseer of the church must be "given to hospitality" or "hospitable" (1 Tim. 3:2) and a "lover of hospitality" or "hospitable" (Tit. 1:8). Both texts use the Greek word *philoxenon*, which means "hospitable, generous to guests, loving toward guests."

Many a preacher has proclaimed that hospitality among God's people is a quickly disappearing quality. For a whole host of reasons, none of which provide sufficient excuse, brethren don't invite people into their homes as they once did.

This is a sad fact, perhaps better described as a sin, which needs remedy. Thus, a man who is going to lead a local congregation toward greater spirituality and righteousness must be a man who has exemplified hospitality before he is appointed to the office.

The Bible teaches us to be hospitable toward other Christians. 1 Peter 4:9 declares, "Be hospitable to one another without grumbling." But, more broadly, Galatians 6:10 says, "Therefore, as we have opportunity, let us do good to all, especially to those who are of the household of faith." However, hospitality goes yet further, demonstrating kindness to strangers. "Do not forget to entertain strangers, for by so doing some have unwittingly entertained angels" (Heb. 13:2).

Now one might categorize hospitality with the domestic qualifications of an elder, and that would be proper enough. One might also suggest it demonstrates the sort of love God has shown for those alien to His fellowship.

But consider that true hospitality bespeaks a loving, kind, and caring disposition key to teaching both the lost and the struggling. Make no mistake, the gospel, not kindness, is the central message of salvation. But people are led to and motivated to listen to that message by people who demonstrate a sincere and loving interest in their welfare.

Think about it. Where a man's home is his castle and the place where he cares for and protects his family, it speaks well of him when he invites an outsider or stranger into that domain. It says a great deal about his attitude and love for the person invited.

The Qualifications as They Relate to the Work of Elders

To "break bread" with another demonstrates a certain degree of intimacy or a desire for such closeness. This is seen clearly in that, when fellowship among brethren is broken by sin, we are commanded "not to eat" with or "keep company" with such a one until he repents (1 Cor. 5:9-11; 2 Thess. 3:14).

In extending hospitality to unbelievers, we express love for them, as Jesus did when He ate with sinners and taught them God's will. And being hospitable links us with the principle of "loving our neighbor" taught in Jesus' story of the Good Samaritan.

It seems that many brethren have lost sight of the fact that the home, not the church building, is the most important center for teaching the lost. The Lord's church critically needs leaders who will use their homes freely in the service of Christ.

Isn't it ironic that, while the typical American's house as doubled, tripled, or quadrupled in average size over the past forty or fifty years, the practice of hospitality has declined in near reverse proportions.

An elder must have a good reputation outside church. One aspect of Christian life critically in need of both teaching and example today is consistency. A Christian must live as such not only on Sundays and before his fellow saints, but daily and in every aspect of life.

Elders, as teachers and leaders, must set forth a pattern of such consistency. Paul wrote, "Moreover, he must have a good testimony among those who are outside, lest he fall into reproach and the snare of the devil" (1 Tim. 3:7). To do otherwise depicts either spiritual immaturity or outright hypocrisy.

A shepherd with a good reputation among unbelievers teaches by example both saint and sinner the ways of God. He is the kind of man people turn to for help and direction when they need it.

Elders Must Be Models

In the same sense as the Apostle Paul wrote, "Therefore be imitators of God as dear children" (Eph. 5:1) and "Imitate me, just as I also imitate Christ" (1 Cor. 11:1), elders must live in such a fashion that they can infer the same to those Christians in their charge. They must, like Paul, be models.

So, to qualify for the job of pastor, a man must be observably "holy" and "just" (Tit. 1:8). The word "holy" suggests being set apart from the practice of sin (pure) and set apart for God's service. Being "just" demonstrates the overseer must seek to deal rightly or righteously with others and to be dedicated to what is right—even strict about it.

These requirements generally don't get the attention some others do in congregational discussions, but it should be clear enough how important they are.

Conclusion

A closer look at the qualifications for elders helps us immensely in seeing that the focus of an elder's work is the spiritual welfare of the local church. If all a bishop needed to oversee was church finances, the Lord could have told us to seek out the best businessman in the congregation. If we needed a "king" to rule us, God could have laid out political, military, and other qualifications. If a men's "business meeting," utilizing both mature men and novices, was God's plan, why did He set forth such comprehensive guidelines for elders?

Two sad facts are apparent. Most congregations are directed by business meetings. And, virtually all these meetings, while able to deal with money matters, building maintenance, and scheduling some annual gospel meetings, fail miserably at spiritual oversight. It probably is not an over-statement to say they are destined to be failures in the spiritual arena.

God is an all-wise and benevolent God. So, He has given us guidelines to find mature, loving, biblically-literate leaders, who have shown they can teach others and live what they teach. This is the pattern God has given us for successful spiritual leadership in the Lord's church. All other models will fail.

The Lord's two lists of qualifications, when combined and assessed, tell us to select men "who by reason of use have their senses exercised to discern both good and evil" (Heb. 5:14). In other words, we need experienced, successful Christian men.

They will be lovers of truth, lovers of their fellow men, and lovers of God. They will be teachers, not mere instructors but men who show others how to do what they are verbally directing.

They will be humble, serving as servants rather than lords. They will have their senses, their mental, moral, and spiritual faculties, under control so that their physical behavior is a model of just, righteous living.

These men may have meetings to discuss various matters, but the board room won't be their primary workplace. Rather, they'll be accomplishing their tasks among the flock, among which the Holy Spirit has made them overseers (Acts 20:28).

There may be money matters or other physical issues that directly relate to the spiritual welfare of the church, which these pastors will need to address. But the deacons can handle most such matters. Elders are commissioned to "watch out for your souls, as those who must give account" (Heb. 13:17).

The Apostle Peter, himself an elder, held out this promise to those who will shepherd God's people faithfully. He said, "and when the Chief Shepherd appears, you will receive the crown of glory that does not fade away" (1 Pet. 5:1-4).

May the Lord open our eyes to envision the true power of spiritual shepherds and our need to both develop and appoint men who can instruct and then demonstrate how to be mature servants of God. Such will be imitators of the "good shepherd," who is Jesus, the Son of God Himself (John 10:11).

Bibliography
General Works

Myers, J. B. *The Church and Its Elders.* Ft. Worth: Star Bible, 1981.

Moore, Charles. *Functioning Leadership in the Church.* Austin: Firm Foundation Publishing House, 1973.

Phillips, H.E. *Scriptural Elders and Deacons.* Bowling Green: Guardian of Truth Foundation Publications, 1959.

Patton, Marshall. *Truth Commentaries: 1-2 Timothy, Titus, Philemon.* Mike Willis, editor. Bowling Green: Guardian of Truth Foundation 2001.

Periodicals

The Spiritual Sword, "The Responsibility of Elders" (October 2009), Vol. 41, No. 1.

Internet

Blackaby, Randy. *Re-thinking Magazine.* Allan Turner, editor (*allanturner.com*). "The Work of Elders is the Critical Matter," January 2006.

_____. *Re-thinking Magazine.* Allan Turner, editor (*allanturner.com*). "Choosing Elders," Parts I, II, III, IV, V, VI, VII, May-December 2006.

_____. *Re-thinking Magazine*. Allan Turner, editor (*allanturner.com*). "Are Business Meetings a Scriptural Expedient in the Absence of Elders?" February 2006.

When Elders Abuse Their Authority
Jerry Blount
Scripture Reading: Acts 20:25-35

And indeed, now I know that you all, among whom I have gone preaching the kingdom of God, will see my face no more. Therefore I testify to you this day that I am innocent of the blood of all men. For I have not shunned to declare to you the whole counsel of God. Therefore take heed to yourselves and to all the flock, among which the Holy Spirit has made you overseers, to shepherd the church of God which He purchased with His own blood. For I know this, that after my departure savage wolves will come in among you, not sparing the flock. Also from among yourselves men will rise up, speaking perverse things, to draw away the disciples after themselves. Therefore watch, and remember that for three years I did not cease to warn everyone night and day with tears. So now, brethren, I commend you to God and to the word of His grace, which is able to build you up and give you an inheritance among all those who are sanctified. I have coveted no one's silver or gold or apparel. Yes, you yourselves know that these hands have provided for my necessities, and for those who were with me. I have shown you in every way, by laboring like this, that you must support the weak. And remember the words of

---

Jerry Blount was born in Enid, OK in 1955. He was raised in Kansas City, MO. He married his high school sweetheart, Teri, in 1974. He was raised in the Christian Church and Teri in the Lutheran Church. He and Teri obeyed the gospel in 1977 through the efforts of John Witt, then of the Hickman Mills congregation in Kansas City. They have three children, two boys and a girl. They have five grandchildren and counting.

He attended Florida College in 1977-79. His first full-time work was with the South Platte congregation in Parkville, MO (N. Kansas City). He has served as the evangelist for Valdosta Street, El Dorado, and Pleasant Valley congregations. Jerry served as an elder for the Pleasant Valley congregation for twelve years. He currently works with the Pillar congregation in Wichita, KS. He has been preaching the gospel for over thirty years. Jerry also publishes "Jerry's Christian Jottings." An e-zine with over 30,000 readers.

the Lord Jesus, that He said, "It is more blessed to give than to receive" (Acts 20:25-35).

Since this passage is the crux of Paul's last admonition to the Ephesian elders, we will use it as the basis our study of the abuse of the eldership. Paul's point is to warn these elders that some from their midst are going to abuse their position as soon as Paul is out of the picture.

Ironically, Paul sets up some things from his own life to serve as the necessary example for them. Unlike Peter, Paul never served as an elder. That being said, in the beginning (Acts 2ff), the apostolic office encompassed the roles of elder, evangelist, etc. As the church went from one congregation (Jerusalem) to several congregations scattered throughout the world, that role began to be divided up. The local men were chosen to serve in their local works.

We can see the process of the apostolic office actually giving way to the eldership in Acts 15. The local church at Antioch had a dispute over circumcision. "And when Paul and Barnabas had great dissension and debate with them" (Acts 15:2).

This dispute was caused by teaching coming in from the outside (Jerusalem reputedly). How did the church handle it? ". . . the brethren determined that Paul and Barnabas and some others of them should go up to Jerusalem to the apostles and elders concerning this issue" (Acts 15:2).

Note that the brethren made this decision. Now when Paul and Barnabus arrived, Peter and the other apostles didn't make the decision in a corner. It was made by the apostles and the elders.

> Then it seemed good to the apostles and the elders, with the whole church, to choose men from among them to send to Antioch with Paul and Barnabas—Judas called Barsabbas, and Silas, leading men among the brethren, and they sent this letter by them, The apostles and the brethren who are elders, to the brethren in Antioch and Syria and Cilicia who are from the Gentiles, greetings (Acts 15:22-23).

It is worthwhile to note that, even with apostles and elders, the church played a role as well. Elders making decisions without the church being kept in the loop, cheat the congregation they lead out of gaining the maturity needed for the next generation.

Paul's first warning or observation was, "I did not shrink from declaring to you the whole purpose of God." Obviously as Paul prioritizes the duties

When Elders Abuse Their Authority

and, by contrast, the failures of the eldership, this ranks at the top of his inspired list.

What is an elder's job? Titus 1:9: ". . . holding fast the faithful word which is in accordance with the teaching, so that he will be able both to exhort in sound doctrine and to refute those who contradict." Both the elder and preacher are placed in a position of trust. Let's ask an obvious question, "What is the absolute worst thing that an elder, as an elder, can do to a congregation?" The answer is this: Let go of some " minor portion" of God's word!

The word can never be whole with some portion missing. "Woe to the rebellious children," declares the Lord, "who execute a plan, but not Mine, And make an alliance, but not of My Spirit, In order to add sin to sin" (Isa. 30:1).

We hear of many things that preachers and elders alike can do, or have done, to fail the trust placed in them. Some regular examples are: having sexual affairs, making shady business deals, making exceptions to the biblically based rules for their families, etc. These are various forms of hypocrisy seen in practice. That said, out of all the possibilities, this simple act of omission (shrinking back) is the most deadly to a church. While hypocrisy can generally be easily spotted, the act of leaving out a portion of God's word can be so subtle (in the beginning), but it leads to all the things that follow in Paul's list.

Not too long ago, a deacon in the Lord's church told me, "We have too many Bible studies around here. I have been talking to several. The people in my generation want more social things."

God's Word is complete and, through its completeness, Jesus leads. Every time a portion of Jesus' leadership is trimmed off, of necessity one discards the wisdom of Jesus, in favor of the wisdom of man.

The point of God's revealing Scripture and giving it to us is that "the man of God may be adequate, equipped for every good work" (2 Tim. 3:16-17). When a portion of Scripture is "shrunk back from," the flock is ill equipped.

One Modern Example of "Shrinking Back"

I recently had a conversation with a local elder regarding marriage, divorce, and remarriage. I had presented an overview of the Bible's teaching. What was his reaction?

Well, I have to agree with you. That is what the Bible teaches on the subject. However, I just don't buy it. I just can't make myself say that . . . and I don't believe the church should get involved in this subject. We should stay out of it and let God sort this out in the judgment.

So, does it matter if an elder "shrinks back" from tough moral issues? The Apostle Paul declares that his consistency in this matter is what freed him from the blood of all men. How many elders in our "liberal" society have the blood of the "ignorantly guilty" on their hands because at a crucial time, those elders cut and run?

Elders Are God's Watchmen

Son of man, I have made you a watchman for the house of Israel; therefore hear a word from My mouth, and give them warning from Me: When I say to the wicked, "You shall surely die," and you give him no warning, nor speak to warn the wicked from his wicked way, to save his life, that same wicked man shall die in his iniquity; but his blood I will require at your hand. Yet, if you warn the wicked, and he does not turn from his wickedness, nor from his wicked way, he shall die in his iniquity; but you have delivered your soul (Ezek. 3:17-19).

The principle is ancient and leads us into Paul's next point. Note Paul's second warning: "Be on guard for yourselves . . . and the flock." In the final analysis, an elder is on guard duty. He is in fact the gate keeper for the local congregation. The apostles were once the gate keepers for the church universal. Jesus told them, "Truly I say to you, whatever you bind on earth shall have been bound in heaven; and whatever you loose on earth shall have been loosed in heaven" (Matt. 18:18).

The church "began" as a large local church in Jerusalem. The "gate" was only open to Jews at the time. What had been "loosed in heaven" was eventually "loosed" on earth (Matt. 16:19) as Peter opened the gate to Gentiles in Acts 10. Peter didn't open the flood gates! In the light of modern circumstances, it worthwhile to note that Peter did not also open the gate to immorality within the body. He opened the gate to the sinners but they must repent of those sins to walk through God's gate of salvation. The church in Corinth seems to have missed that point and Paul specifically commands them to close the gate when they next come together (1 Cor. 5:4).

The apostles "guarded," as they revealed the word. The elders of today "guard" as they use the revealed word. "Obey your leaders and submit to them, for they keep watch over your souls as those who will give an account. Let them do this with joy and not with grief, for this would be unprofitable for you" (Heb. 13:17).

It is devastating to the congregation if they are having to "watch out for" the false teaching and hypocrisy of the elders. Everything is not as it is supposed to be.

An "Orderly" Guard on Duty

The prioritized order of an elder's focus during his shift on guard duty is specified by Scripture. Neither he nor his family is exempt from the scriptural admonitions. In fact, in 1 Timothy 3, there is a focus on him personally and the people closest to him in setting the qualifications necessary for him to be placed in the position of God's gatekeeper in the local church.

Most are familiar with the family qualifications involved. The implication of one of those "other" qualifications is worth noting here: "Not a new convert, so that he will not become conceited and fall into the condemnation incurred by the devil" (1 Tim. 3:6). Obviously, it is not only the new converts who become conceited, self-centered, and fail their flock. Your odds of avoidance are better with seasoned men at the helm, hence the inspired requirement.

Note further that the preacher is given the specific task of being sure that the elder does his job consistently. The preacher is also admonished to be sure the "guarding" that falls to him is done without prejudice.

Checking on the Guards

Do not receive an accusation against an elder except from two or three witnesses. Those who are sinning rebuke in the presence of all, that the rest also may fear. I charge you before God and the Lord Jesus Christ and the elect angels that you observe these things without prejudice, doing nothing with partiality (1 Tim. 5:19-21).

The preacher, Timothy, is admonished to provide a sort of "check and balance" of congregational leadership. If charges of sinning (which would include abuse of his office among other things) come up in an eldership, it was specifically prohibited for Timothy to show partiality in applying the principles of godliness. This prohibition applies, even if it puts him on a collision course with the sinning elders.

There is no way around the fact that it is hard to guard the flock if you are exempting yourself or your family from the various mandates of Scripture (or just plain ignoring them for personal reasons).

But . . . Not My Kids!

Let's illustrate with a current example. One elder whom I believed to be abusing his position thought he had the right to lead a congregation even though an elder is required to have believing children. In his case *all of his kids* were in (and actively promoting) liberal churches. He had also promoted, on behalf of his son, one of the most liberal sponsoring church arrangements around. At the same time, he claimed to be "conservative." The preacher of the congregation defended the elder's promotion of liberal churches as a "personal liberty." It is hard for any man, let alone an elder, to make the appeal to parents to teach them in the Lord's good way, *if his own children (with his blessing!) have rejected such.*

The elder's job is defined by Paul as to hold "fast the faithful word which is in accordance with the teaching, so that he will be able both to exhort in sound doctrine and to refute those who contradict" (Tit. 1:9).

Guarding oneself (and those who are his) is the first step to being a good elder. Excusing oneself is his most likely failure. He must lead rather than drive the group he shepherds. He does this by being out front in following the "Chief Shepherd's" lead.

My Flock or God's?

Note a third danger or example of abuse: "Which He purchased with His own blood." Sometimes it is easy just to overlook the obvious. As the elder leads, protects, and pours his heart into "his" flock, it is easy to forget that the flock isn't really "his"! God has made him an overseer of *God's flock*.

You can do as you choose and lead as you choose, if what you are leading is "yours." In this case when an elder "draws away" disciples, in his heart, he has to have first forgotten whose disciples they are. By nature, Christians (all Christians) must be willing to follow. The elder has the ability, by virtue of his position, to confuse the sheep over which shepherd they are following.

After you have been preaching a while, it is impossible to study such a subject as this without modern examples vividly coming to mind. I know one elder who holds to beliefs on how to derive authority and marriage, divorce, and remarriage that would be deemed unscriptural by faithful brethren. These beliefs have led to two different splits in the same congregation over the years. He generally conceals his beliefs, but they emerge occasionally. When they do, the local church splits. Each time, he has labeled the situation to be the result of stubbornness on the part of his detractors.

He considers the congregation to be "his" flock. In many respects, it really is "his" flock. That flock has proven that it will blindly follow him anywhere. Sheep by nature "choose" not to be aware of their surroundings as they follow *their* leader. The necessity of choosing the right "kind" of leader is essential to the health and safety of a local congregation.

In the pulpit we would call this phenomenon "preacheritus." We don't speak much of "elderitus." The Apostle Paul warns us of "elderitus," nonetheless. It is important to note that "elderitus" is likely the more dangerous of the two forms of "will worship."

Ungodly Methods of Luring the Godly

> Now I urge you, brethren, note those who cause divisions and offenses, contrary to the doctrine which you learned, and avoid them. For those who are such do not serve our Lord Jesus Christ, but their own belly, and by smooth words and flattering speech deceive the hearts of the simple (Rom. 16:17-18).

Over the years, the elder noted above, through his beliefs, has caused the congregation a lot of grief and yet he holds onto his position of leadership.

> Nevertheless the solid foundation of God stands, having this seal: "The Lord knows those who are His," and, "Let everyone who names the name of Christ depart from iniquity" (2 Tim. 2:19).

Note a fourth and fifth element of abuse: "Not sparing the flock, speaking perverse things, to draw away the disciples after them." It is difficult to separate the third, fourth, and fifth elements of an elder's abuse of his trust. I am compelled to make a practical observation. Over the years, I have always seen these three together whenever I have seen any of them.

The flock is partly to blame for all this as they have forgotten where their loyalty lies. This tug between what people want and what they should want has always been a part of leadership. There will always be someone wishing to follow men, and there will always be someone wishing to be followed.

> An astonishing and horrible thing Has been committed in the land: The prophets prophesy falsely, And the priests rule by their own power; And My people love to have it so. But what will you do in the end? (Jer. 5:30-31).

Note that the ancient terminology describing this tug of war is "ruling on their own authority" (or "bearing rule by their means," KJV).

But Elders Said To . . .

How do you define a "perverse thing"? I would submit to you that when an eldership leads a group "away from" or "in defiance of" the Scriptures, that is a perverse thing. Note that the abusing elder uses loyalty "to him" to guide what becomes "his flock" rather than loyalty to Jesus.

Jesus warned us that such leadership would be incredibly effective, albeit ungodly.

> Enter by the narrow gate; for wide is the gate and broad is the way that leads to destruction, and there are many who go in by it. Because narrow is the gate and difficult is the way which leads to life, and there are few who find it. Beware of false prophets, who come to you in sheep's clothing, but inwardly they are ravenous wolves. You will know them by their fruits. Do men gather grapes from thornbushes or figs from thistles? Even so, every good tree bears good fruit, but a bad tree bears bad fruit. A good tree cannot bear bad fruit, nor can a bad tree bear good fruit. Every tree that does not bear good fruit is cut down and thrown into the fire. Therefore by their fruits you will know them (Matt. 7:13-20).

In the late 1800s or early 1900s, when the "progressives" spoke perverse things and urged disciples to follow them, the majority of the churches just went on and followed them. The leadership in place at the time had men "from among" the eldership rise up and they drew Jesus' disciples away from Scripture. Those opposed to those men's innovations were described as "backward."

In the 1950s and 1960s, when the "institutional" and "social gospel" folks spoke perverse things once again, the majority of the churches followed them, this time labeling those opposed as "anti." Again, this group that brought in something new succeeded in drawing away the majority of the congregations.

Today the "forgetting" generation has arisen. Will the leaders who are taking the torch "choose" to remember?

> The people served the Lord all the days of Joshua, and all the days of the elders who survived Joshua, who had seen all the great work of the Lord which He had done for Israel (Judg. 2:7).

Like the elders at Ephesus who served the Lord while under Paul's tutelage, those of the 1950s and 1960s who had to stand for the truth have continued to stand. Paul was concerned as he left them. Why? Paul commended them "to God and to the word of His grace" (Acts 20:32) But he knew both by

When Elders Abuse Their Authority

the spirit and his knowledge of history that the next generation's leadership would struggle over whether to follow God or man. History speaks clearly.

> All that generation also were gathered to their fathers; and there arose another generation after them who did not know the Lord, nor yet the work which He had done for Israel (Judg. 2:10).

As in the generation after Joshua, and the one following Paul, today another generation has arisen who have never had to stand their ground. They don't realize what is really at stake. They have heard the words, but they have not the experience with the words.

Once again God's people find themselves at the next historical crossroads. This generation's version of the "progressives" are now trying to throw off Jesus' leadership. They are once again using the loyalty to "each other" as the fulcrum to pry the untaught, unconverted, and uncaring away from the absolutes of Scripture.

Once again, a very old choice is before the church. Will its leadership go with the flow and follow the pack? Will those speaking of "new" marriage laws succeed? Will those speaking of "new" roles for women succeed? Will those speaking of separate "contemporary" worship services for the young succeed? Is a puppet show really as good as a sermon for teaching God's word? Is watching Andy Griffith reruns really as effective as a Bible study? The sad answer (historically) is that, yes it will succeed.

Speaking as the World Speaks

> That this is a rebellious people, Lying children, Children who will not hear the law of the Lord; Who say to the seers, "Do not see," And to the prophets, "Do not prophesy to us right things; Speak to us smooth things, prophesy deceits" (Isa. 30:9-10).

The reality is that these "modern elders," whether "false" brethren or just "weak" brethren, are driven by worldly pleas and they give the worldly within the church what the worldly wants—a watered down gospel!

> You are of God, little children, and have overcome them, because He who is in you is greater than he who is in the world. They are of the world. Therefore they speak as of the world, and the world hears them. We are of God. He who knows God hears us; he who is not of God does not hear us. By this we know the spirit of truth and the spirit of error (1 John 4:4-6).

To be an elder, one must be willing to serve as an elder! The pleas of the people for a softer gospel cannot be granted. Just as there will always be elders willing to follow rather than lead, there will always be sheep that think they are the shepherd!

There Is Nothing New Under the Sun (Eccl. 1:9)

If you make the ancient pleas for sanity, you will find that most of your conversation is already recorded in Scripture.

> "Why then did you not obey the voice of the Lord? Why did you swoop down on the spoil, and do evil in the sight of the Lord?" And Saul said to Samuel, "But I have obeyed the voice of the Lord, and gone on the mission on which the Lord sent me, and brought back Agag king of Amalek; I have utterly destroyed the Amalekites. But the people took of the plunder, sheep and oxen, the best of the things which should have been utterly destroyed, to sacrifice to the Lord your God in Gilgal" (1 Sam. 15:19-21).

Just as Saul's kingdom was drawn into civil war in ancient times because of Saul's liberalism in following God's instructions, today God's kingdom is forced into warfare as well. The people who have always known the safety of God's word are crying out for the spoils of the world in the form of worldly entertainment, etc.

The voices from the wilderness are again sounding the warning. Today the message is, "Enough already! We should have learned this lesson the first time, or the second or the hundredth or the thousandth time!"

This cycle of things (and God's frustration with it) is not a new thing. It has been around since the beginnings of the human race.

> Hear, O heavens, and give ear, O earth! For the Lord has spoken: "I have nourished and brought up children, And they have rebelled against Me; The ox knows its owner And the donkey its master's crib; But Israel does not know, My people do not consider." Alas, sinful nation, A people laden with iniquity, A brood of evildoers, Children who are corrupters! They have forsaken the Lord, They have provoked to anger The Holy One of Israel, They have turned away backward (Isa. 1:2-4).

If the Lord delays His return, my children will have to make the same decisions (but with different details) as I had to make. In some respects they already have. We shouldn't be in any way surprised by this. Their children will eventually have to do the same.

> If anyone speaks, let him speak as the oracles of God. If anyone ministers, let him do it as with the ability which God supplies, that in all things God may be glorified through Jesus Christ, to whom belong the glory and the

dominion forever and ever. Amen. Beloved, do not think it strange concerning the fiery trial which is to try you, as though some strange thing happened to you (1 Pet. 4:11-12).

If each generation must face this struggle once again, why should we spend our lives worrying about it, preaching on it and resisting it? I have thirty years invested in all this. Was it wasted?

If we know that the majority of each generation after each generation will turn away, why must we continue to try to lead back to the narrow way? God explained the principle to Ezekiel long ago.

> But as for you, son of man, your fellow citizens who talk about you by the walls and in the doorways of the houses, speak to one another, each to his brother, saying, "Come now and hear what the message is which comes forth from the Lord." They come to you as people come, and sit before you as My people and hear your words, but they do not do them, for they do the lustful desires expressed by their mouth, and their heart goes after their gain. Behold, you are to them like a sensual song by one who has a beautiful voice and plays well on an instrument; for they hear your words but they do not practice them. So when it comes to pass—as surely it will—then they will know that a prophet has been in their midst (Ezek. 33:30-33).

It is important that each generation knows that the truth has been in their midst. Our efforts were not wasted. They are our lot in serving God through time. "Therefore, my beloved brethren, be ye stedfast, unmoveable, always abounding in the work of the Lord, forasmuch as ye know that your labour is not in vain in the Lord" (1 Cor. 15:58). God's people from the previous generation has provided the following generation with the opportunity.

Our fellow citizens must know we have spoken from God's word... and that they have the opportunity to step forward and lead!

While the previous generation awaits the outcome of the new generation coming into its own and facing its challenges. The elders among us know that the torch must be passed. Those who have gone before await to see who will take up that torch as the new generation. Each new generation will face its own "crisis in leadership"!

The Work of Deacons
Terrell Dean Bunting
Introduction

This lectureship series is entitled "A Crisis in Leadership" and, in this series, I have been given the topic "The Work of Deacons." From my study of the New Testament, deacons have no authority in or over the church and actually are not in a leadership role by any means. However, they have a unique relationship to the church. In their role of servitude of the Church

---

Terrell Dean Bunting was born December 21, 1957 in Boone, NC. Much of Terrell's early life was influenced by the choices and decisions of his parents, Thomas and Shirley Bunting. They served and worked with churches from Miami, FL up to Sue Saint Marie, Canada as well as overseas in Norway. Terrell attended Florida College from 1976 to 1978. He then transferred to the University of Tennessee in Knoxville where he graduated in 1981 with a BS in Landscape Design and Ornamental Horticulture. He met his wife, Karen, while working in Orlando, FL. They were married in August, 1983. While in Orlando, Terrell decided to go into full-time preaching and moved to Coffee County, TN to work with a rural church there. In January, 1986, Terrell moved to Bergen, Norway. He worked with the Church in Norway for twenty years. He has written several tracts, correspondence courses, and teaching materials for adults and children in the Norwegian language as well as produced a Norwegian Songbook with over 200 songs. Karen and Terrell raised their family overseas. During the last seven years of Terrell's time in Norway he did short term mission work, gospel meetings, and teaching in several countries such as Lithuania, Belgium, Netherlands, Germany, Italy, Spain, South Africa, and Namibia.

In July, 2006, Terrell began working with the Manchester Church of Christ in Manchester, TN. He currently serves the church as their evangelist and one of their elders. Terrell continues his short term mission work to Windhoek, Namibia and tries to go there at least once or twice a year. Terrell and Karen have three daughters, Erika, Renee, and Kristina. Their two oldest daughters are married to Christian men and both live overseas. Erika and her husband, Thayne Washburn, are currently living in Japan; Renee and her husband Heath Robertson, are currently doing mission work in Bergen, Norway. The Buntings just had their first grandchild. Their youngest daughter, Kristina, is still at home.

The Work of Deacons

they become a role model for the membership. Thus, deacons should give much thought to their personal lives, choices and actions while serving because in this role they become an example for all in church. Realizing their important role these men should demonstrate the teaching found in Matthew 6:33 where all disciples are commanded to seek first the kingdom of God and His righteousness. I would advise deacons to make sure that in all aspects of their life and servitude to God and to the church that they are prioritize the kingdom of God. In doing so they leave little or no room for criticism from the Church which they serve. Since deacons are under the leadership of the elders and are an important part in the functioning and work of the local church, a study about them is important in this series.

If one understands the origin of the term "deacon," then he can easily understand why I conclude that a deacon is not in the position of leadership. The Greek word for deacon is *diakonos*. This Greek word primarily denotes a servant, as doing servile work or giving free service. This term is used in the New Testament for domestic servants, civil rulers, Christ, and followers of Christ serving Him as well as serving one another. Servants of Satan are identified by the same word.

The word *diakonos* is used about thirty times in the New Testament and is translated as minister, servant, and deacon. In most English translations, the word "deacon" is only used three or five times in the New Testament (all depending on which English translation one may use). Most of the time that the word *diakonos* is used in the New Testament, it is translated in terms other than "deacon," such as servant.

It is important to distinguish between the Greek words *diakonos* and *doulos*. The word *doulos* is used for a bondservant or slave. *Diakonos* sees the servant in relationship to his **work** and *doulos* pictures the servant in relationship to his **master**. Since the word used for a deacon is *diakonos* the emphasis is on the servant's relationship to the work he is to perform and the role that he fills.

The word *diakonos* is primarily used in reference to all those who are in Christ because all who are in Christ are to be the servants of Christ. We are also to be the servants of one another and our fellowman as well. To give a few examples of how this term is used in the New Testament note the following scriptures: Christ who is called a minister in Romans 15:8, the apostles who are called servants in 2 Corinthians 3:6, evangelists who are called ministers in 1 Timothy 4:6, faithful Christians were called servants in John 12:26, and Christian women who were servants in the church as in Romans 16:1.

In Philippians 1:1 and 1 Timothy 3:8-10 and 13, we see where the word *diakonos* is used in a more unique manner. In Philippians 1:1 the word is used in a unique sense and separate from the term "to all the saints in Christ Jesus which are at Philippi." This indicates that these Christian men were appointed to a specific office for serving and, therefore, they are called "deacon." As for 1 Timothy 3:8-13, there are qualities that must be met prior to the office of servitude. The "deacons" are listed with the "bishops" who also are men who must meet specific qualifications prior to their servitude and position of leadership.

We can, therefore, conclude that the term *diakonos* can refer to a "deacon" who is a servant in a manner different from all Christians who are to be servants. It refers to a man who is *appointed* above the normal duty of all Christians in service. The term emphasizes the relationship this appointed man has to his work of serving. He is a servant in a particular capacity with unique responsibilities to a particular work. The thought here is not a particular position or level in life; the idea is that it identifies the deacon in relationship to the particular work.

Lessons

1. All Christians are to serve. The New Testament clearly identifies the responsibility that each Christian has towards Christ and to His Church (His body). In Romans 12:4, the body has many members and, yet not all members have the same office, but we are all one in Christ. So in one sense, every single Christian is a part of the body and is busy serving the entire body in some form or capacity. God clearly identifies each member of the body as serving the good of the entire body (1 Cor. 12:13-27). God recognizes the diversity in abilities of each member. Each member is to serve in the way he is best suited to serve, whether the hand, feet, eye, or mouth. With ability comes the responsibility that each must perform and serve based upon his ability. This concept is clearly taught in Matthew 25:14-31. In addition to that diversity that exists in the local church, God has identified particular offices or positions of service.

2. Identifying the Specific Office of Deacon. In Philippians 1:1, there is a unique way in which the word *diakonos* is used. Here it suggests an "office" different from the general concept of servants of Christ's body. There are four scriptures that should be looked at in reference to the uniqueness of the

The Work of Deacons

"office" of a deacon. These passages are: Philippians 1:1, 1 Timothy 3:8, 1 Timothy 3:10, and 1 Timothy 3:13. In 1 Timothy 3:13 the expression, "the office of a deacon," is used. In 1 Timothy 3:10 we are told that before a man can be a deacon, he must first be proven and then he may "use the office of a deacon" if he be found blameless. In 1 Timothy 3:8, there is a listing of qualifications that a deacon must have in order to serve the church, which is beyond the requirements of Christians desiring to serve Christ.

Concerning the word "office," used in 1 Timothy 3:10 and 13 in the King James version, I feel that the New King James Version is a better translation. The New King James Version reads "served well as deacons." From this we can see that the Bible does not emphasize the position or the "office"; rather, it emphasizes the work. It is a work to be done, not a position to be filled that is important. It is God's will that there be qualified men for specific works for which men are appointed and called deacons.

The Qualifications of Deacons

The New Testament clearly teaches that those who serve as deacons must be of a certain level of morality and excellence in order to serve the church. Deacons must be and can only be appointed when men are found to be qualified and willing to serve. It is the will of Christ that we fulfill this obligation. I do not plan to use much time in study of the qualifications that must be met but it is useful to at least mention them.

The listing of qualifications as found in 1 Timothy 3:8-13 is as follows:

- Reverent (v. 8)
- Not double-tongued (v. 8).
- Not given to much wine (v. 8).
- Not greedy for money (v. 8).
- Holding the mystery of the faith with a pure conscience (v. 9).
- Husband of one wife (v. 12).
- Ruling their children and their house well (v. 12).

In meeting these qualifications, these men must first of all approve themselves. From this, we understand that the men are to look inward concerning their faith, life, and service before accepting the great role of being appointed to work for the needs of the church. Their own conscience must be clear (1 Tim. 3:5). Then these men need to meet the approval of the church (1 Tim. 3:10), as they are to be tested and be found blameless.

Not as an absolute rule but as an example, we can learn the selection process of deacons from Acts 6:1-5. The church was to look among its membership and find men of honest report, full of the Holy Ghost, and wisdom who could take on the role of meeting this need in the church. If the church is to recognize the qualified men, then these men will be able to function with the full confidence of the church as they serve each and every member of the church. One can see the great wisdom of God in this manner of selection.

The deacon is much more than just an errand-boy or someone who simply carries out the specific instructions of others. The qualifications suggest a large degree of spirituality, responsibility, faithfulness, and trustworthiness both in his public and in his home life. This is someone to whom the church can give an on-going responsibility and work, knowing that it will be taken care of in keeping with the will of Christ, both fairly and expediently. The deacon will be a man who will take charge of the delegated matter and get it done.

What Work Does a Deacon Do?

What kind of service are deacons to perform? What are they to be busy doing? What kind of work are they "appointed" to complete? These questions are not easy to answer because very little is said about the "work" of deacons. God mostly talks about the qualifications needed prior to being appointed to serve the church.

There is more scripture defining the work of the elder. More space is given to the work and the life of an evangelist or preacher and very little is mentioned for the work of a deacon.

Let us first consider what his work is not or should not be. First of all, a deacon has no authority or rule. The deacon is not an elder in training. He does not have the right to rule, lead, or direct the congregation. Secondly, a deacon is not a teacher or preacher. In Ephesians 4:11, there is a list of teachers for the perfecting of the saints. However, a deacon may teach or preach (Acts 6:5; 8:4-5; 21:8).

A deacon is a servant of the church by its very definition. In all probability, Acts 6:1-7 describes men who were deacons serving the church in Jerusalem. What can we learn from this passage? We see that the men selected were men who qualified for this work of serving. We all see that these qualified men were helping with specific needs in the local church. The reason for this was so that the teachers of God's word could continue to focus on teaching and not be distracted or burdened with the physical needs and operation of the church.

The General Nature of a Deacon's Work

We have noticed, thus far, that in the Lord's church there were positions of responsibility to which qualified men were appointed, this being, the office of deacon. These men had to be tested, approved, and then set to the task to which they were appointed. Based upon the meaning of word, the purpose for this office was to serve. A deacon is a *servant* doing servile work, carrying out the needs of others. The example given in Acts 6:1-7 is of seven men who were appointed over the business of caring for the needy widows in the daily distribution in the church in Jerusalem, though they are never specifically called "deacons." Their work is described as "serving tables" in contrast to the "ministry of the word." From this passage one may conclude that these appointed men (possibly deacons) are servants of the church, serving in areas other than teaching and preaching the word of God. In contrast, every Christian is to work towards being able to teach others the word of God. Deacons are not appointed to the office of a deacon in order to teach or preach; they are appointed to this role to serve the physical needs of the church. The deacon is not a preacher or teacher (Eph. 4:11), though he may be capable of teaching and involved in teaching, but his appointment or selection as a deacon is not for the purpose of teaching (Acts 6:5; 8:4-5; 21:8).

Deacons were men appointed to serve in a particular capacity (Acts 6; Phil. 1:1). Elders were appointed to serve in a particular capacity (Tit. 1). Ephesians 4:11 speaks of God "appointing" or giving the church apostles, prophets, evangelist, pastors and teachers for the edifying of the church. In all or any of these roles or works, neither the preacher, elder, prophet, evangelist, teacher nor deacon should accept the appointment if he does not desire and anticipate spending time and energy carrying out the work that belongs to him.

There is not a limit to the number of elders in a church. There is always a need for elders who are in leadership roles to be workers too and not just title holders. The church is not looking for elders who are only decision makers. The church needs workers or servants who have the specific desire to feed the flock, nurture the flock, and to protect and oversee the flock (Acts 20:28-30, 1 Pet. 5:2.)

In like manner, the "deacons" do not simply hold an honorary title or position. They are chosen to serve for the betterment of the church. They are chosen to look to the needs of the church so that those who have the responsibility of the ministry of the word are not hindered from their important responsibility and work.

The preacher should be busy teaching and preaching as the fields are white unto harvest. The preacher does not need to be busy "serving tables." There is much to do in the service of God for *all* Christians. There is a great need for workers in the Kingdom of God, both elders and deacons as well as other kinds of servants. Do not expect to be selected as a deacon and have little to do. It is not an honorary position or title but one that is selected for specific identifiable work that needs to be done in the church. If the church cannot find enough work for deacons, then they are not ambitious enough in the Lord's work and Kingdom. What has blinded our ability to see the needs that are present? I feel so many churches have become indifferent and blinded by selfishness and worldliness to the point that they cannot see the necessity of elders and deacons. There are so many services that deacons are needed to perform. We do not always see the need if we are not looking (as in Acts 6). The problem in Acts 6 was there before the problem came to the attention of the apostles. The problem came to their attention after there arose a fuss in the church among the members. Good leadership will be looking and identifying needs that deacons can be responsible for and thus avoid problems and complaints in the church. Deacons are to serve the needs of the congregation. We do not always do a good job of identifying the needs of the church. This is a great important work elders have and sometimes fail in.

We Have Created a Problem in the Lord's Church.

The truth is that in many churches there is too much shifting of responsibility. The preacher does the work of the elders (visiting, spiritual feeding, guarding, admonishing, planning, evangelistic plans, directing the church, etc.). The elders do the work of the deacons (pursue the business details, budget details, ordering of classroom supplies, maintenance and improvements), and the deacons end up doing what any and every member can and should be doing. The members then don't have anything to do. If this happens we have distorted God's plan for His church and this may even affect whether or not God will bless the church's efforts and work. God may not give the increase because of the problems we have created in His church. Would a church organized or functioning in an unscriptural manner have the full blessings of God?

The Work of Deacons

What Should We Expect Deacons to Do?

When one studies the work of deacons and their duties, as listed in the New Testament, one will notice that the work is not as clearly identified as the work of elders. The information God has chosen to give us is all we have. What God has provided must be considered and, from that, we must conclude that God has given us all He deems sufficient for us to know concerning what deacons are to be involved in. God simply defines the character of a deacon and the nature of his work. From that, Christians are to make judgments as to what kind of work is according to the will of God. We are to use what God has revealed and make good solid conclusions in the application of that God-given instruction.

Deacons are to minister to the *needs* of the church (not teaching). Now what would be included in the description of serving the needs of the church? The physical needs of any church change from time to time. The church's needs will most likely change as there may be changes in the financial situation and social situation of the church members. We know from Acts 6 that deacons are to "care for the needy" of the church. In addition to this, deacons can serve any other kind of need that comes within the scope of the work of the church, worship of the church, and nature of the church.

Consider for a moment what the church is all about. What is the church suppose to be and do? The church is to assemble to worship so, in reference to that, deacons may serve the church in preparation for worship and they may serve in the order and the organization of the worship. The church is to assemble and normally most churches have an assembly place, so deacons can serve the church by taking care of the physical needs and concerns of that assembly place. The church is involved in benevolence, so deacons may identify needs and make sure that the needs are met as well as supervise the distribution of things. The church is to be busy in the work of evangelism. Deacons can serve the church in its efforts in evangelism, in reference to the details, arrangements, advertisements, the facilities, greeting the guests, as well as taking care of any supplies needed for the evangelistic event. Deacons could also serve the church in reference to the collection for the saints. They could be involved in the collection of the money, the treasury, record keeping, budgeting, and reporting. The church is to be a united body. In order for the church to continue to function in unity there must be clear strong spiritual leadership in the area of teaching and protecting the souls of the church. For this work, God declares that the church is to appoint elders to serve. In order for the church to continue to function in unity there must also be a strong physical organization and distribution in the area of meeting the church's physical needs. For this work God declares that the church is to appoint deacons to serve. Deacons can work and help this "need" for unity by keeping each member informed, allowing each member to be heard, and motivating and assisting others towards involvement.

It is not easy to draw a clear, firm line of distinction between what is spiritual and what is physical. There are many physical matters that have strong spiritual influence and effect. How large the lobby of a meeting house should be sounds like a purely physical or material question, but it can have a big impact on the relationship of the members one to another. Of course, one can carry any concern for such things far beyond what is of spiritual value. Rather than dividing between spiritual and physical, why not divide between servants and teachers? The work done in Acts 6 had tremendous spiritual implications and it was more than just the distribution of food!

The work of deacons must be done and maintained on an on-going basis. It takes time, effort, forethought, responsibility, and organizational skills. Let us value deacons and understand the important part they play in serving the church.

All of this must be under the leadership and direction of the elders. They shepherd, oversee, admonish, and exhort. They know the flock and are concerned for the needs of that flock. They can recognize the needs and then delegate the work for serving to the deacons who will then tend to that physical need of the church which the elders have identified. This allows the elders to continue to focus their time, thought, and energy to the work God has appointed them to do.

When things are done God's way, the church will be greatly blessed. Elders are able to focus on what God has given them. Deacons can serve the church as God has commanded them. Then the preacher can give attention to study, meditation, and teaching and not be burdened with trying to do the work of an elder, a deacon, and an evangelist. When it is all done according to the pattern and plan of God, concerning the work of an elder, deacon, evangelist, or teacher, it is all done for the welfare of the church. God knows best! Let us follow His plan.

The Responsibility of the Church to the Deacons

God has appointed these men to this service and work. The church is to gratefully accept it as His will, knowing that this is for their own benefit and good. Deacons are men of particular qualifications who demand our respect.

We respect them for who they are and to the service they are selected and perform. As these men serve as deacons, we need to appreciate their time and effort. We are to understand their weaknesses and need to be careful in our criticism. We are to encourage them and express our appreciation for what they do and finally, we extend to them the same attitude as the Lord does in 1 Timothy 3:13, *"For they that have used the office of a deacon well purchase to themselves a good degree and great boldness in the faith which is in Christ."*

The Morning Classes

Historical Controversies over Leadership:
The Roles of Evangelists and Pastors
Ron Halbrook

And he gave some, apostles; and some, prophets; and some, evangelists; and some, pastors and teachers; For the perfecting of the saints, for the work of the ministry, for the edifying of the body of Christ: (Eph. 4:11-12).

Ron Halbrook was born in Indianola, MS in 1946, moved to Belle Glade, FL in 1951, and grew up and graduated from high school there. He preached for the Southside Church of Christ in Belle Glade in the summer of 1964. During his years at Florida College (1964-67), his preaching continued with the Central congregation near Live Oak, FL (fall 1965), the West Sixth St. church in Pine Bluff, AR (summer 1966), and the Hercules Ave. church in Clearwater, FL (1966-67).

During 1967-73 Ron labored with the Wooley Springs church near Athens, AL, taught high school at Athens Bible School, and finished a degree in history at Athens College (1969). He labored with the Broadmoor church in Nashville, TN 1973-78 (and completed a master's degree in church history at Vanderbilt University, 1979), the Knollwood church in Xenia, OH 1978-82 (with Mike Willis in a two-preacher arrangement), the church in Midfield, AL 1982-84, and the West Columbia, TX church in 1984-97. In August of 1997, he began work in a two-preacher arrangement with Andy Alexander at the Hebron Lane Church of Christ in Shepherdsville, KY. Andy moved to Bowling Green, KY in 2003 and Steven Deaton took his place at Hebron Lane in June 2004. This arrangement allows Ron to hold several gospel meetings and make four trips to the Philippines each year. He has made thirty-eight trips to the Philippines since 1995. Ron's articles have appeared in such religious journals as *Truth Magazine, Searching the Scriptures,* and *The Preceptor.* Other writing includes tracts (*Unity With Christ & Christians; Honorable Marriage*), booklets (*Trends Pointing Toward a New Apostasy; Understanding the Controversy*), and books (*The Doctrine of Christ & Unity of the Saints; Halbrook-Freeman Debate on Marriage, Divorce, & Remarriage*). Ron married Donna Bell in 1967. They have three children: Jonathan, David, and Deborah. Jonathan (married Tanya Bryant; children: Payton, Cole, Paige, Abbie), David (married Starla Page), and Deborah (married Jamie Williams; children: Timothy).

The great plan of redemption created by the grace of God includes the roles of evangelists and pastors. From the moment God revealed His plan, Satan waged all-out war against it. Thus, the roles of evangelist and pastor became one of many battlegrounds from the time God revealed this part of His plan until now. The history of the world is the record of this constant warfare between God and Satan for the souls of men.

God has always organized His people to serve Him and to accomplish things necessary to the fulfillment of His plan of redemption. In the Patriarchal Age God guided His people primarily through patriarchs such as Adam, Noah, and Abraham. During the Mosaic Age God spoke through Moses and the prophets. God leads His people now in the Gospel Age through His Son Jesus Christ, and Christ utilizes servant leaders such as evangelists and pastors.

In the days of the patriarchs, Satan enticed mankind to turn from God and he spread corruption through the sinful exploits of mighty "men of renown" (Gen. 6:4). Even after the terrible judgment of a universal flood, wicked leaders attempted to gain fame and acclaim by building a tower into the very heavens (Gen. 11:1-9).

When God led His people out of Egyptian bondage and into the promised land of Canaan, He blessed them with good leaders. God raised up Moses, but Satan constantly sowed the seeds of distrust, doubt, and rebellion against him. Even his own brother and sister, Aaron and Miriam, envied his unique role of close communication with God and troubled him (Num. 12). The people nearly executed Moses, Joshua, and Caleb for their fearless faith in calling upon them to take the promised land (Num. 14:1-10). Korah and his co-conspirators envied the leadership roles God gave Moses and Aaron, and demanded more authority for themselves by elevation to the priesthood (Num. 16:1-11).

After God led Israel into Canaan, He reigned over them through courageous leaders called judges. Finally, the people rejected God as their sole king and demanded "a king to judge us like all the nations" (1 Sam. 8:1-9, see v. 5). God conceded to the desire of Israel for an earthly king and raised up King Saul, a disappointment, then good King David, "a man after his own heart" (1 Sam. 13:14). Later, David's own son Absalom "stole the hearts of the men of Israel" and usurped the throne (2 Sam. 15:6). The foolish leadership of Solomon's son, Rehoboam, divided the kingdom(1 Kings 12:1-20), and thereafter most of the kings of both Israel and Judah did "evil in the sight of the Lord" (2 Kings 13:11).

The lack of proper leadership was a major factor in the moral and spiritual decline of Israel and Judah, resulting in Israel going into Assyrian captivity in 721 B.C. and Judah into Babylonian captivity in 586 B.C. as stern punishment for their sins and apostasy. Jeremiah 23 pictures the horrible state of God's people with wicked kings: "Woe be unto the pastors that destroy and scatter the sheep of my pasture! saith the LORD" (v. 1). God's heart was broken because the prophets and priests led the people into both doctrinal and moral apostasies (vv. 9-14). Yet, God promised to bring a faithful remnant out of captivity and to raise up a true and righteous king:

> Behold, the days come, saith the LORD, that I will raise unto David a righteous Branch, and a King shall reign and prosper, and shall execute judgment and justice in the earth. In his days Judah shall be saved, and Israel shall dwell safely: and this is his name whereby he shall be called, THE LORD OUR RIGHTEOUSNESS (Jer. 23:5-6).

Jesus Christ rules as a righteous and merciful king for our salvation.

Psalm 68 pictures God leading His people from Mt. Sinai to ascend Mt. Zion, where He would be enthroned as their mighty King. He conquers His enemies and appropriates their riches to bless His own people. "Thou hast ascended on high, thou hast led captivity captive: thou hast received gifts for men; yea, for the rebellious also, that the LORD God might dwell among them" (Ps. 68:18). In spite of all the failings of human leaders, in the end God Himself rules the world so as to fulfill His great plan of redemption. Paul applies this very passage to Christ as the conquering King ordained by God to defeat His enemies and to bless His own people (Eph. 4:7-8).

I. Evangelists and Pastors: Servants for Our Salvation

Saints Growing to Maturity in Christ. Ephesians 4:1-16 beautifully pictures God's plan for nurturing saints to grow to maturity in Christ. The gospel calls upon saints to grow in mutual love and concern for one another that we all may be saved:

> I therefore, the prisoner of the Lord, beseech you that ye walk worthy of the vocation wherewith ye are called, With all lowliness and meekness, with longsuffering, forbearing one another in love; Endeavouring to keep the unity of the Spirit in the bond of peace (Eph. 4:1-3).

The Holy Spirit teaches us this spirit of humble, yielding, patient love for each other which binds us together in unity and peace for the ultimate good of us all. Selfish, proud, demanding, impatient conduct destroys the love and unity which lead us to maturity and final salvation.

True spiritual growth requires the right doctrinal foundation revealed by God:

> There is one body, and one Spirit, even as ye are called in one hope of your calling; One Lord, one faith, one baptism, One God and Father of all, who is above all, and through all, and in you all (Eph. 4:4-6).

All teaching contrary to this true foundation, no matter how eloquently or persuasively presented, undermines our spiritual growth and our ultimate salvation in heaven.

Jesus Christ died for our sins and arose from the grave, then ascended to heaven to rule as our King and Savior. Like a conquering king enriched by the defeat of his enemies, He gives His people gifts which promote spiritual growth and maturity:

> But unto every one of us is given grace according to the measure of the gift of Christ. Wherefore he saith, When he ascended up on high, he led captivity captive, and gave gifts unto men. (Now that he ascended, what is it but that he also descended first into the lower parts of the earth? He that descended is the same also that ascended up far above all heavens, that he might fill all things.) And he gave some, apostles; and some, prophets; and some, evangelists; and some, pastors and teachers; For the perfecting of the saints, for the work of the ministry, for the edifying of the body of Christ: Till we all come in the unity of the faith, and of the knowledge of the Son of God, unto a perfect man, unto the measure of the stature of the fulness of Christ (Eph. 4:7-13).

The work of apostles and prophets was to reveal the great plan of redemption. It was fully revealed by the end of the first century. There are no new apostles and prophets, but we have in the New Testament all the teaching revealed through them for our salvation.

After the message was revealed, it was necessary that it be proclaimed, which is the evangelists' work. This work continues until the end of time, reaping a harvest of souls unto salvation. God ordained that the saved should be gathered into local churches to worship and serve Him under the loving leadership of men called pastors or shepherds. Additional teachers help to provide ongoing instruction. The work of converting souls and edifying them continues until the Lord returns to reward the redeemed.

This perfect plan for our salvation is thwarted when men serve Satan as false apostles and prophets in claiming new revelations of truth. If preachers fail to proclaim the original gospel in its fulness, the plan fails. Souls baptized and then left to drift without the guidance of true pastors will go astray and be lost. When teachers are not equipped to teach or are not sound in what they teach, saints grow weaker rather than stronger.

The growth and maturity of the body of Christ are assured when every member diligently serves and functions under Christ as our head.

> That we henceforth be no more children, tossed to and fro, and carried about with every wind of doctrine, by the sleight of men, and cunning craftiness, whereby they lie in wait to deceive; But speaking the truth in love, may grow up into him in all things, which is the head, even Christ: From whom the whole body fitly joined together and compacted by that which every joint supplieth, according to the effectual working in the measure of every part, maketh increase of the body unto the edifying of itself in love (Eph. 4:14-16).

Our failure to grow invites instability and makes us vulnerable to all sorts of false teachers and false doctrines. Constantly learning and teaching the truth in love delivers us from the devices of Satan. This course puts us on the path of spiritual growth and maturity as we strive to obey and emulate Christ as our Savior and Head.

The Role of Evangelists. The charge of Paul to Timothy clearly defines the role of the evangelist: "Preach the word; be instant in season, out of season; reprove, rebuke, exhort with all longsuffering and doctrine" (2 Tim. 4:2). He must preach "all the counsel of God" without fear or favor toward any man in order to be "pure from the blood of all men" (Acts 20:26-27). He must expose false doctrine and rebuke false teachers, at times specifying their names and doctrines (1 Tim. 1:3; 4:3; 2 Tim. 2:17-18). The faithful evangelist must be bold and straightforward, not ashamed of the truth or of association with other faithful men who suffer for the truth's sake (2 Tim. 1:7-8).

The initial preaching of the gospel results in souls putting their faith in Christ and submitting to baptism, but much follow-up preaching is needed to edify them unto the final salvation in heaven (Matt. 28:19-20). Even the strongest saints need constant reminders, admonitions, and encouragement: "If thou put the brethren in remembrance of these things, thou shalt be a good minister of Jesus Christ, nourished up in the words of faith and of good doctrine, whereunto thou hast attained" (1 Tim. 4:6).

Having received the message of truth through the apostles and prophets sent by God, the evangelist is charged, "These things speak, and exhort, and rebuke with all authority. Let no man despise thee" (Tit. 2:15). The focus of the faithful preacher is not to protect his own ego but to proclaim and protect the truth of the gospel of Christ unto the salvation of souls (Phil. 1:15-18). He does not compete with his fellow soldiers for notice, but directs all his talents and energy to teaching the truth in love in order to save the lost and edify the saved.

The Role of Pastors. God ordained special leaders in local churches and designated them by terms which shed light on the nature of their office and work. They are called *pastors* or *shepherds* because they function as shepherds keeping a flock of sheep, *bishops* or *overseers* because they act as managers over a task or workforce, and *elders* or *presbyters* because they must be spiritually mature to lead properly. The same office is described by all these terms to enhance our understanding of the role or function of these special leaders.

Every congregation is organizationally independent from all others and therefore each one is autonomous in its decisions and work (Acts 14:23). God revealed no additional layers of organization to tie churches together. Furthermore, there are no one-man pastors in a church but a plurality of such leaders in each church (Acts 14:23; Tit. 1:5). Christ authorized the eldership to rule by making decisions within the scope of New Testament principles necessary to oversee the local church, just as He authorized fathers to make decisions in overseeing family life (1 Tim. 3:4-5; 5:17). Pastors function as shepherds under Christ "the chief Shepherd" on behalf of the salvation of the souls committed to their care in the local church (1 Pet. 5:1-4; Heb. 13:17).

Distinct Roles. The roles of evangelists and pastors are separate and distinct. Essentially, evangelists proclaim and teach God's Word and pastors oversee every aspect of congregational life including the teaching program, of which the preacher's work is a part. The evangelist's authority to preach God's Word comes directly from the Lord Himself, and he is not a hireling who must do the bidding of elders in terms of trimming and modifying the truth to please men (Tit. 2:15). Yet, preachers, like all other members, serve God under the oversight of the eldership in regard to all matters of expediency in the work of the church. An evangelist has no more right or authority to defy the decision of the eldership than any other member of the congregation. All members, including the preacher, are commanded to "obey them that have the rule over you" (Heb. 13:17).

Historical Controversies over Leadership

An evangelist can be appointed to serve as one of the pastors in an eldership, if he is qualified. Likewise, a pastor can engage in evangelistic work, if he is equipped to do so. The man who walks this path serves in dual roles, and each role is still distinct. A local church can provide financial support to a man devoting himself wholly to serve the Lord in these dual roles: "Let the elders that rule well be counted worthy of double honour, especially they who labour in the word and doctrine. For the scripture saith, Thou shalt not muzzle the ox that treadeth out the corn. And, The labourer is worthy of his reward" (1 Tim. 5:17-18).

Complementary Roles. Since evangelists and pastors are simply servants of Christ and of their brethren, there is no place for competition in their roles. In fact, their distinctive roles are complementary, each increasing the effectiveness of the other by a division of labor. The model of attitude and action for all of us is the role of a lowly servant, not a self-willed lord, tyrant, or dictator. Christ our Savior and King teaches this by word and example: "And whosoever will be chief among you, let him be your servant: Even as the Son of man came not to be ministered unto, but to minister, and to give his life a ransom for many" (Matt. 20:27-28).

Preachers who diligently devote themselves to their work will not encroach on the role of pastors (1 Tim. 4:15). By word and deed they will demonstrate their love and respect for Christ by fully cooperating with the pastors or shepherds Christ has ordained to oversee the service of his saints. An evangelist's respect for and cooperation with pastors reinforces the effectiveness of their role. The preacher's teaching and conduct encourage all the members to "obey them that have the rule" over the life of the church (Heb. 13:17).

Pastors who focus wholeheartedly on their God-given role and work will not encroach on the role of evangelists. They should not shift their own duties or the work of deacons onto the shoulders of the preacher. As Peter said, "It is not reason that we should leave the Word of God, and serve tables" (Acts 6:2). There must be a proper division of labor in order for both evangelists and pastors to maximize their effectiveness in serving Christ and the brethren. Pastors should not attempt to shackle the conscience of the preacher and prevent him from preaching all the counsel of God in an effort to appease the world, weak members, or outside critics esteemed in some circle of brethren. Pastors should rather demand and support a full proclamation of the truth.

The roles of evangelists and pastors are equally valid and crucial in God's plan for the redemption of sinners and the maturing of saints. The more closely these co-laborers confer and function in their proper spheres, the more effectively they accomplish the work of saving lost souls and edifying the saved unto their final salvation.

God's plan for good leadership will work, if we will work God's plan!

II. Controversy Over the Pastor's Role

The Roman Catholic Model: From Pastor to Priest to Pope. In the second and third centuries, local churches began to elevate one bishop to the new role of "presiding bishop," an office and role unknown to the New Testament. He eventually was designated exclusively by the title "the bishop." Large city churches became centers of power overseeing newer small congregations which were being established, which in turn enhanced the power of "the bishop." The scope of power was enlarged as programs of work were overseen by "the bishop" of a large church in a city, then in a region, and then in a province.

During the second and third centuries, the office of elder evolved into a special priesthood. Elders officiated at the Lord's Supper which lost the simple significance of a memorial and became highly ceremonial and ritualistic. The ceremony was seen as a sacrifice offered by the worshipers, but later as the sacrifice of Christ offered by the bishop-priest. These innovations bred the concept of the clergy as a class with special knowledge and ritualistic power, elevated above the laity.

The bishop of the provincial capitals came to be highly esteemed. The bishops of Jerusalem, Antioch, Alexandria, Constantinople, and Rome were elevated to "Metropolitan Bishop," "Archbishop," or "Patriarch" by the fourth century. In 606, Boniface III of Rome was elected Pope and took the throne in 607, soon proclaiming himself "Universal Bishop" with the backing of Emperor Phocas.

In other words, "the bishop" grew into a very powerful office combining exclusive organizational powers and mystical priestly powers. The simple New Testament office of the pastor became the very powerful office of the bishop and priest, culminating in the pope who claimed universal power and authority over all the churches.

The Denominational Model: Merge Roles of Evangelists and Pastors. Clerical offices, titles, and garb were highly developed and revered in

Historical Controversies over Leadership 175

Roman Catholicism. As the denominations formed beginning in the 1500's (Lutheranism became a separate movement from the Roman Catholic Church about 1530), many of the leaders had been trained as priests, friars, and theologians in the Catholic Church. This is true of Martin Luther (1483-1546), John Calvin (1509-1564), Ulrich Zwingli (1484-1531), John Knox (1505-1572), and most other leaders of the Protestant Reformation. When they left Catholicism, their baggage included many perverted concepts such as confusion about the roles of evangelists and pastors. The denominational bodies they formed essentially combined the roles of preachers and pastors.

Denominational preachers assumed the role of pastors with singlehanded authority to oversee local churches. Typically, "the pastor" in a denominational congregation rules as an autocrat, and he is often viewed with awe as holding mystical priestly powers which qualify him to baptize, conduct worship, and especially administer the Lord's Supper. Some denominations retained the title priest and yet would use "pastor" for the same person, such as the Lutheran Church. The Presbyterian Church utilizes a local board of elders, one of whom is an ordained minister or "the pastor," i.e., the preacher.

Many denominational leaders have viewed church government as a matter of mere expediency. William Paley (1743-1805), able Anglican theologian who wrote on Christian evidences, argued "that Christianity may be professed under any form of church government" which serves to inculcate the truth of the religion.[1] Presbyterians historically have been prolific in presenting the case that their polity is scriptural.[2]

Some denominations distinguish an evangelist as a traveling preacher, whereas the pastor is a preacher who settles down to preach and exercise oversight over a single congregation.

For the most part, denominational bodies and independent congregations with denominational roots merge the roles of preacher and pastor.

Restoring New Testament Christianity. In the late 1700's and early

---

[1] Paley, "A Distinction of Orders in the Church Defended upon Principles of Public Utility," 585-890, see 588.

[2] See, for instance, Thomas Witherow (1824-1890), *Which Is the Apostolic Church?* and Stuart Robinson (1814-1881), *The Church of God as an Element of the Gospel and the Idea, Structure, and Functions Thereof.*

1800's, many denominational preachers became disenchanted with the errors, confusion, and division which prevailed in denominational bodies. In parts of Europe, in the British Isles, and in America, there was a widespread determination to restore or return to New Testament Christianity.

Thomas Campbell (1763-1854) and his son Alexander (1788-1866) were Irish Presbyterians who arrived in America in 1807 and 1809 respectively. They were diligently searching for the old paths of New Testament teaching. In his journal *The Christian Baptist* (1823-1830), Alexander published a thirty-article series on "A Restoration of the Ancient Order of Things," including several pieces on the usurpations of power by the clergy. His examination of denominational practices including the clergy led to the charge that his hand was raised against every man. He answered, "I do oppose, and will, by the grace of God, oppose, not only *almost*, but *altogether*, every thing received as the christian religion, not found in the New Testament, to the utmost of my ability and opportunity."[3]

Alexander lampooned the clergy in "The Third Epistle of Peter to the Preachers and Rulers of Congregations," reminding them to take human titles to elevate themselves: "be ye called Pope, Archbishop, Archdeacon, or Divine, or Reverend, and Right Reverend, or some like holy name."[4] This epistle emphasized the greed as well as the pride of the clergy in a section on "The Clergy's Reward," which said in part, "'In all your gettings' get money!" He continued,

> And when ye shall hear of a church that is vacant and hath no one to preach therein, then be that a *call* unto you, and be ye mindful of the call, and take ye charge of the flock thereof and of the fleece thereof, even of the *golden* fleece.
>
> And when ye shall have fleeced your flock, and shall know of another *call*, and if the flock be greater, or rather if the fleece be greater, then greater be also unto you the *call*. Then shall ye leave your old flock, and of the new flock shall ye take the charge.[5]

In contrast to the pride, greed, and ignorance which characterized much of the denominational clergy, Alexander Campbell insisted on a restoration

---

[3] Campbell, "The Rev. Thomas G. Jones and the Luminary," 99.

[4] "The Third Epistle of Peter to the Preachers and Rulers of Congregations," 244.

[5] *Ibid.*, 247.

of the New Testament pattern for the organization and work of the church. Therefore, he argued, "The standing and immutable ministry of the Christian community is composed of Bishops, Deacons, and Evangelists."[6] Again echoing Scripture, he described the role of bishops as "to preside over, to instruct, and to edify the community—to feed the church of the Lord with knowledge and understanding—and to watch for their souls as those that must give account to the Lord."[7]

After describing deacons as special servants "commissioned by the church," he turned to the evangelist: "His work is to proclaim the word intelligibly and persuasively—to immerse all the believers, or converts of his ministry—and to plant and organize churches wherever he may have occasion; and then teach them to keep the commandments and ordinances of the Lord."[8] Campbell explains that this teaching includes ordaining elders and giving some sort of general supervision to infant churches, but grants the extent of such supervision may be "a question of dubious interpretation."[9] Evangelists ought to be "wholly engrossed" in their work and "fully sustained by their brethren."[10] While affirming the necessity of devoted elders, deacons, and evangelists to perpetuate the gospel system, Campbell avoids all shades of the clergy-laity concept by asserting that any brother may *"preach, baptize, and dispense the supper, as well as pray for all men, when circumstances demand it."*[11]

III. Controversy Over the Evangelist's Role

An Early Strain of Distrust. Some of the men who emerged from denominational and clerical concepts brought with them a strain of distrust of or confusion about the evangelist's role. Many came from Scotch and Irish forms of Presbyterianism via Independent or congregational movements which advocated local church autonomy and sought to escape the clergy-laity distinction. In the 1700's-early 1800's these reforms were advocated by such men as John Glas (1695-1773; left the Church of Scot-

---

[6] Campbell, *The Christian System*, 78.

[7] *Ibid.*, 79.

[8] *Ibid.*, 80.

[9] *Ibid.*, 81.

[10] *Ibid.*, 84.

[11] *Ibid.*, 82; emphasis original.

land to establish an independent congregation in 1728), Robert Sandeman (1718-1771, son-in-law to Glas), Greville Ewing (1767-1841), the brothers James A. (1768-1851) and Robert Haldane (1764-1842), and William Ballantyne. Ballantyne authored *Treatise on the Elder's Office* and James Haldane wrote *A View of the Social Worship and Ordinances Observed by the First Christians*, both advocating a plurality of elders in each church, elimination of the evangelists' role as limited to the first century, and mutual exhortation in the assemblies.

A theologian and linguist of the Church of Scotland, Dr. George Campbell (1719-1796) of Edinburgh, published *The Four Gospels, Translated from the Greek* (1789), which saw a seventh edition by 1834. He lent credence to the idea that evangelists preached "the gospel" but did not teach "the doctrine" in the first century. Some of the Independents embraced this idea and argued that evangelists were a special order of assistants to the Apostles which passed from the scene with the end of the miraculous age. Mutual exhortation is necessary because there are no evangelists today!

Introduced under the name "church order," mutual exhortation bred internal contention and disorder. Several churches which made a hopeful start in Scotland and some in America fell into much strife as ill-equipped men vied to exhort. "Repudiating the clergy and the pope, each member became not only his own pope, but disposed to assume this office in regard to others."[12] This movement largely decimated itself, but a strain of it influenced the thinking of men pleading for a restoration of New Testament Christianity.

Campbell and others bore some measure of this influence, but not in a doctrinaire fashion. He was enamored of Dr. George Campbell's *Four Gospels* and relied heavily on it in publishing a translation of the New Testament he called *The Living Oracles*.[13] For a while Alexander held George's view

---

[12] Richardson, *Memoirs of Alexander Campbell*, II: 128.

[13] The title page of *The Living Oracles* is clear that Alexander Campbell's translation is basically the work of other men with some revisions: *The Sacred Writings of the Apostles and Evangelists of Jesus Christ, Commonly Styled The New Testament*. Translated from the Original Greek. By Doctors George Campbell, James MacKnight and Philip Doddridge. With Prefaces, Various Emendations and An Appendix, by Alexander Campbell (Pittsburgh: Forrester and Campbell, 1839). This was the sixth edition. The first edition appeared in 1826 with slightly different wording on the title page. For the history of this translation, see Thomas,

that there are no evangelists today, but he did not consistently adhere to this position.[14] After claiming in 1827 the work of evangelists was limited to "the apostolic age," he spoke later of his own work "as an evangelist," called Walter Scott "an evangelist," and commended the growing "number of evangelists."[15]

The Necessity of Itinerate Work. Because the gospel spread like wildfire, most of the early preachers were almost constantly on the move by necessity, and some of them thought of themselves primarily as itinerates. Dozens, scores, and hundreds of baptisms were constantly reported in journals published by brethren such as *The Millennial Harbinger, The Christian Messenger*, and *The Evangelist*.[16] J.T. Johnson reported to Stone a meeting at Lawrenceburg, KY in which he participated resulting in thirty baptisms, and adds, "While I was at Lawrenceburg, I heard that C. Kendrick had a most triumphant meeting near Stanford, having gained about 100 in ten or twelve days."[17]

Scott published a plea for help from a small band of brethren in Ohio predicting many conversions if a preacher will come, and a report from Iowa by a church which grew from eight to sixty in two years.[18] Letters from Scott to his wife in 1847 tell of fifteen days labor in Highland County, OH in which "seventy-seven persons . . . were added to the assemblies of Christ, and many hundreds of people heard the word," and seventeen days preaching in Mason County, KY during which "fifty persons . . . believed and were immersed."[19]

Alexander Campbell and His New Version.

[14] For many examples of Campbell's inconsistency in the use of terms like evangelist and preacher, see Halbrook, "At Last . . . Now . . . An Open Confession," 630-634.

[15] Campbell, "Queries," 262 and "Reply," 171-174.

[16] *The Millennial Harbinger* was published 1830-1870. It was ably edited by Alexander Campbell, and after his death by his son-in-law W.K. Pendleton (1817-1899). *The Christian Messenger* (1826-1840) was edited by Barton W. Stone (1772-1844) and *The Evangelist* (1832-1842) by Walter Scott (1796-1861).

[17] "Religious News," 254-255.

[18] "Letters," 119.

[19] Stevenson, *Walter Scott*, 192.

Scott often returned from evangelistic journeys of two to three months after hundreds of conversions only to fall into deep depression compounding his physical exhaustion. B.U. Watkins tells of living with the Scotts, memorizing large portions of the New Testament together, and sharing their privations: "He was very, very poor; while I lived in the family it was not at all uncommon for them to be almost destitute of the common necessaries of life. He was a great believer in prayer, and just at the point of greatest need help always came."[20]

Many churches were being established, but circumstances denied them the much needed attention of full-time preachers, and few had elders. Some met only occasionally when preachers visited while others died a slow death for lack of teaching.

Located Work From the Early Days. There is no question that opposition to denominational clergy coupled with the pressing need to answer Macedonian calls resulted in a strain of discomfort with an evangelist laboring with an established church. Yet, this discomfort was not treated as a doctrinal precept by most brethren. Philip S. Fall (1798-1890) preached regularly for the church in Nashville, TN during the years 1826-1831 and 1858-1877. Jesse B. Ferguson (1819-1870) preached for that same church 1846-1856. A marker at the tomb of Walter Scott says he was the first full time minister for the church at Mayslick, KY, serving 1850-1852.

J.W. McGarvey (1829-1911) worked full time with the Dover church in La Fayette County, MO 1853-1862, at the Main St. church in Lexington, KY 1862-1867, and at the Broadway church in Lexington 1871-1882. McGarvey noted that nearly all preachers had some sideline occupation which was "necessitated by the small salary" churches could provide in Missouri during 1851-1853.[21] Reflecting on changes among Kentucky churches and preachers between 1862 and 1874, McGarvey remembered "only seven congregations in the State . . . that were supporting preachers to labor exclusively in their midst; now I can count twenty-two or twenty-three that are doing so habitually" with adequate support.[22] As the churches grew, they needed more thorough teaching to remain faithful and they were more capable of supporting men.

---

[20] Baxter, *Life of Elder Walter Scott*, 250-251.

[21] McGarvey, *Autobiography*, 19.

[22] McGarvey, "Brother Kendrick on the Cause in Kentucky," 4-5.

Recognizing that pastor, overseer, and elder refer to the same work, Moses E. Lard (1818-1880) warned brethren not to embrace the denominational concept of the "pastorate." He said,

> We have not the least objection to a preacher laboring for the same congregation, if need so require, for one year or ten, as the case may be, but we want him to do so simply as preacher and not as pastor. The modern office of pastor is an office not known in the New Testament; hence the limit of power which may be claimed to belong to it is not therein laid down. . . . the points of resemblance between pastor, priest, and pope are more than the mere circumstance that each word begins with a p. From pastor to priest is only a short step, from priest to pope only a long one; still the step has been taken.[23]

Lamenting the pitiable condition of many aged preachers in 1866, Lard observed that early battles against "the hireling system" sometimes went to extremes which caused collateral damage hindering the just "remuneration of preachers."[24]

Apostasy and Reaction Renew Controversy. For the most part, the growing host of men pleading for a return to New Testament Christianity preached the original gospel including God's plan for the roles of evangelists, pastors, and teachers. In time, this Back to the Bible movement would drift into widespread apostasy as a Back to Denominationalism movement. In 1849 in Cincinnati, OH, the American Christian Missionary Society was formed to centralize the work of evangelism among the churches. In 1859, L.L. Pinkerton (1812-1875) introduced instrumental music into the worship at Midway, KY. These innovations spread rapidly during 1875-1900, precipitating a division between conservative-minded brethren generally gathering under the name churches of Christ and liberal-minded brethren under the names Christian churches and Disciples of Christ.

The societies and the instruments were merely symptoms of a changing mind-set. The more liberal element gradually embraced other practices not authorized by the New Testament including observance of religious holy days such as Christmas and Easter, church sponsored social events such as fairs and festivals, a more worldly lifestyle, and preachers taking titles such as Pastor and Reverend. The denominational pastor system was returning.

---

[23] Lard, "The Work of the Past–The Symptoms of the Future," see section on "Pastors and the Pastorate," *Lard's Quarterly*, II: 258-259.

[24] "The Support of Aged Preachers," 377-382.

Conservative-minded brethren protested these innovations. A watershed gathering of 6,000 brethren occurred August 18, 1889 at the Sand Creek church house in Shelby County, Illinois. Daniel Sommer (1850-1940) thundered against the growing apostasy and many brethren signed the "Address and Declaration" written by Peter Warren summarizing Sommer's stand.[25] If brethren refused to stop the practice of "such abominations," "we *can not* and *will not* regard them as brethren," the document declared. One of the many objectionable practices was the one-man pastorate which was scorned in these words, "*In the entire book of God there is not one fragment of testimony in favor of the imported, one-man, preacher-pastor as the feeder and watcher over the flock after it had been fathered and established.*"

The renewed battle against the denominational one-man pastorate was pressed to an extreme by some men like Sommer so that any preacher working with and being supported by an established church was stigmatized as practicing the pastor system. The issue was discussed on and off among conservative brethren, but, as in the earlier generation, there was a pragmatic reason that many preachers viewed their work as itinerate. The 1906 Census included information on religious groups and reported the Christian churches as having about a million adherents and the churches of Christ about only 160,000. The liberal element swept most of the churches and took most of the property, and the conservative element was reduced to starting over with pioneering efforts like the earlier generation had done. Answering pleas for help far and wide, they scattered out preaching in fields, houses, and borrowed buildings. The nature of the work kept preachers on the move and few churches could afford to support a man.

Strident voices were answered by experienced preachers such as J.D. Tant (1861-1941) and M.C. Kurfees (1856-1931). Tant engaged in much itinerate work but made the common sense observation that the Bible does not regulate whether an evangelist preaches regularly once a week, once a month, or once a year at any certain place.[26] Kurfees traveled widely but was located with the Campbell Street church of Christ in Louisville,

---

[25] The "Address and Declaration" published in the *Octographic Review* was attributed to Sommer but probably written by Warren. For more information about the Sand Creek meeting, the declaration, and Sommer's sermon, see Morrison, *Like A Lion: Daniel Sommer's Seventy Years of Preaching,* 85-104.

[26] Tant, *Gospel Advocate* XLI (July 20, 1899): 449 cited in West, *The Search for the Ancient Order,* III: 72.

KY during most of his life as a preacher (1886-1931). "The wrong in the modern pastor system does not consist in the fact that a preacher is located in one place for an indefinite length of time nor in the fact that the church sustains him for such a time, but it does consist in the relation he occupies to the church and in the work he does," said Kurfees.[27] Just as necessity calls for more itinerate work in some circumstances, necessity calls for more concentrated preaching in established churches to keep them faithful at other times and places.

Factional Voices Cause Division. Daniel Sommer's disposition moderated on the issue of a preacher locating with a church which supports him. In 1932, he expressed his willingness to show more forbearance about such issues which do not change the pattern of the New Testament church by publishing with his endorsement an article entitled, "Can't We Agree on Something?" (*American Christian Review*, June 21, 1932). His protégé, W. Carl Ketcherside (1908-1989), accused his mentor of compromise and generated as much strife and division as possible over the located preacher and over colleges conducted by saints which included the Bible in the curriculum.

Ketcherside pressed the question in his *Mission Messenger* (originally *Missouri Mission Messenger*) and in constant rounds of debates. In 1953, a debate was conducted in Dallas, TX between Flavil L. Colley (b. 1934) and Ketcherside on the proposition, "The securing of a preacher as a minister of a congregation having elders, as generally practiced among the Churches of Christ in Dallas, is Scriptural." Ketcherside affirmed, "The New Testament authorizes an evangelist to exercise authority in a congregation which he has planted until men are qualified and appointed as bishops." Similar propositions were debated with G.K. Wallace (1903-1988) in Paragould, AR in 1952 and in St. Louis, MO in 1953.[28] Ketcherside held other such debates with Rue Porter, Sterl Watson, W.L. Totty, G.C. Brewer, and other men.

---

[27] M.K. Kurfees, "What Does It Mean?" *Gospel Advocate* XLII (July 5, 1900): 418, cited in West, 73.

[28] Both debates also include the proposition, "The organization, by Christians, of schools such as Freed-Hardeman College is in harmony with the New Testament scriptures." In defining his terms, Wallace emphasized, "My proposition says Christians, not churches" *(Wallace-Ketcherside St. Louis Debate*, 176). Ketcherside responded that such schools are sinful whether sponsored by individuals or churches because "it is a human organization doing the work that God intended for the church to do," i.e., teaching the Bible (189).

Leroy Garrett (b. 1918) likewise pressed and debated this issue. In 1954, he debated Bill J. Humble in Kansas City, MO on the proposition, "It is scriptural for a congregation with elders to employ a gospel preacher (evangelist) to preach the gospel regularly to the church."[29] The same year he met George W. DeHoff (1913-1993) on the propositions, "The practice of churches (such as East Main in Murfreesboro) with the elders procuring evangelists like George W. DeHoff to serve as minister to the church is scriptural," and, "Mutual ministry as practiced by me and my brethren is scriptural."

Beginning in the mid to late 1950's, Ketcherside and Garrett swung from their extreme factionalism to extreme ecumenicalism.[30] Many of their brethren followed them down the liberal, ecumenical road, but there are still preachers and congregations who practice so-called mutual edification and condemn the located preacher arrangement. These churches are splintered over other factional views such as the one container for the Lord's Supper, no divided classes, and no divorce for fornication. Their few preachers are active in the U.S., in Africa, in the Philippines, and other places around the world, but their core theory of mutual edification (actually, mutual preaching) breeds strife and confusion everywhere it goes.

In the 1980's-90's I encountered the no-located preacher position in the persons of Roy Hall and Bill Dawson, men preaching in Mingo County, West Virginia and surrounding counties including eastern Kentucky. Thomas G. O'Neal debated Hall in October 1980 in Richlands, VA and then Walter Bailey at Belfast, VA the same month. In July 1985, I debated Bill Dawson for four nights at the Upper Beech Creek Church of Christ in Mingo County. I will summarize and answer their typical arguments here.

1. The Word Game. We are told that "preach" and "teach" are different actions, as "gospel" and "doctrine" are different in content. The "gospel" is the elementary facts about Jesus' life, death, and resurrection and is preached exclusively to sinners. The "doctrine" is all instructions given to saved people as they learn and grow for a lifetime, and is therefore taught exclusively to saints. Therefore, an evangelist cannot preach the gospel to an established church. He appoints elders to teach (not preach) the doctrine (not

---

[29] This debate includes the proposition, "The organization by Christians of schools like Florida Christian College is in harmony with the New Testament."

[30] For a review of Ketcherside's swing from factional extremism to ecumenical extremism, see series by Halbrook, "At Last . . . Now . . . An Open Confession."

gospel) to saints (not sinners) in an established church, while he preaches (not teaches) the gospel (not doctrine) to sinners (not saints) in the world. This is all built on a word game of sophistry by playing on false distinctions in the terms "preach," "gospel," "teach," and "doctrine." Naturally, each word has its own meaning but not so as to distinguish the essential action or message signified.

The terms "preach" and "teach," and "gospel" and "doctrine," differ only in that they each shed more light on the nature of the message and work signified, but not any difference in substance. *Euangelizo* means to announce good news, especially the good news of God's great plan of redemption: "Then Philip opened his mouth, and began at the same scripture, and *preached* unto him Jesus" (Acts 8:35). This message of good news is *euangelion*: "Go ye into all the world, and preach the *gospel* to every creature" (Mark 16:15). The person who brings the good news is *euangelistes*, an evangelist: "do the work of an *evangelist*" (2 Tim. 4:5).[31]

Kerygma is a message proclaimed by a herald: "And my speech and my *preaching* was not with enticing words of man's wisdom, but in demonstration of the Spirit and of power" (1 Cor. 2:4). The *kerux* is the proclaimer who speaks the authoritative word of God: "Whereunto I am appointed a *preacher*, and an apostle, and a teacher of the Gentiles" (2 Tim. 1:11). The action of proclaiming the authoritative message of God is *kerusso*: "Go ye into all the world, and *preach* the gospel to every creature" (Mark 16:15).[32]

---

[31] The primary Greek word *euangelizo* means to announce good news, "*to bring good news, to announce glad tidings . . .* in the N.T. used esp. of the glad tidings of the coming kingdom of God, and of the salvation to be obtained in it through Christ, and of what relates to this salvation," "*to proclaim glad tidings; spec. to instruct* (men) *concerning the things that pertain to Christian salvation*" (Thayer, *Greek-English Lexicon*, 256). The message of good news is *euangelion*, "*the glad tidings of the kingdom of God . . . and . . . of Jesus, the Messiah, the founder of this kingdom,*" "*the narrative of the sayings, deeds, and death of Jesus Christ*" (*Ibid.*, 257). The person bringing good news is an *euangelistes*, "*a bringer of good tidings, an evangelist*" (*Ibid.*, 257). These three terms may used in compound words such as *anangello*, *apangello*, and *katangello* as virtual synonyms.

[32] Another primary word is *kerygma*, "*that which is promulgated by a herald or public crier . . . ; in the N.T. the message or proclamation by the heralds of God or Christ*" (Thayer, 346). The messenger is *kerux*, "*a herald, a messenger vested with public authority. . . . In the N.T. God's ambassador, and the herald*

That which is taught is *didaskalia*: "If thou put the brethren in remembrance of these things, thou shalt be a good minister of Jesus Christ, nourished up in the words of faith and of good *doctrine*" (1 Tim. 4:6). The teacher or instructor is *didaskalos*: "And he gave some, apostles; and some, prophets; and some, evangelists; and some, pastors and *teachers*" (Eph. 4:11). The action of instructing is *didasko*: "And he opened his mouth, and *taught* them" (Matt. 5:2). The instruction taught is also *didache*: "And they continued stedfastly in the apostles' *doctrine* and fellowship, and in breaking of bread, and in prayers" (Acts 2:42).[33]

These words are used as synonyms. The actions called "teach" (*didasko*) and "preach" (*euangelizo*) are used interchangeably in Acts 5:42: "And daily in the temple, and in every house, they ceased not to *teach* and *preach* Jesus Christ." In debating men who make a sharp distinction in these terms, we commonly ask them to teach for five minutes and then preach for five minutes to demonstrate the difference. Who would know when one action stopped and the other began? Paul said in 1 Timothy 2:7 that he was both "a *preacher* (*kerux*)" and "a *teacher* (*didaskalos*) of the Gentiles," thus uniting two terms for one work.

Twice Matthew used identical expressions joining the action signified by teach (*didasko*) and preach (*kerusso*), and making the gospel (*euangelion*) the object of both actions: Jesus was "*teaching* in their synagogues, and *preaching* the *gospel* of the kingdom" (Matt 4:23; 9:35). When He taught, it means He preached the gospel, and when He preached the gospel, He taught. Mark records that Jesus sent the twelve out "to *preach* (*kerusso*)" and to heal, and after they "*preached* (*kerusso*) that men should repent,"

---

or proclaimer of the divine word" (*Ibid.*). To proclaim is **kerusso**, "*to proclaim after the manner of a herald,*" always with the implication of an authority which must be obeyed, "spec. used *of the public proclamation of the gospel and matters pertaining to it*" (*Ibid.*).

[33] The next key word is **didaskalia**, "*teaching, instruction,*" "*teaching* i.e. *that which is taught, doctrine*" (Thayer, 144). The instructor is a **didaskalos**, "*a teacher*; in the N.T. one who teaches concerning the things of God, and the duties of man" (*Ibid.*). To instruct is **didasko**, "*to hold discourse with others in order to instruct them, deliver didactic discourses,*" "*to teach one*: used of Jesus and the apostles uttering in public what they wished their hearers to know and remember" (*Ibid.*). That which is taught is also **didache**, "*teaching,* viz. *that which is taught . . . the doctrine which has God, Christ, the Lord, for its author and supporter,*" "*instruction*" (*Ibid.*, 144-145).

they reported to him "all things, both what they had done, and what they had *taught* (*didasko*)" (Mark 3:14; 6:12, 30). When they preached they taught, and when they taught they preached.[34]

No passage indicates any difference as to the content of the message based on whether the terms "preach" and "gospel" are used, or whether "teach" and "doctrine" are used. Romans 2:21 demonstrates that "teach" and "preach" are used as synonyms, and the content of preaching may be moral instruction rather than being limited to facts about the life of Jesus. "Thou therefore which *teachest* (*didasko*) another, *teachest* (*didasko*) thou not thyself? Thou that *preachest* (*kerusso*) a man should not steal, dost thou steal?" The claim that "gospel" is limited to elementary facts about Jesus and "doctrine" to another body of instruction is baseless. Romans 1:15 shows it is possible to preach the gospel to an established church: "So, as much as in me is, I am ready to preach the gospel to you that are at Rome also."

It makes no more sense to distinguish the content of "gospel" and "doctrine" than to make similar distinctions in the terms "word," "truth," and "gospel." When passages such as Colossians 1:5 refer to "the word of the truth of the gospel," the one divine message of salvation is signified by three terms. It makes no more sense to distinguish the content of "gospel" and "doctrine" than to make similar distinctions in the terms "law," "testimony," "statutes," "commandment," "judgments," "ways," "precepts," and "words." When Psalms 19 and 119 use these expressions, the one divine revelation of Old Testament Scripture is signified by all of these eight terms. Each term simply sheds light on the nature of God's Word.

God's message of salvation is "gospel" because it is good news and it is "doctrine" because it is conveyed to the human heart by teaching. God ordained that we must "preach" or "proclaim" the message, or to say it another way, we must "teach" it. It is foolish, factional, and futile to build a theology on subtle distinctions in these terms.

1 Timothy 6:4-5 warns of the false teacher who flatters himself with the conceit that he possesses knowledge others are ignorant of, yet actually he "knows nothing. He has an unhealthy interest in controversies and quarrels about words that result in envy, strife, malicious talk, evil suspicions and

---

[34] Many such examples are given in Halbrook, "At Last . . . Now . . . An Open Confession: What Saith the Scriptures," *Truth Magazine* XX, 39 (Sept. 30, 1976): 616-619.

constant friction" (NIV). Word games and sophistry are detrimental to the peace and unity of God's people.

2. No Stay, No Pay. The so-called mutual edification faction insists that it is sinful for a preacher to locate with an established church and to receive financial support for his labors. Preachers who do so are hirelings and one-man pastors.

How long an evangelist labors in any one locality or with any congregation is purely a matter of judgment according to his assessment of needs and opportunities for teaching. When Barnabas and Paul preached together at Antioch, "a whole year they assembled themselves with the church, and taught much people" (Acts 11:26). When Paul went to Corinth, "he continued there a year and six months, teaching the word of God among them" (Acts 18:11). He reminded the Ephesian elders of his work at Ephesus: "by the space of three years I ceased not to warn every one night and day with tears" (Acts 20:31). It seems "Philip the evangelist" was located at Caesarea for over twenty years (Acts 8:40; 21:8).

We are told that a preacher can stay for an extended period of time with a congregation only if it has no elders, but the church at Ephesus had elders and yet Paul told Timothy "to abide still at Ephesus" (1 Tim. 1:3). The response given is that this is permissible when the eldership is weak, unqualified, and corrupt, but there is no evidence of this at Ephesus. False claims are backed up with more false claims, not with Scripture.

The assertion is made that, when an established church (meaning a church with elders) arranges to support a preacher while he labors with it, all parties to this arrangement sin. In fact, this arrangement is stigmatized as the one-man pastor system or the hireling system. In other words, the preacher is accused of usurping the authority of the eldership as denominational preachers do and of preaching for the love of filthy lucre. Paul warned that false teachers would prop up their case by judging motives and by "evil surmisings" (1 Tim. 6:4).

Paul argued at length that, while he labored at Corinth, he had a right to be supported by that church, but he did not exercise it for reasons of expediency (1 Cor. 9:1-18). "Even so hath the Lord ordained that they which preach the gospel should live of the gospel," is very plain (v. 14). Was Paul teaching preachers to labor for the love of filthy lucre as hirelings? Bill Dawson argued that the passage authorizes support only for inspired men specially called to preach such as Paul was, but Paul in the context speaks

Historical Controversies over Leadership

of general rights of all brethren such as marriage, not exclusive privileges for people with a miraculous call. All of us are called by the gospel to spread the gospel (Matt. 28:19-20; 2 Thess. 2:13-14). The Lord ordained that "they which preach the gospel," not exclusively they which are inspired by a miraculous call, "should live of the gospel."

We are told a preacher's pay must be spontaneous and not stipulated or agreed upon. This is another human rule not revealed in Scripture. When Paul spoke of receiving "wages" for his labors, he used a term for a stated recompense or stipend (2 Cor. 11:8; cf. 1 Cor. 9:7).[35]

Arrangements between a congregation and an evangelist for his length of stay and wages are matters of judgment not legislated by God.

3. Evangelistic Oversight. Advocates of so-called mutual edification assert that a preacher can work regularly with a church only when it has no elders. He exercises evangelistic oversight which includes the power to appoint and to dismiss elders. Several churches may be under his oversight at any time.

The main passage misused to manufacture this claim is Titus 2:15, "These things speak, and exhort, and rebuke with all authority. Let no man despise thee." The passage says nothing about an evangelist exercising oversight over a congregation but rather instructs him to speak the authoritative Word of God in its fulness without hesitation, fear, or favor toward any man. We are told Paul gave Titus oversight of the churches on Crete because he instructed him to "set in order the things that are wanting, and to ordain elders in every city" (Tit. 1:5). Yes, but the means for accomplishing this mission is given in Titus 2:15: fully and forcefully teach the truth.

The pattern for appointing officers is found in Acts 6:1-6 where the Apostles instructed the brethren concerning the qualifications and allowed them to select qualified men, and then they were appointed or ordained. If the inspired Apostles did not presume to handpick officers, why do men today imagine they can usurp this authority without inspiration?

Power to dismiss elders is claimed from 1 Timothy 1:3, interpreted to mean that Paul told Timothy to take over the oversight of the church

---

[35] The Greek word ***opsonion*** refers to "a soldier's pay, allowance" including rations and money (Thayer, 471). It means "provisions; a stipend or pay of soldiers," "wages of any kind," "due wages, a stated recompense" (Wigram, *Greek Lexicon*, 297).

at Ephesus and dismiss its corrupt elders. Paul gave no such instruction! Timothy was told to "charge some that they teach no other doctrine," and he was to inculcate respect for and submission to the rule of the elders (1 Tim. 1:3; 5:17-19).

It is ludicrous and ironic that evangelists working with churches and focusing on their scriptural role are smeared as one-man pastors ruling the roost by men who advocate an evangelist personally taking the oversight of any number of churches! And handpicking their elders! And dismissing them if they displease him! Such a theory makes evangelists not only one-man pastors but also little popes.

The role of evangelists is evangelism, not the oversight of churches.

4. Mutual Edification Legislated. The Bible requires mutual edification but gives no examples of the located preacher arrangement, it is argued.

A favorite passage appealed to is Ephesians 4:16: "From whom the whole body fitly joined together and compacted by that which every joint supplieth, according to the effectual working in the measure of every part, maketh increase of the body unto the edifying of itself in love." The primary mistake is equating edification exclusively to preaching. Paul wrote in 1 Corinthians 12:18-19, "But now hath God set the members every one of them in the body, as it hath pleased him. And if they were all one member, where were the body?" The whole body is not a mouth, as if mutual edification meant mutual preaching. If it teaches mutual preaching, the women must preach in the assemblies because they are also members of the body, and the passage speaks of the activity of "the whole body," "every joint," and "every part."

Christians edify each other both in and outside our public assemblies. Faithful attendance at worship edifies the body. Each member participating in the worship, each one according to his or her proper role and talents, edifies the whole. Preaching is only one very limited facet of edification.

The demand for a specific example in Scripture of the located preacher with a congregation supporting him betrays ignorance of how to establish and apply Bible authority. Some things are authorized but not specified. Gospel preaching is authorized but all the possible methods and details are not specified, including a one week's gospel meeting or the located preacher arrangement.

Furthermore, various details constituting Bible authority may be gleaned from several passages but may not all be found in one passage. All of the following are essential in God's plan of redemption but all are not found in one verse: God's grace, Christ's sacrifice, the necessity of preaching, and the conditions of pardon which include hearing, believing, repenting, confessing Christ, and submitting to water baptism.

All of the following provide authority for the located preacher arrangement but all are not found in one verse: We can read that the preacher's duty is to "preach the word" (2 Tim. 4:1-5). Sometimes he may need to "abide still" in one location, depending on the circumstances (1 Tim. 1:3). Local churches are authorized to provide financial support to faithful preachers (1 Cor. 9:14). The amount of support may be stipulated as "wages" (2 Cor. 11:8).

Conclusion: Use Our Gifts to Glorify Our King!

By the love and wisdom of God, Jesus Christ died for our sins and arose again to effect the plan of redemption. When He ascended to His throne in heaven, He gave gifts to bless His people and bring the plan of redemption to its full fruition.

> **And he gave some, apostles; and some, prophets; and some, evangelists; and some, pastors and teachers; For the perfecting of the saints, for the work of the ministry, for the edifying of the body of Christ: (Eph. 4:11-12).**

Satan is doing everything he can to wreck this plan and to doom our souls. We can honor and glorify our great King and defeat Satan by using our gifts as Christ intended we should.

Let evangelists, pastors, deacons, and all the saints find our God-given roles and use our talents to serve the Lord and each other. Let us approach our work with proper attitudes of humble love and mutual patience. Let us settle in our hearts the truth about the one body, one Spirit, one hope, one Lord, one faith, one baptism, and one God and Father of all. Then, let us give ourselves fully to our work in a spirit of coordination and cooperation like the members of a healthy body, not the carnal spirit of competition, envy, and strife.

Avoiding the winds of false doctrine and foolish controversy which destroy the church, let us set our minds to speak "the truth in love" that we "may grow up into him in all things, which is the head, even Christ; From whom the whole body fitly joined together and compacted by that which every joint supplieth, according to the effectual working in the measure of every part, maketh increase of the body unto the edifying of itself in love."

Bibliography

Baxter, William. *Life of Elder Walter Scott*. Nashville, TN: Gospel Advocate Co., reprint of Cincinnati, OH: Bosworth, Chase & Hall, 1874.

Campbell, Alexander. *The Christian System in Reference to the Union of Christians and Restoration of Primitive Christianity as Pled by the Current Reformation*, 4th ed. Bethany, VA: A. Campbell, 1857. (1st ed. published under the title *Christianity Restored*, 1835; 2nd ed. and subsequent editions published under the title *The Christian System*, 1839.)

_____. *The Living Oracles. The Sacred Writings of the Apostles and Evangelists of Jesus Christ, Commonly Styled The New Testament*. Translated from the Original Greek. By Doctors George Campbell, James MacKnight and Philip Doddridge. With Prefaces, Various Emendations and An Appendix, by Alexander Campbell. 6th ed. Pittsburgh: Forrester and Campbell, 1839.

_____. "Queries from Different Sources." *Christian Baptist* IV, 12 (July 2, 1827): 262.

_____. "Reply to Epaphras, No. 7." *Millennial Harbinger* IV, 4 (April 1833): 171-174.

_____. "The Rev. Thomas G. Jones and the Luminary." *The Christian Baptist* I, 5 (Dec. 1, 1823): 98-100.

_____. "The Third Epistle of Peter to the Preachers and Rulers of Congregations." *The Christian Baptist* II, 12 (July 4, 1825): 243-247.

Colly, Flavil L. and W. Carl Ketcherside. *Colly-Ketcherside Debate*. Dallas, TX: Flavil L. Colly, 1954.

DeHoff, George W. and Leroy Garrett. *DeHoff-Garrett Debate*. Murfreesboro, TN: DeHoff Pub., 1955.

Halbrook, Ron. "At Last . . . Now . . . An Open Confession." *Truth Magazine* XX, 37-40 (Sept. 16-Oct. 7, 1976): 583-586, 598-602, 616-620, 630-634.

Haldane, James A. *A View of the Social Worship and Ordinances Observed by the First Christians*. Edinburgh, 1805. Reprint by Springfield, MO: Yesterday's Treasures, 1997. This was reprinted by men interested in upholding the mutual edification faction.

[Wigram, George V.] *The Analytical Greek Lexicon*. New York: Harper & Row Pub., [1960]. Originally published by London: Samuel Bagster & Sons, 1852, subsequently revised.

Humble, Bill J. and Leroy Garrett. *Humble-Garrett Debate*. Oklahoma City, OK: Telegram Book Co., 1955. Reprint by Bowling Green, KY: Guardian of Truth Foundation, 2005.

Johnson, J.T. "Religious News." *The Christian Messenger* XII, 8 (June, 1842): 254-255.

Lard, Moses E. "The Work of the Past–The Symptoms of the Future." *Lard's Quarterly* II, 3 (April 1865): 251-262.

_____. "The Support of Aged Preachers." *Lard's Quarterly*, III, 4 (Oct. 1866): 377-382.

McGarvey, J.W. *The Autobiography of J.W. McGarvey (1829-1911)*. Special Issue of *The College of the Bible Quarterly* XXXVII, 2 (April 1960).

_____. "Brother Kendrick on the Cause in Kentucky." *Apostolic Times* VI, 33 (Nov. 19, 1874): 4-5.

Morrison, Matthew C. *Like A Lion: Daniel Sommer's Seventy Years of Preaching*. Murfreesboro, TN: DeHoff Publ., 1975.

Paley, William. "A Distinction of Orders in the Church Defended upon Principles of Public Utility." *Sermons on Public Occasions*, in *The Works of William Paley*. London: T. Nelson and Sons, 1860.

Richardson, Robert. *Memoirs of Alexander Campbell*, 2 vols. Philadelphia: J.B. Lippincott & Co., 1870.

Robinson, Stuart. *The Church of God as an Element of the Gospel and the Idea, Structure, and Functions Thereof.* Philadelphia: Joseph M. Wilson, 1858.

Scott, Walter. "Letters." *The Evangelist* VII, 5 (May 1, 1839): 119.

Sommer, Daniel. "Address and Declaration." *Octographic Review* XXXII, No. 36 (Sept. 5, 1889).

Stevenson, Dwight E. *Walter Scott: Voice of the Golden Oracle, A Biography*. Joplin, MO: College Press, [1980]; reprint of St. Louis, MO: Christian Board of Publication, 1946.

Thayer, Joseph Henry. *Greek-English Lexicon of the New Testament*. Marshallton, DE: National Foundation for Christian Education.

Thomas, Cecil K. *Alexander Campbell and His New Version*. St. Louis, MO: The Bethany Press, 1958.

Wallace, G.K. and W. Carl Ketcherside. *Wallace-Ketcherside Debate*. Longview, WA: Telegram Book Co., 1952.

_____. *Wallace-Ketcherside St. Louis Debate*. Longview, WA: Telegram Book Co., 1954.

West, Earl Irvin. *The Search for the Ancient Order*. Vol. 3. Indianapolis, IN: Religious Book Service, 1979.

Witherow, Thomas. *Which Is The Apostolic Church? An Inquiry at the Oracles of God as to Whether Any Existing Form of Church Government Is of Divine Right.* Philadelphia: Presbyterian Board of Education, 1856.

Women in Business Meetings
Tom M. Roberts

During the months August and November, 1994, a written debate was conducted in the *Guardian of Truth* magazine between Vance Trefethen and Tom Roberts. The first proposition, affirmed by brother Trefethen stated:

> "Resolved: The Scriptures teach that the pattern of decision-making in matters of congregational judgment must always include the whole church (including women) under male leadership in all local churches (both with and without elders)." Affirm: Vance E. Trefethen; Deny: Tom M. Roberts

The second proposition, affirmed by brother Roberts, states:

> "Resolved: The Scriptures teach that the elders of a local church are authorized to assemble privately to make decisions in matters of judgment for the local church before and without calling together the whole congregation." Affirm: Tom M. Roberts; Deny: Vance E. Trefethen.

The occasion for the debate was set in motion by a booklet written by

---

Tom Roberts was born in Gladewater (northeast), Texas on February 8, 1935. He married Pauline Kelley the year he graduated and attended Florida College during the 1954-55 school year. Together, they had three children: Curtis (1956), Tommy, Jr. (1957), and Paula (1964). Tommy was accidently killed in a motorcycle accident in 1981 at twenty-three years of age. Tom and Pauline have been married over fifty-six years (1953-). They currently reside in Arlington, TX where he works with the Northside church in Mansfield, in the Dallas-Fort Worth metroplex area.

Tom began preaching full time in 1956 in south Texas and has preached continually since then, having lived in North Carolina (twice), Texas, and Florida. He has been a staff writer for *Truth Magazine*, co-editor for *Watchman Magazine,* and co-author and editor of *Neo-Calvinism in the Church of Christ.* He has preached in gospel meetings across the nation, preached on radio and television, and helped start congregations in Sherman, TX, Morehead City, NC, and Fort Worth, TX.

brother Trefethen entitled *Confusion or Consensus* (New Horizon Books, Montgomery, AL, 1993). In that publication, he advocated a certain *pattern* of "congregational decision-making in matters of judgment" that required "an increased role for women in the decision-making processes of local churches" (3). Additionally, he asserted that private decision-making by elders to be "without authority" (6), thus sinful. In his attempt to substantiate his views, he stated that "Acts 15 is the only Bible pattern there is on the matter" (32). Certainly all this had to be addressed.

The ensuing debate has been published and is available for your consideration.

The Detrimental Effects of This Error

During the intervening years since 1994, several churches have experienced confusion and unrest over the issue of women in the business meeting and the subject needs our continued attention. Other preachers besides brother Trefethan have taken up this cause and have been very vocal in attempting to advance the practice. I have been asked by two congregations to address this subject because of aggressive members who insisted on changing their business meetings to a format that would include women in decision-making. I know of other congregations that have experienced unrest in the membership over this issue, so it is of current interest.

A number of factors contribute to continued unrest. First, there are some preachers who have zealously pursued this approach and have produced printed materials and sermons which promote the idea. Second, there are social changes in America that have elevated the subject of women's liberation to the status of civil liberties. It is popular today to throw the mantle of "civil liberties" over every perceived notion and pass legislation to make it national policy. A new generation of young women in the church has been educated in public schools where this advanced notion has been taught and are now reflecting their new-found equality in areas of spiritual service. Third, aggressive feminists are no longer satisfied with submissive roles and seek to enlarge their areas of service. There are many examples of women's meetings throughout the nation in which women take leadership roles and preach to and teach other women. We certainly recognize that it is biblical for women to teach women (1 Tim. 2:12; Titus 2:3-5), as reflected in this current lectureship. We have seen the development of an aggressive feminism occur nationally, and cultural practices are often carried unwittingly into the Lord's church. As ladies in the church have found increased occasions for public speaking, some are no longer content to sit idly in the background as their husbands discuss the internal matters of a local congregation. My first real introduction to this issue occurred in Virginia, prior to 1994, where a militant sister in the church demanded her place as an equal in the business meeting and left the congregation when she was not given that right. Certainly, these changes in society indicate that our subject in not a moot point among brethren today.

Needed Disclaimers

Before addressing the pros and cons of our subject, there need to be some clarifications stated that should be evident to all (but may not be).

1. Women are equal to men in quality and value. Let no one imagine that this discussion suggests otherwise. When we discuss whether or not women should be present in the decision-making process of a local congregation, we are talking about *place of service*, not *value*. One is not demeaned when God assigns a place of service and any one should find complete fulfillment in the place of assignment, not in the assignments of others, as did Paul (2 Cor. 10:12-18).

For example, men are lower than angels (Heb. 2:7). Should we be bitter against or jealous toward angels simply because they are above us? Hebrews 1:14 reveals that they are "ministering spirits sent forth to minister for those who will inherit salvation." Men are assigned different roles of service to God than angels. Neither is demeaned in accepting their place of service and doing it in their love for God. We are warned, in fact, that "angels who did not keep their proper domain, but left their own habitation, He has reserved in everlasting chains under darkness for the judgment of the great day" (Jude 6). We would do well to heed that warning in this instance, as well.

Women are to be in submission to men (1 Cor. 11:3; 1 Tim. 2:11-15; Tit. 2:3-5). This is a biblical fact that cannot be denied by any Bible-believing person. Paul explains much of the background of this relationship as he wrote to Timothy, invoking the creation as proof. But a place of submission is not to be confused with *value or worthiness*. We have no better example of submission of one to another than that of Jesus Christ becoming submissive to the Father in order to save mankind.

> Let this mind be in you which was also in Christ Jesus, who being in the form of God, did not consider it robbery to be equal with God, but made himself of no reputation, taking the form of a servant, and coming in the likeness of men. And being found in appearance as a man, he humbled

himself and became obedient to the point of death, even the death of the cross (Phil. 2:5-8).

What an example of service! Did Jesus lose His value when He submitted to the Father? No, rather He enhanced it and was "highly exalted" because of His submission (v. 9). Ladies, in like manner, you are assigned a place of service and it is not insulting to you to suggest that your place is not in the decision-making function of a local congregation.

2. There is a difference between the decision-making process and making a decision itself. We understand this in the home. It is healthy and right for a family to receive input from every member about those matters that affect them. There are times when disagreements occur. A husband and wife may have a wide-ranging discussion about an important matter that is before them. A husband who loves his wife will certainly take into consideration the wisdom and experience of his spouse and not ignore her feelings and thoughts. However, God has assigned the husband to be the head of the wife (1 Cor. 11:3) and she is to be submissive to him (Eph. 5:22-24). Thus, when all the discussion is over and some one must make a decision, God has assigned that role to the husband. Yes, the wife is included in the decision-making process, but the final responsibility to decide lies with the husband. This godly arrangement is not dictatorial and abuses (which have certainly happened) do not negate the wisdom of including others in the decision-making process.

Now, apply this to the local congregation. Surely there can be opportunities for elders (or men of the business meeting) to receive input from the whole congregation (including the women) on important matters that must be resolved. Wise elders realize that both men and women in the church have knowledge, wisdom, and experience in many things. In the interest of harmony and understanding, an arrangement can be made to receive advice from all the members. But God has assigned elders the responsibility of leading, guiding, and overseeing the flock (these scriptures will be discussed separately) and, when all is said and done, the elders must make the final decision. This avoids the danger of "lording it over the flock" (1 Pet. 5:3), while including and respecting the (sometimes opposite) views of the members.

Brother Trefethen's solution for "consensus" (general agreement) among matters of judgment was to provide the vote for every member (including the women). The fallacy of this should be evident to all. If the vote is one vote for every person, when there is a plurality of women, the women control all the decisions of the church. Likewise, the vote of a newly baptized twelve-year-old boy would carry the same weight as an elder who had given his life to the study of God's word. Consensus in the home and in the church cannot be decided by the vote, brethren. Four teenagers can outvote Mom and Dad and 100 women and girls can outvote five elders!

3. We need to also be aware that our discussion relates to matters of judgment, personal opinions, and liberties. To be true to God, a congregation yields to the pattern of God's word in matters of faith (Jude 3). No business meeting or eldership can overthrow a matter of faith. However, outside of that realm of revealed truth, many matters of judgment often test our harmony. Since all collectives must have a means of reaching decisions, so also must the church. Within the framework of seeking input from all the members, a final decision is made by the men's business meeting or the eldership.

Two Types of Proofs Presented to Sustain My Position

In the process of argumentation, I will try to produce valid positions to sustain the truth of what I believe. First, there will be a consideration of scriptural passages which are pertinent to the discussion. Secondly, we will consider *definitions* given in the Bible for those who are given oversight by God in local congregations to see if women can be included in these definitive terms.

Is There A Pattern For Women in Business Meetings?

It has been asserted that Acts 15 is the only pattern to be found on the matter before us. Since a pattern allows no deviations, if it can be shown that a single deviation to the pattern exists, there is no pattern! The same holds true for all those who advocate a certain position. I respect and acknowledge the pattern principle of God's word. "Hold fast the pattern of sound words which you have heard from me, in faith and love which are in Christ Jesus" (2 Tim. 1:13). Timothy was sent to Corinth by Paul to "remind [them] of my ways in Christ, as I teach everywhere in every church" (1 Cor. 4:16). The pattern principle applies to all of us, but a pattern cannot exist if alternate principles can be shown to lead in a different direction.

Also, it must be recognized that certain factors included in Acts 15 make it impossible to replicate the entire situation as it existed in Jerusalem, thus limiting it as a pattern for us today. The presence of the apostles, prophets and the Holy Spirit, by which divine guidance was revealed cannot be a pattern for today. The uniqueness of that meeting limits it to a first century context. That women were present when some of the events took place cannot be denied. But they never took a leadership role in the revelation of divine truth. If some continue to assert that women in Acts 15 participated as leaders, they must be able to explain how women remained in subjection, yet maintained equal roles with elders, prophets, apostles, and the Holy Spirit.

Another consideration also limits Acts 15 as a pattern for today. Present in the assembly in Jerusalem were members of the church at Antioch. These members met with the apostles, elders, and prophets and were involved in producing the letter which was sent to area churches also troubled by the Judaizing teachers. Would any contend that non-members of a local church could attend a local business meeting today and participate in decision-making, much less co-authoring letters telling area churches what God had revealed to them? The principle of local autonomy would prohibit such actions, except in the unique situation at Jerusalem by which God made His will known by revelation.

Contextually, Acts 15 cannot be stretched wide enough to include women in the *decisions* that were made. While women were included in the "whole church" (Acts 15:22) that heard the vital discussion relating to Jews and Gentiles in fellowship, we must remember that the contention is that it is a sin for *private meetings* and *private decisions* to be made without women being included. But that is exactly what happened! Acts 15:6 states plainly that the "apostles and elders came together to consider this matter." Sometimes, the whole church was together. Sometimes, the apostles and elders met without the whole church. This is realized by simply looking at the text. But this violates the "pattern" doesn't it? Is it a sin for elders to meet privately, apart from the whole church, including the women, to consider matters to be decided? Not if you read the chapter.

But Acts 15 should be read alongside Galatians 2 which refers to the same meeting. Paul relates in Galatians 2:1-2: "Then after fourteen years I went up again to Jerusalem with Barnabas and also took Titus with me. And I went up by revelation and communicated to them the gospel which I preach among the Gentiles, *but privately* (emp. mine, tr) to those who were of reputation, lest by any means I might run, or had run, in vain." Privately, brethren, and not before the whole church (including the women). Who were included in that private meeting? Paul tells us in verses 7-9 that it included James, Cephas (Peter), and John, along with himself and Barnabas. Did

Women in Business Meetings 201

they sin by not including the whole church in the discussions? To ask the question is to answer it!

Other Passages to Consider

Actually, rather than Acts 15 being the only (sole, single) passage that teaches concerning congregational action, there are many scriptures that give us additional insight.

1. Acts 4:34-37. From the beginning, decisions were made privately (not secretly, as some imply). (*Secretly* implies an attempt to hide something from others; to be surreptitious; *privately* suggests a need to limit a discussion to a smaller group than the whole church.) Private meetings by leaders are not "new" doctrine, but historical in the Bible. Disciples brought gifts to the apostles "and they distributed to each as anyone had need." This "apostolic example" showed male leadership making private decisions about who the needy were, how much each received, and how long they were to receive it, without congregational meetings. The rule of "consensus" would imply that they sinned!

2. Acts 6:1-6. This passage clearly asserts the right for private decisions to be made without involving the whole church. The apostles *privately* decided to change previous practices and to put in place a ministry for the poor, *privately* decided among themselves to stop serving tables, *privately* decided to appoint seven men (not women) to this ministry, and what they decided *privately* pleased the whole multitude. Here is an example of the traditions of the apostles (2 Thess. 2:15; 3:16) which do not agree with the new-found "pattern" of consensus. If ever there were a case in which women would take a leadership role in decision-making, this would have been an ideal case, because those being served were women. But, the Spirit-guided Apostles led the congregation in appointing men to oversee the work of ministering to the poor widows.

Vance labeled all private decisions by males as "lording it over" (*Ibid.,* 15-16; cf. Matt. 20:25-27). The disciples had been arguing about who was "greatest" in the kingdom. "Overlording," not decision-making, was sinful and Jesus rebuked them. The apostles made decisions later and were not guilty of abusing authority (1 Cor. 7:6, 25, 40; 2 Cor. 1:23-2:1) like Diotrephes (3 John 9).

3. Acts 9:26-28. The apostles sat in *private* judgment on behalf of the church at Jerusalem concerning Paul's membership, making a private decision to receive a brother without the whole church, including the women, being present. Again, no sin was involved. It would be entirely appropriate today for elders to interview a prospective member in a local church in order to determine his faithfulness. In such a manner, they "watch" on behalf of the congregation.

4. Acts 11:27-30. Local elders acted *on behalf of* the needy brethren as they received the benevolent funds to relieve the needy. Inherent in "oversight" is the ability to "see over" a work (*Bishop:* "An overseer, a man charged with the duty of seeing that things to be done by others are done rightly," Thayer, 243). (Note: Judgments may be done "rightly" [expediently] or "wrongly" [inexpediently] without sin being charged.) Oversight is not innately overbearing but may, in fact, be benevolent. Authorized private meetings are not sinful when they act as an agency for the local church. Elders acted as authorized agents for the church, being duly appointed by the Holy Spirit and the local church for this very purpose.

5. Acts 13:1-3. Prophets and teachers were "in the church" but were not "the church." Yet these men *privately,* before and without calling the entire congregation together, and without the women, fasted, prayed, and laid hands on Barnabas and Saul and sent them away. Their private functions as males were directly ordered by the Holy Spirit and clearly show that males may act on behalf of the congregation, as do elders.

6. Acts 15:1-31; Gal. 2:1-10. Paul, Barnabas, Titus, and the apostles and elders at Jerusalem made *private* (not secret) decisions on behalf of the church concerning the Gentiles (Gal. 2:2; Acts 15:6). The whole church enjoyed the benefits of the private meetings and was included in sending the letter to Antioch. It is poor exegesis to deny that private meetings occurred on behalf of, before and without calling the congregation together. It is specifically stated that, even when the congregation was included (as in chapter 15), the "decrees" (letters) "were determined by the apostles and elders at Jerusalem" (16:4). James also confirmed this (Acts 21:25) by stating ". . . we have written and decided. . . ." Private (not secret) decision-making by authorized men was a New Testament practice.

There are other considerations concerning the uniqueness of the Jerusalem meeting that prohibit it from being a pattern for decision-making today. Present in Jerusalem were prophets and apostles who, under the direct guidance of the Holy Spirit made the decision which was accepted by the church. "The multitude kept silent" (v.12) and were taught the will of God. It is certainly true that women were included among the "multitude" that attended the gathering, but it is also true that common men and women do not have the authority to act as prophets or apostles in direct contact with the Holy Spirit (2 Pet. 1:20-21). Acts 15 is profitable to us today as an example of how brethren should submit to an inspired revelation, but not as a pattern for making un-inspired decisions. This pattern requires guidance of the Holy Spirit, which we do not have today.

Additionally, in attendance in Jerusalem were Paul, Barnabas "and certain others" (Acts 15:3), members of the church at Antioch. They went to Jerusalem to consult with "the apostles and elders, about this question." This consultation was to be done "privately, to those "who were of reputation," not the whole multitude, including the women. It is important to note that Paul also relates in Galatians 2:2 that he also took Titus with him and that he went to Jerusalem "by revelation." This clearly destroys the contention that "all decision-making must be inclusive of women, even when there are elders." But let us not forget that men from one congregation (Antioch) were present (by revelation) at the decision-making meeting of Jerusalem, a separate congregation, and were involved in preparing a letter that was sent to other congregations who were agitated by Judaizing teachers. I would like to hear those who contend for Acts 15 to be a "pattern" for decision-making today deal with local autonomy and the events at Jerusalem. Would Acts 15 provide authority for men from another congregation to attend business meetings at another church and participate in deliberations and decisions? Can a congregation today, composed of brethren from more than one local church, send an inspired message to other congregations to "settle" issues before the brotherhood? Clearly, when a passage is isolated from its context, dangerous precedents can be established which have far-reaching consequences.

7. Acts 20:17-36. I do not want to be overly repetitious, but we need to keep in our minds the full contention that is being made. First, that Acts 15 is the only pattern to learn of congregational meetings. Secondly, that it is a sin for the men of the congregation (even when there are elders) to have a private meeting without including the whole church (including the women). Now, with this in our minds, compare it to Scripture. When the apostle Paul came to Miletus on his return journey to Jerusalem, he met with the elders of Ephesus at the seacoast town. Please notice the text. "From Miletus, he sent to Ephesus and called for the elders of the church" (v. 17). The rest of the passage relates the instructions of Paul to *the elders who met with Paul privately, without the whole church (including the women).*

Can there be a plainer passage? Should there be any misunderstanding about what is written?

8. Acts 21:15-26. Even after Acts 15, concerning Gentiles in the church, Paul's presence in Jerusalem threatened to disturb the church. He, therefore, "went in" (v. 18), a *private* (not secret) meeting with "James and all the elders" to discuss how the church would be affected, for "the assembly must certainly meet, for they will hear that you have come" (vv. 20, 22). The elders "took heed" and "watched" (Acts 20:28, 31) on behalf of "the assembly," being concerned for the unity and peace of the church. In their eldership capacity, they "assembled privately to make decisions in matters of judgment for the local church before and without calling together the whole congregation," and advised Paul what to do so that "all may know" (v. 24). This was not "individual action" (*Ibid.*, 97). The elders' advice was binding on Paul as a judgment (v. 23) as they represented and shepherded the flock through a perilous time. Some are denying elders' right to do what we are clearly taught that they did do. Remember God's reaction to Miriam, who was not afraid to speak against ordained authority (Num. 12:1-8).

Our Second Proof: Word Study

Words are vehicles of thoughts and inspiration has chosen the exact words to explain the scope of the elders' authority, the congregation's relationship to elders, and woman's subjection. *"Which things also we speak, not in words which man's wisdom teacheth, but which the Spirit teacheth; combining spiritual things with spiritual words"* (1 Cor. 2:13). When one is a "bishop" and exercises "oversight," he is and does expressly what the Holy Spirit teaches. Divine concepts ("spiritual things") are expressed through divine precepts ("spiritual words"). Human concepts (congregational decision-making) are expressed through human precepts (consensus, voting) and constitute "human wisdom."

Elder, presbyter (Gk: *presbuteros*; Acts 14:23; 20:17, 28; Phil. 1:1; 1 Tim. 5:17; Tit. 1:5). "(3) in the Christian churches, those who, being raised up and qualified by the work of the Holy Spirit, were appointed to have the spiritual care of, and to exercise oversight over, the churches" (Vine, Vol. II, 21).

Bishop, overseer (Gk: *episkopos;* 1 Tim. 3:2; Tit. 1:7). "An overseer, a man charged with the duty of seeing that things to be done by others are done rightly, any curator, guardian, or superintendent . . . spec. the superintendent, head or overseer of any Christian church" (Thayer, 243). "Lit, an overseer

... 2) ... is rendered ... 'office of a bishop,' lit. 'overseership,' there is no word representing office. *Note*: The corresponding verb is *episkopeo*, which, in reference to the work of an overseer, is found in 1 Pet. 5:2 ... 'exercising the oversight ... taking the oversight'" (Vine, 129).

Pastor, shepherd (Gk: *poimen*): "a shepherd, one who tends herds or flocks (not merely one who feeds them), is used metaphorically of Christian 'pastors,' Eph. 4:11. Pastors guide as well as feed the flock; cp. Acts 20:28, which, with v. 17, indicates that this was the service committed to elders (overseers, bishops); so in 1 Pet. 5:1-2, 'tend the flock, exercising the oversight'; this involves tender care and vigilant superintendence" (Vine, 167).

Feed (verb, Gk: *poimaino;* Acts 20:28; 1 Pet. 5:2). "To act as a shepherd" (quoting Trench), "The tending (which includes this) consists of other acts, of discipline, authority, restoration, material assistance of individuals, but they are incidental in comparison with the feeding" (Vine, 87, 88)

Appoint (Gk: *kathistemi*): "prop. to set down, put down ... (a) to set one over a thing (in charge of it), Acts 6:3 ... (b) to appoint one to administer an office, Tit. 1:5" (Thayer, 314). Compare its usage: Matthew 24:45, 47; Acts 6:3; Tit. 1:5."

Rule (Gk: *proistemi:* 1 Thess. 5:12; 1 Tim. 3:4; 5:17). "To set or place before; to set over. a. To be over, to superintend, preside over, rule," (Thayer, 539); (*hegeomai*), Heb. 13:7, 17: "to lead, is translated to rule" (Vine, 307).

These words clearly define that elders have the *authority of God* to oversee, exercise the oversight, see that things are done rightly by others, to be set over, to be a leader, to rule. There is no ambiguity here. It is inconceivable that elder oversight excludes the ability to make even *one decision,* much less that they sin by doing so. The Holy Spirit "makes" bishops (Acts 20:28) by the qualifications in 1 Timothy 3 and Titus 1 and defines their authority by these words that describe them. It is ludicrous to use the terminology without applying the definitions. To admit oversight and superintendency is not to stretch a single word from its meaning or context. This is what elders are and what they do, *not in name only.* To strip elders of decision-making ability is to deny elders what they do by definition: "exercise the oversight." It is notable that the same word "appoint" used in Acts 6:3 authorizing "deacons" to decide about tables is also used in Titus 1:5 regarding elders. Are deacons permitted to do that which is forbidden to elders: make decisions about their work? Elders are not to "lord it over the flock," nor act as Gentile masters, but there is *legitimate oversight* (else words have no meaning), not to be confused with abuse (1 Pet. 5:3; Luke 22:25-26). As a father rules his house, so an elder rules the "house of God" (1 Tim. 3:4-5). Must a father rule by consensus or by majority vote without the ability to make a single decision unless the whole family, including the children, are in agreement? In any collectivity (whether a family or a congregation), information may be sought from every member by the overseer, but someone must make a final decision. In the family, this is the father (Eph. 5:23). In the church, these are elders.

Congregation's role toward elders: **Submit** (Gk: *hupeiko*): "To resist no longer, to give way, yield, metaph. to yield to authority and admonition, to submit, Heb. 13:17" (Thayer, 638). **Obey** (Gk: *peitho*): "1. To persuade, i.e. to induce one by words to believe; . . . 2.a. to be persuaded, to suffer one's self to be persuaded . . . b. to listen to, obey, yield to, comply with, Acts 5:36-39; 23:21; 27:11; Ro. 2:8; Gal. 3:1; 5:1; Heb. 13:17; Jas. 3:3" (Thayer, 497). Study the cited scriptures carefully. Elders cannot be excluded from this work since it applies to those who are to "rule" over the church and elders are specifically charged with this duty. They are the only scripturally qualified men so charged.

Woman's subjection (Gk: *hupotage;* 1 Tim. 2:11). "1.The act of subjecting, 2. obedience, subjection, to arrange under, to subordinate, to subject, put in subjection" (Thayer, 645). Brethren must make up their mind whether women have decision-making authority or not. In those congregations with a majority of women, the men must either submit to the authority of the women or over-ride their decision-making authority. If elders are present, they must defer to the women, if the women decide to go against the judgment of the elders. If this is not true, women have no decision-making authority. The Bible requires women to be in subjection; some require them to have decision-making authority. If "being in subjection" allows decision-making authority, why would not "being in subjection" also allow women to serve the Lord's table, preach, or teach mixed adult classes so long as they did so "under male leadership"?

Does Voting Solve the Problem?

Vance Trefethen made an interesting admission in the debate that will afflect all those who insist on consensus. He noted that Alexander Campbell was on record as approving of voting to achieve "consensus." He was willing to allow voting even when elders were present in a congregation.

The fatal flaw in this principle is that the church is not a democracy but a spiritual body with Christ as its head and the **law of Christ** is **eldership oversight**, not **consensus**! Though not in his proposition, consensus is taught repeatedly in his book and was the heart of the debate. Later in the debate, he went beyond **consensus** and **specifically endorsed church voting** instead of eldership oversight. Of course, consensus as a process of decision-making, demands voting. One person/one vote is a subversion of truth! Every voting person has an absolutely equal voice. Most adherents of consensus deny believing in feminism but a church vote knows no gender, acknowledges no maturity, and respects no submission. *Voting changes female participation to female leadership and female majority gives women control of the church.* One cannot give women the vote in one breath and deny them leadership with the next. Subjection does not exist in the church ballot box. Consensus might include persuasion, but voting is raw majority rule, removes women from their subjection to men (1 Tim. 2:11-15) and the congregation from submission to elders (Heb. 13:7, 17). Once the **principle** of female leadership is introduced, the door cannot be shut. Others will allow men and women team-teaching in Bible classes, women serving the table, or preaching.

Conclusion

Throughout the centuries, changes to the biblical pattern have been introduced and they all have led away from truth and into apostasy. If one should compare the momentous changes which led to Catholicism, women in the business meetings might seem rather tame. However, apostasy takes small steps that result in major movements. We must not be blind to the effect of the women's liberation movement and what it has done in society as multitudes have embraced this "civil liberty." We have seen how this has impacted liberal churches of Christ as well as denominations (including the Catholic Church). In denominational churches, many have fomented for women priests, women to take part in public worship as leaders, and, of course, women preachers in many churches. Agitation among churches of Christ has led to women elders, women who serve the Lord's supper, women lead singing, and women participating in business meetings as equals with men in decision-making. The Bible does not authorize women in such places of service and oversight. Angels, men, and women have been appointed places of service in the kingdom of God and we must not leave our "places of habitation" (Jude 6) lest we bring confusion into congregations and suffer the same consequence as the angels who were not satisfied where God placed them.

The Authority of Elders: Do They Rule Only By Example?

Tom O'Neal

To the Corinthians, the Apostle Paul wrote, "But let all things be done decently and **in order**" (1 Cor. 14:40). Whatever God has done has been "in order." The practice of man has been to rebel at the order of God.

I. Men Have Opposed God's Order

God appeared to Moses at Horeb in a burning bush and said to him, "Come now therefore, and I will send thee unto Pharaoh, that thou mayest bring forth my people the children of Israel out of Egypt" (Exod. 3:10).

Tom O'Neal was born May 2, 1938 in Washington, D. C. where his father was a member of the Washington, D. C. Metropolitan Police Force. Upon his retirement in 1947, the family moved to Lawrenceburg, Tennessee, which was the home of his mother. While in high school, Tom studied Bible each day at the Christian Home Bible School under brother E. O. Coffman, a Gospel Preacher who had been Principal of the Lawrence County High School for 38 years and was highly respected in educational circles in Tennessee. Tom went on to Freed-Hardeman College (now University), Livingston State College (now West Alabama University), Middle Tennessee State University, and the University of Alabama at Birmingham. He has done local work with Butler, Jasper, Bessemer, and Ensley, Alabama churches; in Murfreesboro, Tennessee with both Westvue and North Meadow Churches; and with Orlando, Largo, and Tampa, Florida churches. He has led singing for many Gospel Meetings, engaged in a number of debates, and preached on a number of radio stations. His articles have been published in *The Gospel Guardian, Sword of Peace, Truth Magazine, Vanguard, Searching The Scriptures,* and *Back To Basics,* as well as his own paper, *Walking In Truth*. With both of their spouses deceased, he met and married Carolyn Osborne LaCoste in 1999. Tom's daughter, Meg and husband Keith Pritchard have given them two grandchildren, Koen and Kiersten; Carolyn's son Tim LaCoste and wife, Ariel, have given them two, Autumn and Ayden. Presently Tom and Carolyn live in Tampa, Florida where Tom preaches for the Central Church of Christ.

The Authority of Elders: Do They Rule Only By Example?

When Moses went to Egypt and led the children of Israel out of Egyptian bondage, he was challenged by Korah, Dathan, and Abiram along with two hundred and fifty princes of the children of Israel who said, "Ye take too much upon you" (Num. 16:3). Moses replied by saying, "Hereby ye shall know that Jehovah hath sent me to do all these works; for I have not done them of mine own mind" (Exod. 16:28). The Lord punished Korah, Dathan, and Abiram by having "the ground clave asunder that was under them; and the earth opened its mouth, and swallowed them up, and their households, and all the men that appertained unto Korah, and all their goods. So they, and all that appertained to them, went down alive into Sheol: and the earth closed upon them, and they perished from among the assembly" (Num. 16:31-33). Moses said these men were "sinners" (Num. 16:37), "despised Jehovah" (Num. 16:30), and were "wicked men" (Num. 16:26). That is how men who oppose God's order are viewed by the Holy Spirit.

After the children of Israel had entered the promised land and been ruled over by judges, they came to Samuel and wanted a king like the nations about them (1 Sam. 8). The elders of Israel said to Samuel, "Thou art old, and thy sons walk not in thy ways: now make us a king to judge us like all the nations" (1 Sam. 8:5). When Samuel took the matter up with God, he was told, "They have not rejected thee, but they have rejected me, that I should not be king over them" (1 Sam. 8:7). To reject God's rule or order was to reject God. Those who want to reject God's rule of elders today would do well to remember this.

II. Over/Under Relationship

Men whose agenda is to deny an eldership the right to rule can write all they want, talk all they want, or preach all they want, but when they get done, the New Testament still teaches an *over* and *under* relationship in the Lord. Look at some passages.

1. Acts 20:28. "Take heed therefore unto yourselves, and to all the flock, *over* the which the Holy Spirit hath made you *over*seers, to feed the church of God, which he hath purchased with his own blood."

2. Hebrews 13:7. "Remember them which have the rule *over* you, who have spoken unto you the word of God: whose faith follow, considering the end of their conversation."

3. Hebrews 13:17. "Obey them that have the rule *over* you, and submit yourselves: for they watch for your souls, as they that must give account, that they may do it with joy, and not with grief: for that is unprofitable for you."

4. Hebrews 13:24. "Salute all them that have the rule *over* you, and all the saints."

5. 1 Peter 5:2. "Feed the flock of God which is among you, taking the *oversight* thereof, not by constraint, but willingly; not for filthy lucre, but of a ready mind."

6. 1 Thessalonians 5:12. "And we beseech you, brethren, to know them which labor among you, and are *over you* in the Lord, and admonish you."

III. Despots and Tyrants Rejected

From the reading that I have done, it appears that some brethren have the idea that there are those of us who believe the authority that elders have is an arbitrary dictatorship, despotic, tyrannical rule as overlords, and are iron clad bosses that compare to rulers of the pagan world. I do not know of any brother who believes such, teaches such, practices such, or would defend such. Such a view is a misrepresentation of good brethren.

Brethren over the years have rejected such a view.

1. Brother Colly Caldwell said, "If elders see their function as institutional executives or 'business managers' they have missed the point of their service in the Lord's body."[1]

2. Brother N. B. Hardeman in 1942 preached in the *Hardeman Tabernacle Sermons,* "Now, let it be understood that elders should never be dogmatic nor arbitrary."[2]

3. Brother J. Ed Nowlin quoted the above from brother Hardeman in his Florida College lecture in 1982, showing he agreed with what brother Hardeman said forty years before.[3]

4. I wrote, "New Testament elders are not lords, tyrants or despots. If, and when, they ever become such, they cease to be New Testament elders and should be removed by the congregation. The congregation has no obligation to obey such men. Peter said elders were not 'lords over God's heritage' (1 Pet. 5:3). Of the word 'lord' Thayer says 'to hold in subjection, to be

---

[1] G. C. "Colly" Caldwell, *Guardian of Truth* [Oct. 4, 1990], 3.

[2] N. B. Hardeman, *Hardeman's Tabernacle Sermons,* V: 132.

[3] J. Edward Nowlin, *Their Works Do Follow Them,* 1982 Florida College Annual Lectures, 102.

The Authority of Elders: Do They Rule Only By Example?

master of, exercise lordship over' (332). MacKnight says 'this is a strong word, denoting that tyranny which the men of this world often exercise, when they have obtained offices of power."[4]

5. I had written earlier, "The Bible teaches that elders are to rule in the flock of God (1 Pet. 5:1-4; Acts 20:28; Heb. 13:7, 17; 1 Tim. 3:4-5). Elders are to take the oversight of the flock; but that does not give them the right of tyrannical rule. Peter said elders are not to be 'lords over God's heritage' (1 Pet. 5:3). Of the Greek word 'lord' — *katakurieuo* — Thayer said, "b. to hold in subjection, to be a master of, exercise lordship over' (332). Vine says, 'of the evil of elders lording it over the saints under their spiritual care' (II: 333). When elders make decisions without due consideration being given to the desires of the congregation they are headed for trouble. When elders are afraid to openly announce before the whole congregation what they have decided, there is something wrong with their decision. When members of the church do not feel close enough to the elders that they can sit down and discuss problems with them, there is something wrong with the relationship between the elders and the flock and the elders should examine their attitude to see if they are the problem. When elders think they can make decisions and, regardless of what it is, the church must accept it, they have the attitude Peter said they must not have. The congregation selected them to serve as elders and if they get to be 'lords' the congregation has the responsibility to select to withdraw them out of the eldership. Some elders need to think of this when they get so tyrannical and despotic. Serious problems will always result when elders become 'lords over God's heritage.'"[5]

6. In 1950, brother E. R. Harper said, in a tract published by the Firm Foundation Publishing House of Austin, Texas, "Of course we understand they are not to rule as 'lords over God's heritage' for Peter says in 1 Peter 5:2: 'Feed the flock of God which is among you, taking the oversight thereof, not by constraint, but willingly; not for filthy lucre, but of a ready mind; neither as lording it over God's heritage, but being example to the flock.' This shows plainly that you are not 'bosses' in the sense of a Stalin, or a Pope, that the church must bow to your every demand regardless; but you are to lead, to teach, to tend, to draw, to influence by your godly life and to cause them, from watching your sincere and humble life, to be happy to follow you and do the work of the church. Too often elders become 'lords over

---

[4] Tom O'Neal, *Walking In Truth* [Oct.-Nov.-Dec., 1991], 8.

[5] Tom O'Neal, *Walking In Truth* [Feb., 1977], 3-4.

God's people' and the church is never considered and the men of influence in the church, men of much ability, are shunned and even reprimanded for offering suggestions that might make more attractive the services of the Lord or might lift the vision of the church to greater things. He rules well who serves his people best. Even Christ said, 'I am not come to be ministered to but to minister.' And 'he that is greatest is the servant of all.'"[6]

7. In an exchange of articles with brother Dale Smelser, brother Mike Willis said, "I concur with him in objecting to rule by elders or business meetings that is lordly, tyrannical, and dictatorial. On this we are agreed."[7]

8. Brother Tom Roberts in a written debate with brother Vance Trefethen in *Truth Magazine* wrote, "Elders are not to 'lord it over the flock,' nor act as Gentile masters, but there is *legitimate oversight* (else words have no meaning), not to be confused with abuse (1 Pet. 5:3; Lk. 22:25-26)."[8]

9. Brother Roy E. Cogdill wrote of elders, "They have the 'rule' of the church committed into their hands by the Holy Spirit. It must not be done by their own arbitrary will, or by lording it over the church, but God had committed to them the 'oversight' of the flock and charged them with the responsibility of directing its affairs in harmony with His will."[9] "Arbitrary, dictatorial, and tyrannical authority breeds rebellion in addition to being unchristian. Elders who want to make every little decision without taking into consideration the preferences, judgments, and counsel of others are not fit to be elders."[10]

IV. Acts 20: Elders, Bishops, Pastors

In Acts 20, the Apostle Paul called the Ephesian elders to meet him at Miletus. In verse 17, they are called "elders," in verse 28 they are called "bishops" and are said "to feed" (pastor) the flock of God. All three words picked by the Holy Spirit are used in this one context. A knowledge of these words and what they mean will help one in understanding the oversight that elders have of the congregation where they are members.

---

[6] E. R. Harper, *Elders, Their Work and Qualifications* (8) which is a sermon he preached at the Broadway Church of Christ, Lubbock, Texas, October 20, 1950.

[7] Mike Willis, *Truth Magazine* [March 5, 1998], 24.

[8] Tom Roberts, *Truth Magazine* [Nov. 17, 1994], 11.

[9] Roy E. Cogdill, *Truth Magazine,* [Nov. 13, 1975], 3.

[10] Roy E. Cogdill, *1968 Florida College Lecture Outlines*, 38.

The Authority of Elders: Do They Rule Only By Example?

1. Elders. Of the Greek word, *presbuteros*, translated "elder," Thayer says, "elder; used 1. Of age; a. where two persons are spoken of, the elder . . . Lk. 15:25. B. univ. advanced in life, an elder, a senior . . . 2. A term of rank or office; as such borne by, a. among the Jews, a member of the great council or Sanhedrin (because in early times the rulers of the people, judges, etc., were selected from the elderly men); . . . B. those who in the separate cities managed public affairs and administered justice: Lk.7:3. B. among Christians, those who presided over the assemblies (or churches): Acts 11:30, 14:23, 15:2, 4, 6, 22; 16:4, 21:18, I Tim. 5:17-19, Titus 1:5, II John 1; III John 1: I Pet. 5:1-5. . . . that they did not differ at all from the (*episkopoi*) bishops or overseers is evident from the fact that the two words are used indiscriminately, Acts 20:17-28, Titus 1:5-7, and that the duty of presbyters is described by the terms *episkopein*, I Peter 5:1 sq., and *episkope*....The title *episkopos* denoted the function, *presbuteros* the dignity:"[11]

Vine says essentially the same thing Thayer does in definitions one and two. Then the number three definition says, "3. in the Christian churches, those who, being raised up and qualified by the work of the Holy Spirit, were appointed to have the spiritual care of, and to exercise oversight over, the churches. To these the term bishops, *episkopoi*, or overseers, is applied (see Acts 20, ver. 17 with ver. 28, and Tit. 1:5 and 7), the latter term indicating the nature of their work, *presbuteroi* their maturity of spiritual experience. The Divine arrangement seen throughout the N. T. was for a plurality of these to be appointed in each church, Acts 14:23; 20:17; Phil. 1:1; 1 Tim.. 5:17; Tit. 1:5. The duty of elders is described by the verb *episkopeo*. They were appointed according as they had given evidence of fulfilling the Divine qualifications, Tit. 1:6-9; cf. I Tim. 3:1-7 and I Pet. 5:2."[12]

From the definition of the word "elder" we learn that they were "elderly men" who had "advanced in life" with a "maturity of spiritual experience" and had "the spiritual care of" the churches as "overseers." These men "presided over the assemblies (or churches)" and "exercise[d] oversight over, the churches." No, they were not despots, but they exercised authority or oversight over the congregation where they were elders.

2. Bishops. Of *episkopos* Thayer says, "an overseer, a man charged with the duty of seeing that things to be done by others are done rightly,

---

[11] J. H. Thayer, *Thayer's Greek-English Lexicon of the New Testament,* 535-536.

[12] W. E. Vine, *Expository Dictionary of New Testament Words,* II: 21.

any curator, guardian, or superintendent . . . hence in the N. T. . . . .guardian of souls, one who watches over their welfare . . . spec. the superintendent, head or overseer of any Christian church."[13]

Of **episkope** Thayer says, "oversight i.e. overseership, office, charge . . . spec. the office of a bishop (the overseer or presiding officer of a Christian church); 1 Tim. 3:1, and in eccl. writ."[14]

Of **episkopeo** Thayer says, "to look upon, inspect, oversee, look after, care for: spoken of the care of the church which rested upon the presbyters."[15]

W. E. Vine says the same thing by way of definition of these words.[16]

Inherent in the word "bishop" is the idea of "seeing that things to be done by others are done rightly." That means that, if they are not "done rightly," it is the bishop's responsibility to correct the way they are being done and the Holy Spirit has authorized elders to do whatever is necessary to see that things are "done rightly." That does not mean bishops have "despotic or tyrannical authority." Bishops are superintendents and they cannot do this only by example. They are the "presiding officers" of the church. Some "officers" they would be if they had no "authority" to "care for" or "oversee" the congregation. Officers, yes, but not in the sense of political positions of the world. The word "office" is used in connection with elders in 1 Timothy 3:1 but the verse goes on to explain by "office" is meant "work" or function. The "office" of elder or bishop is the work, function, or service of bishop.

3. Pastors. Of *poimen* Thayer says "a herdsman, esp. a shepherd . . . the presiding officer, manager, director, of any assembly: so of Christ the Head of the church. . . .of the overseers of the Christian assemblies [A. V. pastors]."[17]

Of *poimaino* Thayer says "to feed, to tend a flock, keep sheep, to rule, govern: of rulers . . . of the overseers (pastors) of the church . . . .B. to furnish pasturage or food; to nourish."[18]

---

[13] J. H. Thayer, *Thayer's Greek-English Lexicon of the New Testament,* 243.

[14] Thayer, *op. cit.,* 242-243.

[15] Thayer, *op. cit.,* 242.

[16] Vine, *op. cit.,* I: 128-129; III: 152.

[17] Thayer, *op. cit.,* 527.

[18] Thayer, *op. cit.,* 527.

Vine defines the words in essentially the same way.[19]

Words either have meaning or they do not. If they do not have meaning, then one can ever determine what is being said. With words not only having meaning, but understanding that the Holy Spirit selected the very words of the New Testament (1 Cor. 2), we can come to a definite conclusion as to what the New Testament teaches.

The elders in the church of the New Testament are older men who have gained experience and insight into the affairs of life that the younger or novice has not had time to obtain. Their knowledge and their wisdom should not only be respected, but should be appreciated and used in the service of the Lord. Is this not what the Apostle Paul had in mind when he asked the Corinthian brethren, "What cannot there be found among you one *wise man* who shall be able to decide between his brethren?" (1 Cor. 6:5).

These wise men or elders are charged with seeing that things are done in a right manner or order. This, in and of itself, gives them the "authority" to see to the affairs of the congregation. There is a work to be done by the congregation and somebody must see to it. Who is it that is charged by the Holy Spirit to oversee this work? Decisions of various kinds have to be made concerning the work that the congregation does. Who is to make those final decisions? There is an old saying, "What is everybody's business is nobody's business." This is true with the Lord's church. Where everybody is responsible, nobody is responsible.

Have we learned nothing from those who say there should be "mutual edification"? Among those brethren who truly practice such, the brethren who preach are sometimes limited in ability and have little opportunity to prepare their lessons because of the demands of a full-time job. The result is preaching which does not meet the needs of the congregation. What is everybody's business turns out to be nobody's business and the church is not edified adequately.

There are some among brethren who contend that there are no elders today because elders were only for the days of inspiration. They do no want elders so they come up with an argument that they think sounds scriptural to eliminate elders. If there are elders today to oversee the church, to guide and direct it, then these individuals "do not get to have their say" as to how the church will operate.

---

[19] Vine, *op. cit.*, III: 167; IV: 19.

When brethren say elders rule only by example and have no authority over the church, it is a good way for them to claim that the entire congregation should decide matters in meetings in which the entire congregation is engaged. Thus, they get to have their say in what is done or not done. Any way they argue for congregational business meetings making decisions, they are arguing against the rule and oversight of elders.

When I mention the authority of elders, I am not talking about some concept foreign to the New Testament, even though there are some brethren who think so. Brother Maurice Barnett, in a Florida College Lecture, said, "Some insist that elders have no authority *whatever.* However, that observation depends on what one means by authority. Luke 22:24-26 teaches just that no Christian is a ruler over others *as* the kings and lords of the world are over physical nations. Christians are not just abject citizens of the elders' domain. 1 Peter 5:3 forbids them to 'lord it over' the charge allotted to them. Thus there are limits to what elders can do. . . .The position of elders is that of ruling by leadership, not of ruling by authoritative command. Their role lies between the two extremes of authority of lordship and having no authority at all. The Scriptures clearly show what they are authorized to do."[20]

My Freed-Hardeman College (now University) classmate, Jay Lockhart wrote, "Based upon this text (1 Pet. 5:2, TGO), some brethren have taken the position that elders have no authority and can lead only by example. Being an example is an important attribute of elders (1 Pet. 5:3), but we should not overlook the fact that every command of God carries with it the authority to do whatever is necessary in obeying that command. Since elders are to be overseers, they have the authority to do whatever is necessary in overseeing, that is, 'seeing that things are done rightly,' being guardians 'of souls,' and 'watching over their welfare' (Thayer, 243). Elders are not dictators (lords over the church), but they are leaders who have the authority to do whatever is necessary as they seek the welfare of the church."[21]

In 1961 brother Charles A. Holt, Jr. moved from the East Florence, Alabama Church, where he had been the preacher, to Wichita Falls, Texas. In the church bulletin that Charles published in Texas, he began to print material on the eldership by brother Homer Hailey. Charles moved further down the

---

[20] Maurice Barnett, *Reemphasizing Bible Basics in Current Controversies,* The 1990 Florida College Annual Lectures, 95-96.

[21] Jay Lockhart, "Take Care of the Church," *The Spiritual Sword* [Oct. 2009], 26.

The Authority of Elders: Do They Rule Only By Example? 217

road from brother Hailey's position on elders by writing that there was no such thing as elders in the church, except the older men and women; there was no such thing in the New Testament as a "church"; there was no church treasury taught in the New Testament; we do not have a correct translation of the Bible; that the Lord's Supper was observed on any day of the week, that instrumental music could be used in worship; there was a leadership role for women in the church and played around with Olan Hicks and his false teaching on marriage, divorce, and remarriage. Charles started two papers, *Sentinel of Truth* and *The Examiner* in which he advocated these views.

V. Quotations of Others' Positions

1. Brother Homer Hailey's views on elders has been published among brethren.[22] Of elders, brother Hailey says, "their rule is by guidance through moral persuasion" (528). He talks of "moral suasion" (527). "Their rule was to be oversight by example" (528). "In the realm of judgment or opinion an elder has no *authority* more than another individual or the congregation" (534). He says that an elder's influence is "exerted by moral persuasion" (530).

Brother Hailey goes on to say, "The 'rule' of elders is in the realm of faith" (534). "When men have been made overseers by the Holy Spirit (Acts 20:28), and duly appointed by the church to that duty, one rebels against God when he rebels against them" (539). How does one rebel against an example? "Let the watchman warn the wicked who go astray, and with a firm hand and in a positive manner discipline them, and there will be less within the church at which to be pointed with scorn by those outside, and there will be a holier disposition on the part of faithful members to overlook the many deficiencies in their qualifications" (541). "A firm hand and in a positive manner discipline" certainly implies more than just an example.

Reading these statements it appears to me that there are two different concepts set forth by brother Hailey. One time he has elders ruling by example only and at another time ruling by "a firm hand." It can't be both ways! If elders rule only by example, then they do not have any kind of authority to rule with a firm hand. If elders rule with authority, then they do not rule only by example.

At the 1968 Florida College Lectures, brother Roy E. Cogdill spoke on "The Nature and Structure of the Church" for three days. These lectures

---

[22] Homer Hailey, *Hailey's Comments*, II: 526-545.

were a review and an exposé of both brother Hailey's views and also brother Charles Holt's on the rule of elders.[23]

2. Closely associated with brother Hailey at Florida College was brother Clinton Hamilton. Whether either of them obtained his views about elders from the other or was influenced by the other in this regard, I do not know. I do know that brother Hamilton believed very similar views to brother Hailey. Brother Hamilton spoke to The Sower's Club on the campus of Florida College on February 14, 1966 on the subject of the rule of elders. Some objected to his presentation and this caused much discussion. The next week, brother H. E. Phillips was invited to speak on the rule of elders with a different view from that of brother Hamilton and did so on February 21, 1966.

In his presentation on the rule of elders, brother Hamilton emphasized that elders watch for *souls* and matters of a physical nature, like who is cutting the grass at the meeting house or what color a wall is painted, have nothing to do with his soul. The implication is that elders have no authority to make judgment decisions about matters of a physical nature, anymore than another male member would have. Brother Hamilton went on to say that the "only time elders can tell me what to do is what the word of God says." He further said that an elder "only can use moral suasion. When he gets through with this, he doesn't have anything."[24]

---

[23] Roy E. Cogdill, "The Nature And Structure of the Church" (a 24-page outline) in the 1968 Florida College Lectureship Outlines. Brother Hailey was present in Hutchinson Memorial Auditorium, front row, second seat, to hear Cogdill deliver his lectures. Because brother Cogdill reviewed brother Hailey's position on the rule of elders publicly in brother Hailey's home territory could well be one of the reasons brother Hailey did not really care for brother Cogdill. Brother David Edwin Harrell, Jr. quoted brother Hailey as saying to him in an interview with him in Tucson, Arizona on July 16, 1998, "I have never been an admirer of Roy Cogdill. I could tolerate him but I was never close to him. . . .He was a lawyer and he had a *legalistic* spirit. . . .Everyone else admired him so I never said much" (*The Churches Of Christ in the 20th Century*, 367, 448).

[24] The two presentations on the rule of elders to The Sower's Club by brethren Hamilton and Phillips were recorded by brother H. E. Phillips. He gave me a copy of the tape containing both lessons. Not wanting to make a big issue of this on campus in 1966, he asked that I not circulate the tape, which I have not. He and brother Hamilton had private conversations at the time between them. Brother Phillips told me that he asked brother Hamilton in the course of their

The Authority of Elders: Do They Rule Only By Example?

3. In more recent years brother Dale Smelser has said a good bit about the rule of elders. Some material from his pen has appeared in *Think On These Things* (July-Sept, 2000, page 2), *Truth Magazine* (Mar. 5, 1998), in a tract entitled *The Rule of Elders* in 1993, in a series of four articles in *Focus Magazine* (Jan.-April, 2000), and in other places.

Trying to nail down specifically brother Smelser's position on this question has been very difficult for me. I find several things that he does say that are confusing. Some of what he does is equivocation. He, like the institutional brethren of a generation ago, uses one word to mean several different things.[25] Brother Smelser uses the word "authority" in relation to the rule of elders to mean (a) whatever authority he is willing to say elders have and then uses "authority" or "authoritarian" to mean (b) despotic, tyrannical, arbitrary, ruling overlords. One time elders have authority and at other times they do not have any authority. Which way is it? It cannot be both ways. He wrote, "Elders must not act with the authority of a boss or board of directors, making all the decisions and imposing them by announcement. Those who advocate that have misunderstood the elder's role."[26] Now, who believes that? Brother Smelser did not tell us who it is that believes that nor did he document this supposed position. Wonder why? Brother Smelser goes on to say, "Lording it over the flock and being authoritarian are the same thing."[27] Elders "lording" it over the flock, no; elders being over the flock or overseeing the flock, yes. Again, brother Smelser says, "Jesus forbids the exercising of dominion and authority by some over others in the kingdom."[28] Previously I have quoted passages from the New Testament that show there

---

conversations, "Clinton, do you think any of us believe elders should use a baseball bat in their rule?" Brother Hamilton should have known that brother Phillips did not agree with his erroneous view on the rule of elders for brother Phillips discussed this on pages 47 and 48 of his book, *Scriptural Elders and Deacons*. Brother Hamilton had read the manuscript before its publication some seven years earlier (introduction page to *Scriptural Elders and Deacons*).

[25] They used the word "home" and never explained which definition they were attaching to it in a given sentence. Sometimes in one sentence they used the word "home" to mean [a] a house, [b] a family relationship, and [c] a board of directors of a human corporation.

[26] Dale Smelser, tract *The Rule of Elders,* 7.

[27] Dale Smelser, *op. cit.,* 6.

[28] Dale Smelser, *op. cit.,* 6.

is an *over/under relationship* in the Lord and I will look at them in more detail before the end of this lecture. Brother Smelser is still hung up on this matter of authority for elders. He says, "The other thing Jesus prohibited is *authority.*"[29] I expected better of him than that. Just like I have respected brethren Hailey and Hamilton through the years, I have respected brother Smelser since we were young preachers living not very far from each other forty-five to fifty years ago in the Birmingham, Alabama area.

Brother Smelser does not believe elders are limited to ruling by example only. He wrote, "Elders leading only by example is not my view."[30] I do not want to misrepresent him and would quickly correct anyone I heard misrepresenting him on this point. His view of elders is a little different twist to ruling by example only.

He believes that the "rule" that elders have is in "leading" the congregation in a meeting of the entire congregation to come to what he calls a "consensus" on a matter. Hear him. "It takes special leadership to bring about consensus and that kind of respect" and "If the consensus they bring about should conflict with my personal preference this time, let me yield, retiring my preference, and likewise act for the good of the flock."[31] If the decision of the entire congregation with women present is at odds with brother Smelser's preferences, yet he could yield his preference to them, why could he not yield his preference to the decision of the elders when his preference was at odds with them? Of elders, brother Smelser says, "They lovingly watch over the spiritual community of believers in their midst, to secure each soul and bring scriptural and practical consensus through their Christ devoted leadership."[32]

Brother Smelser wrote, "Rather than asking if women may attend business meetings, the better question is: May the whole church be present to consider congregational matters, with or without elders?"[33] Brother Smelser uses Acts 6 to prove that the whole Jerusalem church assembled to choose the men to oversee the distribution to the needy widows. He further says

---

[29] Dale Smelser, *op. cit.,* 7.

[30] Dale Smelser, *Think On These Things* [July-August-September, 2000], 2.

[31] Dale Smelser, tract, *op. cit.,* 10.

[32] Dale Smelser, *Sentry Magazine* [Dec. 31, 1987], 2.

[33] Dale Smelser, *Sentry Magazine* [Dec. 31, 1987], 2.

The Authority of Elders: Do They Rule Only By Example?

"the whole church was present for the discussion and its resolution." He goes on to say, "we see the whole church present to solve the logistics of ministering" and that "this justifies the presence of the congregation" and then asks, "Where is a passage that justifies a business meeting that prohibits the presence of women?"[34] "Choosing is a decision. And the whole multitude chose."[35] "The whole multitude chose in Acts 6. Therefore the whole multitude made a decision."[36] From these statements of brother Smelser, if the whole congregation is to have a part in the decisions that are made for the congregation, and women are to be in those congregational meetings, why would it not follow that women participated in the decision making for the congregation?

VI. Authority for the Rule of Elders

Having set the stage for the "why" of this particular lecture, I want to turn to the New Testament. What some brother believes or does not believe about the rule of elders is of little importance. However, what the New Testament teaches on this topic is of supreme importance.

1. Acts 20:28. "Take heed therefore unto yourselves, and to all the flock, over the which the Holy Spirit hath made you overseers (bishops, ASV), to feed the church of God, which he hath purchased with his own blood."

This passage teaches that those men who were designated as "elders" in Acts 20:17 were told by the Apostle Paul that thy were "over" the "flock"! Where is the passage that teaches some "other arrangement" is "over" the flock of God? If, as has been claimed, the "whole congregation" is to have a part in the decisions for the congregation along with the elders, and women are a part of the "whole congregation," why would it not follow that women have a part in the oversight and decisions for the congregation? Brethren need to stop this "double talk" and playing the "cat and mouse" game with the word of God and with good brethren. Such does nothing but create doubt and confusion in the minds of brethren.

The elders who are bishops or overseers are defined by Thayer as ones who "managed . . . affairs" and "administered justice." In New Testament churches they "presided over the assemblies" or the congregation. How does one "manage," "administer," and "preside over" just by example?

---

[34] Dale Smelser, *Truth Magazine* [Mar. 5, 1998], 16.

[35] Dale Smelser, *Truth Magazine* [Mar. 5, 1998], 22.

[36] Dale Smelser, *Truth Magazine* [Mar. 5, 1998], 22.

Of the word "bishop" Thayer says, "an overseer, a man charged with the duty of seeing that things to be done by others are done rightly" and is the "overseer of any Christians church." How does one see that others do things rightly just by setting a good example? How does one oversee anything just by example?

Of another form of the Greek expression translated "bishop," Thayer says it means "to look upon, inspect, oversee, look after, care for." I raise the question, "How does one inspect by example?" The inspector with the United States Department of Agriculture does not inspect beef, pork, chicken, etc. by just setting a good example. Would you want to eat fish, pork, beef, and chicken if you knew the inspector with the Department of Agriculture had only been a model citizen on the job? No, you would not. And brethren are foolish to play their little "cat and mouse" games in regard to elders overseeing the church. They should be ashamed of themselves for bringing up such foolishness and straining at the definitions of words to make the New Testament teach something that the Holy Spirit never intended. When good brethren take the time not being intimidated by their good words and fair speech, to settle down and make a serious investigation of words and their meaning, brethren will see the error of these little "cat and mouse" games.

Of *poimano* translated "to feed" in Acts 20:28, Thayer says "to rule, govern," "of the overseers . . . of the church," and the "manager, director, of any assembly: . . . of the overseers of the Christians assemblies."

When brethren think in terms of elders, pastors, bishops, ruling in the church of God and the only thing that they can think of is an arbitrary boss, a dictator, a despot, a tyrannical ruler, an overlord, and an iron-clad boss like those in the Gentile world, they are not thinking in terms of the New Testament. They need to get their act together and stop acting like there are brethren who want to make elders fit their perception.

2. 1 Timothy 3:4-5. "One that ruleth well his own house, having his children in subjection with all gravity; (For if a man know not how to rule his own house, how shall he take care of the church of God?)."

The Holy Spirit makes ruling well his own house equal to taking care of the church of God. An elder does not rule his own house only by example and neither does he do it by consensus. Many a man has ruled his own house when others members were in total disagreement with what he was doing. When such happens, that does not mean he is being a dictator or some tyrannical boss. It means that he recognizes his responsibility to lead, rule, and guide the house and is doing so for the good of his family.

Of "ruleth" (*proistamenon*) in 1 Timothy 3:4, Thayer says, "to be over, to superintend, preside over." How does one do that by only an example or consensus? When he so superintends, presides over, he is not being a tyrant. He can so rule without being tyrannical.

Of "ruleth" in 1 Timothy 3:5 Thayer says, "To take care of a person or thing (*epi*) denoting direction of the mind toward the object cared for...."

3. 1 Timothy 5:17. "Let the elders that rule well be counted worthy of double honor, especially they who labour in the word and doctrine."

Of "rule" in 1 Timothy 5:17, Thayer says, "to be over, to superintend, preside over" and then gives 1 Timothy 5:17. Do elders who "rule well" demonstrate that by setting a better example than the elder who just sets a good example? How does an elder "rule well" by consensus? If one elder does a *good* job ruling by consensus and another elder "rules well," does he have *more consensus* than the other elder who just rules? If one has *consensus*, can another have *more consensus*?

4. Titus 1:7. "For a bishop must be blameless, as the steward of God; not selfwilled...." Of "selfwilled" (*authades*)**,** Vine says, "self-pleasing (*autos,* self, *hedomai*, to please), denotes one who, dominated by self-interest, and inconsiderate of others, arrogantly asserts his own will, 'self-willed,' Tit. 1:7, 2 Pet.2:10 (the opposite of e*pieikes,* gentle, e.g., 1 Tim. 3:3)," "one so far overvaluing any determination at which he had himself once arrived that he will not be removed from it."[37]

When an elder is not a "self-willed" person, he will not be a tyrant, a despotic individual. Thy Holy Spirit knew how to weed out the despotic, tyrannical individual from being an elders before such a concern ever came up. If brethren would just follow the teaching of the Holy Spirit, a lot of our problems would be eliminated before we ever had to deal with them.

5. Hebrews 13:7, 17, 24. "Remember them which have the rule over you, who have spoken unto you the word of God: whose faith follow, considering the end of their conversation. . . . Obey them that have the rule over you, and submit yourselves: for they watch for your souls, as they that must give account, that they may do it with joy, and not with grief: for

---

[37] Vine, *op. cit.,* III: 342.

that is unprofitable for you. . . .Salute all them that have the rule over you, and all the saints."

Here are three verses in Hebrews 13 that says someone has the rule over someone else. Because these verses do not specifically mention elders, some have concluded that elders are not under consideration. That is a convenient position to take. By taking that position, they eliminate elders being over the church. However, some use these verses to show that elders are just over the souls of Christians and not over the work of the church. By doing so, they admit that the ones who are over others are elders.

Of the word "rule" Thayer says, "a. to go before; b. to be a leader; to rule, command; to have authority over; in the N. T. so only in the pres. ptcp. . . . a prince, of regal power . . . governor, viceroy . . . leading as respects influence, controlling in counsel, . . . over whom one rules, so of the overseers or leaders of Christian churches; Heb. xiii, 7, 17, 24."[38]

Of this word "rule" in Hebrews 13, Presbyterian commentator James MacKnight (1721-1800) says something that I would have thought brethren would have read, digested, and understood. But evidently some haven't. MacKnight said, "Though the word *ruler* properly signifies *a ruler* or *commander*, we should recollect, that the authority of Christian bishops and pastors, of whom the apostle is speaking, is not of the same kind with that of civil rulers, 1 Pet. V. 3, being founded, not on force, but in the fidelity with which they discharge the duties of their function, and in the esteem and affection of their flock."[39]

6. 1 Peter 5:2. "Feed the flock of God which is among you, taking the oversight thereof, not by constraint, but willingly: not for filthy lucre, but of a ready mind: Neither as being lords over God's heritage, but being ensamples to the flock."

The Apostle Peter tells the elders among the brethren in Pontus, Galatia, Cappadocia, Asia, and Bithynia to "feed the flock" and they are to take the oversight of the flock of God among them. Here again is an under/over relationship. Somebody is over somebody else. Preachers can argue all they want about it, but when all is said and done, there are still some people who are over others. Who are those who are over others? The text says it is the "elders."

---

[38] Thayer, *op. cit.,* 276.

[39] James MacKnight, *MacKnight on the Epistles,* V: 501.

The Authority of Elders: Do They Rule Only By Example?

Again, the Apostle Peter says while the elders are to have the oversight, they are not to "lord" it over the heritage of God. Of the word "lord," Thayer says, "b. metaph. The presiding officer, manager, director, of any assembly . . . of the overseers of the Christian assemblies [A.V. *pastors*]."[40] MacKnight says of this word "lord," "This is a strong word, denoting that tyranny which the men of this world often exercise, when they have obtained offices of power."[41]

Some brethren use 1 Peter 5:2 and tie the expression "neither as being lords over God's heritage, but being ensamples to the flock" with a statement of Jesus in Matthew 20. Jesus said, "You know that the rulers of the Gentiles lord it over them, and those who are great exercise authority over them. Yet it shall not be so among you; but whoever desires to become great among you, let him be your servant. And whoever desires to be first among you, let him be your slave—just as the Son of Man did not come to be served, but to serve, and to give His life a ransom for many." (Matt. 20:25-28).

The first thing I need to point out is that Jesus was not speaking these words in a context of the rule of elders in the New Testament Church. In fact, Jesus spoke these words before there were any elders in the New Testament Church or even the New Testament Church.

The second thing that needs to be noticed is Jesus spoke these words regarding a controversy among the disciples as to who would be the greatest in the kingdom when it did come. Jesus showed the greatest person in His kingdom would be the one who rendered the greatest humble service.

The third thing that needs to be pointed out is that the kind of "lording" done by the Gentiles is not the same kind of ruling that the elders of the New Testament Church do.

What some brethren have done is presumed, assumed, and asserted that New Testament elders rule the church just like Gentile lords rule. It is one thing to make such a charge and it is another thing to prove it is true. Brethren who have charged others with defending despotic and tyrannical rule of elders should be ashamed of themselves for misrepresenting their brethren over something that has caused so much unrest.

The authority that an eldership has is not to make laws for the kingdom

---

[40] Thayer, *op. cit.*, 527.

[41] James MacKnight, *op. cit.*, V: 501.

of God. The law of God has been settled in heaven (Psa. 119:89). Elders cannot formulate some creed for faith and morals to which brethren must bow. They do not have the power to change God's plan for anything. They cannot changed the worship or organization of the church or pervert the function of the church. Brethren are to submit to them only as they submit themselves and their rule to the authority of Christ. "Consensus" which is just another name for majority rule or a democracy within the church puts matters concerning the church in the hands of those who are untaught in the word of God, therefore, ignorant for the most part of the Scriptures, the inexperienced, the untrained, and the fleshly and carnally minded individuals.[42]

---

[42] Roy E. Cogdill's comments summarized from the 1968 Florida College Lectures, 35-36.

The Ladies Classes

Qualifications of Elders' and Deacons' Wives

Sherelyn Mayberry

The qualifications of elders, deacons, and their wives are given in 1 Timothy 3 and Titus 1 and must be evident before a man is appointed to the office. The wife of an elder or deacon impacts his ability to fulfill some of his qualifications and she, also, has qualifications she should satisfy as his wife. Her husband's ability to serve in this capacity will be affected by his early years in marriage, continuing through mid-life, and his later years. Therefore, let us look at her specific stipulations and then address her part in helping him meet the conditions of his office.

Specific Qualifications of the Wives

Even so must their wives be grave, not slanderers, sober, faithful in all things (1 Tim. 3:11, KJV).

Women must likewise be dignified, not malicious gossips, but temperate, faithful in all things (1 Tim. 3:11, NASB).

Sherelyn Mayberry was born on August 20, 1956, in Wichita Falls, Texas. She, along with her parents, Ernest and Frances Finley, two sisters and a brother lived in Oklahoma and Texas as her father preached in different locations. She married Mark Mayberry in 1978. He has preached in Apollo Beach, FL, Groveton, Tyler, and Cooper, TX, and Clarksville, TN. Her husband currently preaches for the Adoue Street Church of Christ in Alvin, TX where they have lived for eleven years. Mark has also served as an elder for the local church for six years. She and her husband have two sons: Nathan (24), married to Sarah Smith and father of Kaelyn and, as of this writing, is expecting another child in March, and Ryan (18), a high school graduate who loves music, photography, and computers and plans to attend Texas Tech University. Both sons are active faithful members of the Lord's church. Sherelyn has assisted her husband in the Lord's work and taught Bible classes for young children, teenage girls, and adult women for many years.

Even so must their wives (KJV); Women must likewise (NASB). The Greek word *gune*, here translated "wives" (KJV) or "women" (NASB), occurs over 200x in the NT. Thomas says it refers to "a woman." BDAG offers the following meanings: "(1) an adult female person, woman (virgins are included); (2) a married woman, wife; (3) a newly married woman, bride, to be considered in some contexts."

The marginal note in the NASB says, "i.e. either deacons' wives or deaconesses." Some have taken the position that there is an office of a deaconess, but the context in 1 Timothy 3 centers around the qualifications of elders and deacons and what is required of their wives. The other scripture that refers to a woman "deaconess" is found in Romans 16:1 and pertains to Phoebe who was a servant of the church at Cenchrea, of many, and of Paul. However, she does not function in an official position or capacity.

Be grave (KJV); be dignified (NASB). The Greek word *semnos*, here translated "grave" (KJV) or "dignified" (NASB), occurs 4x in the NT (Phil. 4:8; 1 Tim. 3:8, 11; Tit. 2:2). BDAG say it pertains "to evoking special respect; (1) of living entities; (a) human beings worthy of respect/honor, noble, dignified, serious. . . .(2) of characteristics, states of being, and things honorable, worthy, venerable, holy, above reproach."

> Finally, brethren, whatever is true, whatever is ***honorable***, whatever is right, whatever is pure, whatever is lovely, whatever is of good repute, if there is any excellence and if anything worthy of praise, dwell on these things (Phil. 4:8, NASB95).

> Deacons likewise must be ***men of dignity***, not double-tongued, or addicted to much wine or fond of sordid gain (1 Tim. 3:8, NASB95).

> Women must likewise be ***dignified***, not malicious gossips, but temperate, faithful in all things (1 Tim. 3:11, NASB95).

> Older men are to be temperate, ***dignified***, sensible, sound in faith, in love, in perseverance (Tit. 2:2, NASB95).

A related word, *semnotes*, occurs 3x in the NT (1 Tim. 2:2; 3:4; Tit. 2:7). Thomas says it describes "seriousness." BDAG defines it as "a manner or mode of behavior that indicates one is above what is ordinary and therefore worthy of special respect; (a) of a human being, dignity, seriousness, probity, holiness = Latin *Gravitas*; (b) of a deity holiness."

This characteristic is required of disciples in general (1 Tim. 2:2; Phil. 4:8), the children of elders/overseers (1 Tim. 3:4), deacons (1 Tim.

Qualifications of Elders' and Deacons' Wives

3:8), their wives (1 Tim. 3:11), older men (Tit. 2:2), and evangelists (Tit. 2:7).

> First of all, then, I urge that entreaties and prayers, petitions and thanksgivings, be made on behalf of all men, for kings and all who are in authority, so that we may lead a tranquil and quiet life in all godliness and *dignity* (1 Tim. 2:1-2, NASB95)

> Finally, brethren, whatever is true, whatever is *honorable*, whatever is right, whatever is pure, whatever is lovely, whatever is of good repute, if there is any excellence and if anything worthy of praise, dwell on these things (Phil. 4:8, NASB95).

> He must be one who manages his own household well, keeping his children under control with all *dignity* (1 Tim. 3:4, NASB95).

> Deacons likewise must be *men of dignity*, not double-tongued, or addicted to much wine or fond of sordid gain (1 Tim. 3:8, NASB95).

> Women must likewise be *dignified*, not malicious gossips, but temperate, faithful in all things (1 Tim. 3:18, NASB95).

> Older men are to be temperate, *dignified*, sensible, sound in faith, in love, in perseverance (Tit. 2:2, NASB95).

> . . . in all things show yourself to be an example of good deeds, with purity in doctrine, *dignified*, sound in speech which is beyond reproach, so that the opponent will be put to shame, having nothing bad to say about us (Tit. 2:7-8, NASB95).

The wife of an elder or deacon should conduct her life in a manner that engenders respect. She is worthy of honor. "Strength and dignity are her clothing." Her husband and children praise her noble character (Prov. 31:25, 28, 29). Crudity and coarse jesting are not a part of her demeanor (Eph. 5:4). She is joyous, but dignified and serious; as a result, her husband's reputation is upheld and others have confidence in her.

Not slanderers (KJV); not malicious gossips (NASB). The Greek word *diabolos*, here translated "slanderers" (KJV) or "malicious gossips" (NASB), frequently refers to the devil himself. Thomas defines it as "slanderous, accusing falsely." BDAG say it "(1) pertains to engagement in slander, slanderous; (2) substantively, one who engages in slander." Normally it refers to Satan (1 Tim. 3:6, 7; 2 Tim. 2:26); occasionally it is used of men and women (1 Tim. 3:11; 2 Tim. 3:3; Tit. 2:3).

> . . . and not a new convert, so that he will not become conceited and fall into the condemnation incurred by the *devil* (1 Tim. 3:6, NASB95).

> And he must have a good reputation with those outside the church, so that he will not fall into reproach and the snare of the ***devil*** (1 Tim. 3:7, NASB95).
>
> . . . and they may come to their senses and escape from the snare of the ***devil***, having been held captive by him to do his will (2 Tim. 2:26, NASB95).
>
> Women must likewise be dignified, not ***malicious gossips***, but temperate, faithful in all things (1 Tim. 3:11, NASB95).
>
> . . . unloving, irreconcilable, ***malicious gossips***, without self-control, brutal, haters of good (2 Tim. 3:3, NASB95).
>
> Older women likewise are to be reverent in their behavior, not ***malicious gossips*** nor enslaved to much wine, teaching what is good (Tit. 2:3, NASB95).

The following passages warn against the sin of gossip and slander:

> He who conceals hatred has lying lips, And he who spreads slander is a fool (Prov. 10:18, NASB).
>
> He who goes about as a slanderer reveals secrets, Therefore do not associate with a gossip (Prov. 20:19, NASB).
>
> And just as they did not see fit to acknowledge God any longer, God gave them over to a depraved mind, to do those things which are not proper, being filled with all unrighteousness, wickedness, greed, evil; full of envy, murder, strife, deceit, malice; they are ***gossips***, slanderers, haters of God, insolent, arrogant, boastful, inventors of evil, disobedient to parents, without understanding, untrustworthy, unloving, unmerciful (Rom. 1:28-31, NASB).
>
> For I am afraid that perhaps when I come I may find you to be not what I wish and may be found by you to be not what you wish; that perhaps there will be strife, jealousy, angry tempers, disputes, slanders, ***gossip***, arrogance, disturbances; I am afraid that when I come again my God may humiliate me before you, and I may mourn over many of those who have sinned in the past and not repented of the impurity, immorality and sensuality which they have practiced (2 Cor. 12:20-21, NASB95).
>
> At the same time they also learn to be idle, as they go around from house to house; and not merely idle, but also ***gossips*** and busybodies, talking about things not proper to mention (1 Tim. 5:13, NASB).
>
> But realize this, that in the last days difficult times will come. For men will be lovers of self, lovers of money, boastful, arrogant, revilers, disobe-

dient to parents, ungrateful, unholy, unloving, irreconcilable, ***malicious gossips***, without self-control, brutal, haters of good, treacherous, reckless, conceited, lovers of pleasure rather than lovers of God, holding to a form of godliness, although they have denied its power; Avoid such men as these (2 Tim. 3:1-5, NASB).

Older women likewise are to be reverent in their behavior, not ***malicious gossips*** nor enslaved to much wine, teaching what is good, so that they may encourage the young women to love their husbands, to love their children, to be sensible, pure, workers at home, kind, being subject to their own husbands, so that the word of God will not be dishonored (Tit. 2:3-5, NASB).

The wife of an elder or deacon should always speak the truth in love (Eph. 4:15). She should assist her husband in building up the body of Christ. Sometimes she is in a position of knowing facts that do not need to be spoken of to others. Furthermore, she should never spread hearsay or falsehoods about others. An elder or deacon's wife must control her tongue or great damage can be done.

Sober (KJV); but temperate (NASB). The Greek word *nephalios*, translated "sober" (KJV) or "temperate" (NASB), occurs 3x in the NT (1 Tim. 3:2, 11; Tit. 2:2). Thomas defines it as "sober." BDAG say it "(1) pertains to being very moderate in the drinking of an alcoholic beverage, temperate, sober. For prohibition of strong drink to priests when engaging in official duties see Leviticus 10:8-11; (2) pertains to being restrained in conduct, self-controlled, level-headed, a figurative extension of 1."

An overseer, then, must be above reproach, the husband of one wife, ***temperate***, prudent, respectable, hospitable, able to teach (1 Tim. 3:2, NASB95).

Women must likewise be dignified, not malicious gossips, but ***temperate***, faithful in all things (1 Tim. 3:11, NASB95).

Older men are to be ***temperate***, dignified, sensible, sound in faith, in love, in perseverance (Tit. 2:2, NASB95).

The Lord then spoke to Aaron, saying, "Do not drink wine or strong drink, neither you nor your sons with you, when you come into the tent of meeting, so that you will not die—it is a perpetual statute throughout your generations—and so as to make a distinction between the holy and the profane, and between the unclean and the clean, and so as to teach the sons of Israel all the statutes which the Lord has spoken to them through Moses" (Lev. 10:8-11, NASB95).

A related word, *nepho*, occurs in the following six passages in the NT and means "to be sober" or "to abstain from wine" [Thomas]:

> . . . so then let us not sleep as others do, but let us be alert and *sober* (1 Thess. 5:6, NASB95).

> But since we are of the day, let us be *sober*, having put on the breastplate of faith and love, and as a helmet, the hope of salvation (1 Thess. 5:8, NASB95).

> But you, be *sober* in all things, endure hardship, do the work of an evangelist, fulfill your ministry (2 Tim. 4:5, NASB95).

> Therefore, prepare your minds for action, *keep sober* in spirit, fix your hope completely on the grace to be brought to you at the revelation of Jesus Christ (1 Pet. 1:13, NASB95).

> The end of all things is near; therefore, be of sound judgment and *sober* spirit for the purpose of prayer (1 Pet. 4:7, NASB95).

> Be of *sober* spirit, be on the alert. Your adversary, the devil, prowls around like a roaring lion, seeking someone to devour (1 Pet. 5:8, NASB95).

An elder's or deacon's wife should show level-headedness that will help her say the proper words necessary for edification (1 Pet. 4:7). Self-control will cause her to maintain restraint through difficult situations, so she is a support, instead of a hindrance, to her husband. She does not partake in alcohol, because it may cause her to lose self-control and act in a way unbecoming of a faithful Christian.

Faithful in all things (KJV & NASB). The Greek word *pistos*, occurring 67x in the NT, refers to one who is "faithful" or "reliable" [Thomas]. BDAG define this adjective as "(1) pertaining to being worthy of belief or trust, trustworthy, faithful, dependable, inspiring trust/faith; (2) pertaining to being trusting, cherishing faith/trust."

Faithfulness is required of disciples in general (Luke 12:42-44; 16:10-13), and teachers in particular (1 Tim. 1:12-13; 2 Tim. 2:1-4). It is reflected in the lives of Christian women, such as Lydia (Acts 16:14-15) and the wives of elders and deacons (1 Tim. 3:11).

> And the Lord said, "Who then is the *faithful* and sensible steward, whom his master will put in charge of his servants, to give them their rations at the proper time? Blessed is that slave whom his master finds so doing when he comes. Truly I say to you that he will put him in charge of all his possessions (Luke 12:42-44, NASB95).

Qualifications of Elders' and Deacons' Wives

> He who is *faithful* in a very little thing is *faithful* also in much; and he who is unrighteous in a very little thing is unrighteous also in much. Therefore if you have not been *faithful* in the use of unrighteous wealth, who will entrust the true riches to you? And if you have not been *faithful* in the use of that which is another's, who will give you that which is your own? No servant can serve two masters; for either he will hate the one and love the other, or else he will be devoted to one and despise the other. You cannot serve God and wealth (Luke 16:10-13, NASB95).
>
> I thank Christ Jesus our Lord, who has strengthened me, because He considered me *faithful*, putting me into service, even though I was formerly a blasphemer and a persecutor and a violent aggressor. Yet I was shown mercy because I acted ignorantly in unbelief (1 Tim. 1:12-13, NASB95).
>
> You therefore, my son, be strong in the grace that is in Christ Jesus. The things which you have heard from me in the presence of many witnesses, entrust these to *faithful* men who will be able to teach others also. Suffer hardship with me, as a good soldier of Christ Jesus. No soldier in active service entangles himself in the affairs of everyday life, so that he may please the one who enlisted him as a soldier (2 Tim. 2:1-4, NASB95).
>
> A woman named Lydia, from the city of Thyatira, a seller of purple fabrics, a worshiper of God, was listening; and the Lord opened her heart to respond to the things spoken by Paul. And when she and her household had been baptized, she urged us, saying, "If you have judged me to be *faithful* to the Lord, come into my house and stay." And she prevailed upon us (Acts 16:14-15, NASB95).
>
> Women must likewise be dignified, not malicious gossips, but temperate, *faithful* in all things (1 Tim. 3:11, NASB95).

The wife of an elder or deacon should be reliable and trustworthy. She can be counted on to uphold the Lord's cause "in all things." Her faithfulness is evident toward God, her husband, her family, and members of the church. Those who know her have confidence in her and recognize her to be dependable. She fulfills her responsibilities and seeks opportunities to serve. She is an asset to her husband and the Lord's work.

Supporting Qualifications of the Wives

The husband of one wife (KJV & NASB). For a man to be qualified to be an elder or deacon, he must be married lawfully in God's eyes. He is married to a woman who has a right to marry him and he, also, has a right to be married to her. He has only one wife and is not a bachelor (1 Tim. 3:2, 12; Tit. 1:6).

Given to hospitality/A lover of hospitality (KJV); hospitable (NASB). Hospitality is evident in the home of an elder and his wife. They are generous with their guests, whether strangers, acquaintances or close friends. They evidence this characteristic without complaint (1 Pet. 4:9; Heb. 13:2). Such couples open their home for food and lodging. This qualification shows an active good will for others. Visitors can learn and be encouraged by the godly couple, and an elder and his wife can enjoy making new friends to remember in years to come.

One that ruleth well his own house (KJV); one who manages his own household well (NASB). An elder or deacon must rule his house well. He is in charge of his home and is responsible for what goes on therein. His wife supports him in his role as head and also helps to guide the family unit (1 Tim. 5:14). His children function under his management and oversight. The home is the proving ground for an elder overseeing the church (1 Tim. 3:5; 1 Thess. 2:7-11).

Having his children in subjection with all gravity (KJV); keeping his children under control with all dignity (NASB). An elder's children should learn that their father is one of their authority figures and they are to be subject to him. The wife also assists the father in teaching this subjection and sets an example to the children by submitting herself. Children are to honor their father and mother, and fathers are to train their children in the instruction of the Lord (Eph. 6:1-4). God does not approve of insolence in children. Rebellious and unruly children evidence a lack of control in the home. Both husband and wife must take their parental responsibilities seriously.

Having faithful children (KJV); having children who believe (NASB). Having been taught subjection by the father, an elder's children evidence their respect for God's will by becoming Christians. The wife of an elder will have a tremendous effect on the faithfulness of her children by living a godly life herself. She will not tear down her husband's influence, but will uphold his hands by helping him train the children in God's way (Prov. 22:6).

Not accused of riot or unruly (KJV); not accused of dissipation or rebellion (NASB). As the elder leads his family, the wife reinforces his rule with diligence. This gives their children the groundwork for making proper choices as they grow and mature (Prov. 29:15). In such a home, children will not be given to rebellion or disobedience.

Good report of them which are without (KJV); good reputation with those outside (NASB). An elder must have a good reputation among those outside the church (Prov. 31:23). His wife has an effect on that reputation and she must be an asset to his good name. She should not bring reproach on his standing in the community.

A lover of good men (KJV); loving what is good (NASB). An elder must love what is good. Choosing his wife because of her goodness evidences this characteristic (Rom. 12:9). She will be a godly servant of the Lord, uplifting him in their married life. Also, her life will be characterized by acts of nobility toward her fellow man.

Conclusion

The wife of an elder or deacon has a great impact on her husband's ability to effectively serve in the Lord's church. Some of the qualifications of an elder or deacon depend upon his wife doing her part. If she possesses the godly qualities described above, she will be a wonderful helper to her husband and a great example to those with whom she comes in contact. If she lacks these qualities, an otherwise good man will be prohibited from serving the local congregation. Therefore, I encourage you to become the woman that God desires you to be, so the church can function according to His plan and pattern.

Bibliography

BDAG = Arndt, W., F. W. Danker, and W. Bauer. *A Greek-English Lexicon of the New Testament and Other Early Christian Literature*. 3rd Edition. Chicago: University of Chicago Press, 2000.

KJV = *The Holy Bible: King James Version.*

NASB = *New American Standard Bible: 1995 update*. LaHabra, CA: The Lockman Foundation, 1995.

NT = The New Testament of Jesus Christ.

Thomas = Thomas, R. L. *New American Standard Hebrew-Aramaic and Greek Dictionaries: Updated edition*. Anaheim: Foundation Publications, Inc., 1981, 1998.

Women's Role in the Church
Kate Mitchell

At the time of this writing, we are living in the middle of the worst crisis in the history of our United States of America. Our freedoms, liberties, and religion are being challenged more and more every day. It is more legal to curse God than to praise Him or to pray to Him in Jesus name. Our president is like the kings of old who "did that which was evil in the sight of the Lord," following after strange gods. As in the Bible, historians have, through the years, recorded how all of our past leaders and presidents have conducted themselves and what their accomplishments have been. Statistics and events relating to our economy, population, weather, temperatures, and

---

Kathleen (Kate or Kathy) Mitchell was born in Fort Collins, CO on April 7, 1952. She grew up on the family farm outside of a little town called Wellington. She attended schools there and graduated from Poudre High School in 1970. After attending college in Wichita, KS for one year, she came home and met her husband, Thomas Mitchell. Kate became a Christian, being converted from denominationalism to the Lord's body, the church of Christ. She and Tom have been married for thirty-seven years and have lived in Wellington, CO; Laramie, WY; Pocatello ID; and Blackfoot, ID where they presently have lived on a small farm for thirty years. They have three children: Chad (1979), Angela (1981), and Casey (1983). Casey was nineteen years old when he passed away due to a farm accident in 2002. They have three beautiful grandchildren, thanks to Chad and his wife, Kassandra: Paxton (4), Tessa (2), and Jacey (born Nov. 30, 2009). Angela is married to Timothy Woodside and they are now residing in Reno, NV. Kate graduated from Idaho State University in 1997 with an Elementary Education K-8 Bachelors of Science teaching degree. Due to the demand of a rising custom fabrication welding shop, Industrial Metal Enterprises LLC, which they started in 1993, Kate was only able to substitute teach for a while. Kate and Tom both keep busy with the shop and their farm where they raise cattle and horses. They presently work and worship with the church in Blackfoot, ID and have been able to attend all of the Truth Lectures. Each year has been a source of great edification to both of them. Kate is humbled to be able to personally participate this year.

diseases have been written down by men for us to see and compare, up to this very day.

We are fortunate to live in a time where we can read about our past history and see the good choices and the mistakes of those who have lived before us. Through the course of time, we have had God's book, in the form of scrolls and, later the Bible, written and unchanged for us by the one true God of heaven. In it God preserved for us accounts of human activity showing the choices people made for good or evil. Recorded for us are the events, sins, and victories of God's people. Of all generations of people with God's written word readily available to us in the form of the whole Bible, along with the technology of computer Bible programs and the internet available to us with the touch of just a few keys on a keyboard, we should have enough knowledge and wisdom to *not* violate the laws of God. We have no excuses.

To the world, the Bible has lost potency and strength. Those who have lost the recognition of this power and strength, tell us that the Bible is just a good storybook and that we must "go beyond" what we have previously been taught. We cannot let the influences of these people of the world, Satan's domain, overpower us.

If God chose to write about us and our generation, as He did those of ancient times, what would He write? What does God see when He looks on His creation today? What are His people in churches of Christ doing now that is worthy to be preserved in history? Does He see a people who are heavily influenced by the world in the way they dress, how they talk and act, and by the activities they themselves engage in? Do they hide their religion? Is their treatment of others done with recognition that all who are of the world are in a lost condition? Are His people genuine watchmen providing warning against the evil enemies in Satan's army? Does He see those who are submissive to His authority? In our age, I'm convinced that He sees a rebellious and perverse generation.

Moses wrote about the corruption of the Israelites who were God's chosen people. "They have corrupted themselves, their spot is not the spot of his children: they are a perverse and crooked generation" (Deut. 32:5). David speaks to us about God's people turning from His ways as being a rebellious generation. "And might not be as their fathers, a stubborn and rebellious generation; a generation that set not their heart aright, and whose spirit was not stedfast with God" (Psa. 78:8). We must take warning from this and be on guard for rebellion and corruption of ourselves today.

The role of women in the church today is becoming a "controversial" subject, which is leading to a crisis in leadership against God's planned purpose for the woman. We must go back to the old paths, which have woven their way through out the history of God's people and diligently study to gain knowledge, wisdom, and understanding of His laws governing the roles of men and women both then and now.

What Is Meant by a "Crisis"?

Do you know what the word "crisis" means? *Webster's Dictionary* defines it as "a turning point, as in a sequence of events, for better or for worse; a condition of instability that leads to a change."

Now, looking back in time, we will investigate the definition of *crisis* as a *"turning point"* and as a *"sequence of events."* This is when we can look back and see what we can learn from "hindsight." Some of us may well remember when the ERA (equal rights amendment) movement and "woman's lib" was starting to get popular. These woman's liberation movements started the ball rolling towards greater social, economic, and political rights for women. They have undermined the home and distorted the male/female, husband/wife roles. Think about the two words "woman's liberation." The root word "liberate" is defined as: *"to set free, to be free from control of social and economic constraints or discriminations; arising from traditional role expectations."* This puts the man and woman in direct competition. Women wanted to be their own boss and independent. They did not want to be in subjection to man. When women choose to follow in this direction, this puts them in disobedience to the scripture stating: "but they (women) are commanded to be under obedience (or submission) as saith the law" (1 Cor. 14:34). Since the 1960s women have fought for equal pay and job opportunities. This has resulted in the reality of women in non-traditional positions as welders, astronauts, pilots, heavy equipment operators, soldiers, and such like. Today women are thrust to the front as leaders in the business world and politics. Forgotten and ignored is the commandment given in 1 Timothy 2:12 that women are not to usurp the authority God has given to men. Can you see the "sequence of events" taking shape? Women have gotten use to being in the lead and want things to stay that way in all aspects of their lives. Men have gotten use to the woman being in charge and that has brought about instability in their role as men and has *"led to a change"* as is the second definition of a "crisis."

As a result, we can see these ideas and beliefs creeping into the Lord's churches across the land.

This makes it crystal clear why there is a *"crisis in the role of women in the church."* Women want to have a say in what goes on in their local congregation and want to be involved in decisions made by attending the men's business meetings. They want to lead prayers, wait on the table, lead the singing, and be a deaconess or preacher. Men, who have turned into marshmallows with no backbone, and who do not want to correct or "stir the waters" and enrage the women who can make it very uncomfortable at home, are allowing this sad state of affairs. So, consequently, *the role of women in the home affects the role of women in the church* and has an impressionable imprint on the body of Christ (the church). It is hard to separate the role of the woman at home, with husband and family, from the role of women in the church. The attitude of the woman towards God, husband, elders, and most importantly, the authority of the Bible affect both places. In his book *Women Professing Godliness,* Donnie V. Rader states, "Most, if not all, of the problems to arise among brethren are due to lack of respect for the authority of God's word." Yes, this is a dangerous crisis we find ourselves sitting in the middle of. This issue of the woman's place and role in the church is a symptom of a turning point leading to change and we find ourselves not addressing the heart of the problem by treating it lightly and ignoring the consequences it will bring upon us. Once the gate is opened, there is no stopping what comes out of it, nor what is to follow.

The Pattern of Order

God is the creator of the world and all things in it. "In the beginning God created the heaven and the earth" (Gen 1:1). Never have so few words said so much! This brief summary of the story of creation of the whole universe in its magnitude and incredible wisdom and power was put together according to a *pattern of order* and beauty to provide a home for man. God created man first, then woman was created from man. "So God created man in his own image, in the image of God created he him; male and female created he them" (Gen. 1:26). Woman was created to be a complement to man. Genesis 2:18 calls her a "helpmate." It takes a woman to fill this role, as there are no substitutes! Man and woman were created equal in the sight of God. One has no superiority over the other as to their worth to Him or to one another. But, God did create them with differences in anatomy, biochemical and emotional makeup. God created them this way. Both the man and woman have a different capacity in service to Him. These differences allow each one to "serve with excellence in the different roles designed for his or her fulfillment" (*Answers For Our Hope,* by M.E. Patton). In 1 Corinthians 11:3 these roles are explained. "But I would have you know that the head of every man is Christ; and the head of every woman is the man; and the head of Christ is God." So, as the ranking of the divine order goes, God the Father is the head over Christ, Christ is the head over man, and man is the head, or leader, over the woman.

As women, we must recognize the rule and authority that God has given to the elders in the church. "Take heed therefore unto yourselves, and to all the flock, over the which the Holy Ghost hath made you overseers, to feed the church of God, which he hath purchased with his own blood" (Acts 20:28). As the elders are instructed to feed the flock (spiritual food from God's word), women must be willing to eat thereof. As elders are to lead, we must follow. As elders are to set the example, we women must imitate it in an appropriate way. As elders are to teach, women must learn from them. Women must recognize their relationship to the elders, as part of the flock they are leading. A congregation must have both leaders and followers as each has its own place. It is hard to lead those who don't want to be led. The woman's role would be to teach other women to recognize and submit to this relationship. Hebrews 13:17 says, "Obey them that have the rule over you, and submit yourselves: for they watch for your souls, as they that must give account, that they may do it with joy, and not with grief: for that is unprofitable for you." First, and foremost, in all of this is that God would be pleased. We recognize that even elders are human and can err. We also need to be aware that there must be a "thus saith the Lord," and "book, chapter, and verse" to back all decisions made by the eldership.

The First and Worst Crisis

The first crisis between a man and a woman came in the book of Genesis. Adam and Eve established the first home within the paradise of the "Garden of Eden." God had provided everything that they would possibly need or want. Everything that was pleasant to the sight and good to eat was growing where the first woman began her role as wife and homemaker. Man and woman were created as free will moral agents, with the intelligence to exercise freedom and power of choice. Then came Satan, disguised as a serpent, giving Adam and Eve the opportunity to exercise their free moral agency. Being deceived by his lies, the woman yielded to the tempter and ate of the forbidden fruit. "And when the woman saw that the tree was good for food (the lust of the flesh), and that it was pleasant to the eyes (the lust

Women's Role in the Church

of the eyes), and a tree to be desired to make one wise (the pride of life), she took of the fruit thereof, and did eat, and gave also unto her husband with her, and he did eat" (Gen. 3:6; 1 John 2:16). This was the beginning of sin in the world. In eating from the forbidden tree, they transgressed God's law and brought upon themselves and all the generations to follow the penalty of death. "Wherefore as by one man sin entered into the world, and death by sin; and so death passed upon all men; for that all have sinned" (Rom. 5:12). The woman was the first to transgress, then the man. God's curse to the woman was that of submission and pain in childbirth. "Unto the woman he said, I will greatly multiply thy pain and thy conception; in pain thou shalt bring forth children; and thy desire shall be to thy husband and he shall rule over thee" (Gen. 3:16). And unto Adam he said, "Because thou hast hearkened unto the voice of thy wife, and hast eaten of the tree, of which I commanded thee, saying, thou shall not eat of it; cursed is the ground for thy sake; in sorrow shall you eat of it all the days of your life" (Gen. 3:17). After hearing the consequences of their sin, God drove them out of the beautiful garden to fend for themselves among the thorns and thistles, which would come forth among the herb of the field (Gen. 3:18). Yet, amongst the dark clouds of doing wrong, there was a ray of hope for mankind in the words that God told the serpent, "I will put enmity between thee and the woman, and between thy seed and her seed: he shall bruise thy head, and thou shalt bruise his heel" (Gen. 3:15). God was making reference to the time when Jesus would destroy the power of Satan over mankind, when He gave Himself as a ransom for our sins on the cross of calvary and was raised from death and the grave.

The Influence of Evil Women of the Bible

Now that sin had entered the world, let us consider a few biblical examples written regarding some of the crises that evil women caused and the lives they touched. *Delilah* has left her legacy as a temptress who accepted monetary bribery, though she claimed "true love" for Samson. Judges 16:16 tells us that she "pressed him daily with her words and urged him, so that his soul was vexed unto death: that he told her all his heart." In today's terminology, we would call her a "nag." This resulted in the loss of his profound strength and the departure of the Lord from Samson, allowing the Philistines to take him as a prisoner. Later on in his life, with his last burst of strength given him from God, Samson took thousands of Philistines with him to their death, when he destroyed the house of Dagon, their god, as a result of Delilah's betrayal of Samson to his enemies.

Next we see the heartless, wicked *Queen Jezebel*, whose influence on her husband made him even more wicked, if that is possible. She influenced her husband *toward the worship of idols* and *away from God*. She knew Ahab would please her and acquiesce to her demands, as he would not stand up against her wishes. She was the cause of the death of many of God's prophets and sought diligently to kill Elijah. Through her influence and leadership as a queen, she took matters into her own hands and devised the murder of Naboth, using false accusations and lies. This enabled King Ahab to get his way and have the vineyard that rightfully belonged to Naboth's family. "But there was none like Ahab, which did sell himself to work wickedness in the sight of the Lord, whom Jezebel his wife stirred up" (1 Kings 21:7). Jezebel was in the position to exercise a strong influence for good or evil. She chose to exercise evil upon and through her husband. She now has her reward in the lake of fire.

In the book of Esther we read about the devastating influence of *Zeresh* on her husband, Haman. With the encouragement of his wife and friends, Haman built the gallows to hang the despised Mordacai. "Then said Zeresh his wife and all his friends unto him, Let a gallows be made, that Mordecai may be hanged thereon. And the thing pleased Haman and he caused the gallows to be made" (Esth. 5:14). The king discovered how Mordacai had saved his life. When Queen Esther, who was a Jew, exposed Haman's plan to murder all of the Jews, the King ordered Haman to be hanged on his own gallows, along with his ten sons. "So, they hanged Haman on the gallows that he had prepared for Mordecai" (Esth. 7:10). The evil influence of his wife contributed to his death and the death of her ten sons, which in turn, made her a widow and childless.

Job was reduced to a state of utter despair and pain after Satan brought upon him boils from the "sole of his feet to the crown of his head." His wife came to him and said, "Dost thou still hold fast thine integrity?" ("Integrity" means "uncompromising, moral and ethical principle" *[Webster's Dictionary]*.) "Renounce God and die" (Job 2:9, 10). Rebuking her, Job replied, "Thou speak as one of the foolish women speaks." Now keep in mind that Job's wife had also endured the loss of their children, and was down and out physically, financially, emotionally, and, undoubtedly, was very discouraged. But to outwardly encourage her husband to curse God and blame Him for all the evil that had come upon them was sinfully bad advice. Job goes on to say, "What? Shall we receive good at the hand of God, and shall not receive evil? In all this did not Job sin with his lips." Job did not heed to his wife's disrespect to God. *Job's wife* showed a real lack of faith in God and she wanted to blame him for all their misfortune and pain. Despite this, God blessed them with ten more children and twice as many possessions in the end, but credit is due to Job, not his wife (Job 42:10).

The Devil Seeks to Draw Us Away

All of the above women took it upon themselves to advise the men in their lives what should be done, producing a crisis in leadership. This is not the role God intended for women. The devil is seeking to lead us astray and he is not a respecter of persons. "Be sober, be vigilant; because your adversary the devil, as a roaring lion, walketh about, seeking whom he may devour. Whom resist steadfast in the faith, knowing that the same afflictions are accomplished in your brethren that are in the world" (1 Pet. 5:8, 9). Satan is constantly working to draw us away from God's plan in any way he can. The influence of the world can have an alluring effect on us, persuading us to depart from God's intended role for women in the church. We must not be ignorant of Satan's tactics: "Lest Satan should get an advantage of us: for we are not ignorant of his devices" (2 Cor.2: 11).

Women Influencing for Good

In contrast, there are many women mentioned in the Bible who had a good influence over those with whom they came in contact. It would be difficult to mention all of them in this lecture, but let us notice a few. It is interesting that one insignificant woman, whose name was not even mentioned, played an enormous role towards the preserving of mankind. *Noah's wife* had to be a big influence on the whole family because Genesis 7:7 states, "Noah went in and his sons and his wife, and his sons' wives with him, into the ark, because of the waters of the flood." Only eight were saved and "became the heir of the righteousness which is by faith" (Heb. 11:7). It would have taken the backing of a strong woman to help Noah through all the criticism he must have faced as a "preacher of righteousness" (2 Pet. 2:5), warning the people of God's wrath which would come upon them. I can just imagine what was said about building an ark where there was no, or little, water! It is evident that she had her part in raising their children to love God. A loving and diligent attitude was needed to teach their sons during the evil times in which they lived as they grew to the age of marriage. All three boys married well, having wives who were obedient unto God. All eight of them had to believe in the one true God or they, too, would have perished in the waters of the flood.

A Prophetess and a Judge of Israel

Deborah poses a different approach to the role of a woman, as she was much more a leader than most women of this time. She was a *prophetess* and a *judge of Israel*. She was a famous, patriotic woman who was married to Lapidoth of whom the Bible says nothing more. She apparently was more gifted than her husband, but this unusual woman kept her place as a wife. Nowhere do we read of her displaying an air of superiority or having the attitude of being dominant. "Now, as a judge, she sat quietly under a palm tree giving counsel to those who came to her" (Judg. 4:4, 5). As a prophetess, she accompanied Barak, the leader of Israel's army, to give him moral support. She tried to talk Barak out of taking her into battle, but he said he would not go if she did not go with him. After the battle was over, they sang a song of thanksgiving to God for delivering of Israel from their enemy (Judg. 5:1-3). She was looked upon as a woman of God who was obedient in all her ways. Her only word of self-praise was that she arose as a "Mother in Israel" (v. 7).

Ruth, called *"woman of strength,"* was a good example of a constant, submissive, loving woman who made a wise choice. Her attitude and heart were right, as she had to deal with widowhood. She must have adored her mother-in-law in order to leave her own people and country. Naomi and her family had taught Ruth the truth of God's laws. Ruth wanted to follow Naomi and her God wherever she went. Ruth said to Naomi, ". . . for whither thou goest, I will go; and where thou lodgest, I will lodge, thy people shall be my people, and thy God my God" (Ruth 1:16). Because of her diligence and unselfish love and concern, Ruth found favor with Boaz, the wealthy landowner where she was gleaning in the barley fields (Ruth 2:11, 12). Boaz said unto her, "It hath fully been showed me, all that thou hast done unto thy mother in law since the death of thine husband: and how thou hast left thy father and thy mother, and the land of thy nativity, and art come unto a people which thou newest not heretofore. The Lord recompense thy work, and a full reward be given thee of the Lord God of Israel, under whose wings thou art come to trust." What a beautiful phrase, "under whose wings thou art come to trust." After her marriage to Boaz, she had a son, Obed, who was the grandfather of David. This put her in the linage of Christ. Though she was a stranger in the land, without a husband, and looked upon as a poor woman, she found grace in the eyes of God through her obedience. We can learn much from this woman, Ruth.

Seek the Old Paths

There is a great need in the Lord's church today to go back to the word of God and the Old Paths. "Thus saith the Lord, Stand ye in the ways, and see, and *ask for the old paths, where is the good way, and walk therein*, and ye shall find rest for your souls." "But they said, 'We will not walk therein'" (Jer. 6:16). Do we see a crisis in leadership here? Why can we not learn from these "old paths" recorded for our learning that rebellion towards God will only make things harder for us? "Wherefore, beloved, seeing that ye look for such things, be diligent that ye may be found of him in peace, without spot, and blameless" (2 Pet. 3:14). We need to study diligently the roles God has given to women. And, Ladies, may God help us to be content to obey and abide by the limitations God has placed upon us. He has given us enough responsibility and commands to keep us plenty busy, if we heed His word. There are many facets of the role women can work in the church today. Let us begin to seek out exactly what women are required to do.

We have examples of women in the Bible who served to the best of their capacities all the days of their lives. Anna, the prophetess, was of a great age and had been a widow for eighty-four years. She "departed not from the temple, but served God with fastings and prayers night and day" (Luke 2:36-38). I have heard people say, "I've been a Christian for fifty years. I've done my share of teaching, and the like, now I'm going to let the young folks take over." I fear that this is the prime way apostasy creeps into a congregation, when the older members "bow out of the way," bringing about a *"turning point"* and in comes "new ideas"—a *"sequence of events"* introduced into the way things are done, *"leading to a change."* We are back to the definition of a *crisis!* This also shows the lack of respect for the Word of God. Do we have a biblical example of quitting or retiring and standing back watching others work? The only "retirement plan" I find in the Bible is that of the promise of a home in heaven, if we have diligently followed His ways unto the end of our days. "Be thou faithful unto death, and I will give thee a crown of life" (Rev. 2:10b). We do not want to be found guilty like those in Jeremiah's day, when he reminded them of the old paths, "We will not walk therein." They were not faithful unto death. This surely leads to the destruction of souls. We must not quit, no matter what our age is, as long as we have the strength and ability to still serve our Lord.

The Architect Must Be Consulted

It is a woman's role, as the "Queen of the house," to build these strong homes with the "blueprint" God has written down for us. Hebrews 3:4

says, "For every house is builded by some man; but he that built all things is God." The wise King Solomon told us the materials we need to build a strong house in the Lord. "Through *wisdom* is an house builded; and by *understanding* it is established: And by *knowledge* shall the chambers be filled with all precious and pleasant riches" (Prov. 24:3-4). The architect (God) drew up the plans (Bible) that must be consulted throughout the entire building of the home. In his book, *Building Strong Homes,* Robert Harkrider defines "wisdom" as "seeing earthly matters from heaven's point of view." We view what is *really* there as God sees it. "Understanding" is "responding with depth of insight." Something we previously took personally, which may have offended us, we learn to overlook and take it in stride showing selflessness. "Knowledge" is to " learn with perception." This means being more aware of what we see and how we respond to it, in every-day life experiences, than to what we can learn from facts in "book learning," man's own wisdom.

Marriage Is from God

The foundation to a strong home in the Lord is to be married. "Marriage is honourable in all, and the bed undefiled: but whoremongers and adulterers God will judge" (Heb 13:4). Marriage was designed in heaven and was carried out on earth. Mark 10:7 reads, "For this cause shall a man leave his father and mother, and cleave to his wife." In today's culture, the popular thing to do is to live together for a while to see if the man and the woman are compatible. Note that the passage in Hebrews says that God is the founder of marriage and those who do not comply will be adulterers in his eyes. And God is the Judge, not the man at the courthouse who follows man-made laws.

A happy marriage doesn't just happen. It is gained through patient striving between two human beings with all their faults and weaknesses and strengths. It is an 80-20% give and take for each partner. There needs to be *commitment* to each other, between both the man and the woman. I have heard it said that, if this marriage doesn't work out, "I'll just get another wife/husband." God says that He hates "putting away" or divorce (Mal. 2:16). "Wherefore they are no more twain, but one flesh. What therefore God hath joined together, let not man put asunder (divorce)" (Matt. 19:6). I firmly believe that the key to any and all relationships in our lives is *communication* and a *love for God* and *love for each other.* I also believe that there is no problem that cannot be worked out in a marriage, as long as both partners are honest with themselves, each other, and God. Do not be afraid to talk *to* each other, not *at* each other. When you fell in love and married, you gave your life to each other. Your life together should not end just because of some frivolous unimportant thing that has not been thoroughly talked about. A lot of times, disputes arise because of misunderstandings, which may not surface unless it is talked about. Marriages have to be lived out on earth among all the trials and temptations common to man. So, try with all your might to make your marriage pleasant and happy. This is pleasing to God.

Follow Your Husband in All Subjection

Wives are to be in subjection to their husbands and are to let them "wear the pants in the family" and be the "head of the house." The wife is to be involved with events and definitely has a right to her input concerning decisions, but ultimately, the husband has the final say. "For after this manner in the old time the holy women also who trusted in God, adorned themselves, being in subjection unto their own husbands" (1 Pet. 3:5, 6). "*Sarah* obeyed Abraham, calling him lord" (v. 6). We are told she was a beautiful woman, was full of faith, and showed godly subjection. The title of "lord" indicates authority or rulership, showing that Sara recognized Abraham's God-given rank above her. Sarah also revealed her attitude of respect and reverence. Through her son, Isaac, would come the fulfillment of God's promise to Abraham to be the "Father of all nations" (Gen.17: 4). "As for me, behold, my covenant is with thee, and thou shalt be a father of many nations." Sarah helped her husband gain the promise from God.

A Disobedient Submission for Evil and Good

Submission can also have its down side. The only reason authorized not to show submission to man is if it goes against God and His laws. As we see in the story of Ananias and *Sapphira*, her submission was in *disobedience to God's laws* as an accomplice to a lie. This account is told us in Acts 5:9, "Then Peter said unto her, how is it that ye have agreed together to tempt the Spirit of the Lord? Behold, the feet of them which have buried thy husband are at the door, and shall carry thee out." The price she paid for agreeing to her husband's wish to lie to the Lord and to Peter was her very own life and soul. Though she was in submission to her husband, she made the choice to follow what was wrong.

Queen Vashti is an example of *a courageous wife with morals*, taking a stand against her husband, in a matter in which he was in the wrong. She refused to follow the command of King Ahasuerus, her husband, to expose herself before him and the drunken lords, who wanted to gaze upon her beauty with lustful eyes. This was a direct disobedience to the king's command, showing negative submission and a bad example for the wives of all of the men in the land. This conduct would not be tolerated. As a result, she was deposed as the queen. She lost her position in life, but did not participate in sin.

Older Women Are to Teach the Younger Women

"God has chosen *teaching* of the truth and its application in life as the means of building strong character and finding true happiness" (*Train the Young Women*, by Ruth Thompson). "Character" is defined as *"the sum total of the qualities that distinguish one person from another."* One is not born with character, but it is something that is developed and acquired over time as one matures. "All of life's events and trials and triumphs along the way, help to build our character. It has been said that religion is the strongest influence in the development of a good character. A diligent study of God's word along with much prayer will help provide that influence" (*The Woman of God*, by Hallie Adams Kellogg).

Titus 2:3-5

One of the most complete scriptures that form the foundation defining the role of both the older women and the younger women is in Titus 2: 3-5. These verses contain every phase of the work, responsibilities, and duties of women. "The aged women likewise, that they be in behavior as becometh holiness, not false accusers, not given to much wine, teachers of good things; *That they may teach the young women to be sober, to love their husbands, to love their children, to be discreet, chaste, keepers at home, good, obedient to their own husbands, that the word of God be not blasphemed."* In 1 Timothy 5:14, the directive to younger women is given: "I will therefore that the younger women marry, bear children, guide the house, give none occasion to the adversary to speak reproachfully." Within these words one can learn how to achieve *goodness* and *happiness,* and know that they are compatible. In these two scriptures, we can see that there is an equal command for the older women to teach the young women, and that the younger women are to listen to what the older women can teach them. Today, we find ourselves amidst the "Me Generation" who think they know everything there is to know. I'm not sure why they would be able to know everything of importance at such a young age, but I guess, maybe, because of all the modern technology we have at our fingertips. Even at my age, I still do not know all I need to know. Most tend not to want advice and take offence if even a suggestion in this direction is given. The respect for our elders and the authoritative figures, especially God, is sadly lacking in many of our young people. So, today more than ever, we need strong homes with a love and respect for God and for each other, regardless of age.

1. Love Their Husbands. Because of the restraint of time, I would like to focus on what the older women are to teach the younger. These truths are the backbone of the role of women in the church. If they are followed as closely as possible, there will be harmony in the home and unity in the church. The aged women are to *train* the young women to *"love their husbands."* You might say that you love your husband, but there are many different ways you can show your love. As wives being of all different ages, we need to be aware of how we *really* treat our husbands. Men have certain God-given qualities and, unless we know what these qualities are and learn how to deal with them, we will not know how to understand or appreciate the man we have chosen to be our life-long companion. Needing to be truly loved is one of these qualities. The love a woman shows her husband at home also shows forth in her conduct at church. Love is not just doing laundry, fixing food, and cleaning the house for him. There is a deep, sincere love that affects the emotions and there is a surface love (which is lacking in sincere love and warmth). We need to make sure what we do for him is done in sincerity and with love from the heart.

The first commandment God gave to woman after her fall was, "Thy desire shall be to thy husband and he shall rule over thee" (Gen. 3:16). The attitude a wife has towards being submissive is prompted by the knowledge of the God-given role of the headship given to husbands and by a love for the God who gave the commandment. Obedience prompted by a feeling of "duty" is one thing; but obedience prompted by "love from the heart" is another. God prefers the latter, which brings its rewards with it.

> Ill thrives the hapless family that shows
> A cock that is silent and a hen that crows,
> I know not which live the most unnatural lives
> Obeying husbands or commanding wives (Francis Quarles).

As wives, and women without regard to our marital status, we need to strive to be as the woman described in Proverbs 31. In verse 10 we read, "Who can find a virtuous woman? Her price is far above rubies." "The heart of her husband doth safely trust in her, so that he shall have no need of spoil. She will do him good and not evil all the days of her life." Verse 30 says, "Favor is deceitful, and beauty is vain: but a woman that feareth the Lord, she shall be praised." Our goal in life should be to conduct ourselves in such a way that we can be as valuable as a ruby to our husbands. We want to be an asset to him, as this woman was, not a hindrance or an embarrassment. To be commended by her husband for her virtues shows his appreciation and love, and her devotion, love, and obedience. "Her children arise up, and call her blessed; her husband also, and he praiseth her" (v. 28). We all need to pattern ourselves after this woman in Proverbs who was honest, obedient, thoughtful, kind, wise, industrious, a willing worker, not a busy body, but tending to the things of her own household. She helped the poor and needy and did not eat the "bread of idleness." What an example she is!

The change in marriages today is a result of "role changing." As a fellow worker, the wife has much more limited time to spend with her husband and children. The demanding chores of the home still have to be done, but in a much more limited time frame. Frustration can take its demeaning toll on the welfare of the marriage and the home. Money matters are the cause of most of the divorces today. In some cases, the husband is the "keeper at home" while the wife goes off to work. This "turning point" and "change of events" leads us down the road to a "crisis" in the role of women at home, thus affecting the role of the woman in the church. What are our children being taught in these situations? This is not God's pattern or intent for the way the home should be.

Attitude and actions go hand in hand. Not a word has to be spoken to show how a wife feels towards her husband and what he feels for her. Our actions speak volumes to those around us without saying a word. Women's attitudes at the church building help set the atmosphere for the worship. In my opinion, women can make or break a church. Why the women? Because their attitude reflects in their husband and children, which in turn reflects to the other members. If these attitudes are negative and not checked, they cause problems that turn into cankers which can split the local church. So, a positive attitude towards our husbands and families creates a better environment in which to serve and worship our Lord. As women, we need to be watchful and careful to be pleasing to God with our attitudes. This is what we need to strive for as Christ prayed for the church to have unity in John 17:21: "That they all may be one; as thou, Father, art in me, and I in thee, that they also may be one in us; that the world may believe that thou hast sent me."

2. Love Their Children. Another commandment given for the older women to teach the younger women is to *"love their children."* Oh, the blessings of motherhood. "Lo, children are an heritage of the Lord: and the fruit of the womb is his reward" (Psa. 127:3). John states, "A woman when she is in travail hath sorrow, because her hour is come: but as soon as she is delivered of the child, she remembereth no more the anguish, for joy that a man is born into the world" (John 16:1). Eve did bring pain into our lives in childbirth, but blessings are also a part of this, as our children enrich our lives. "Children are an heritage of the Lord: and the fruit of the womb is his reward. As arrows are in the hand of a mighty man; so are children of the youth. Happy is the man that hath his quiver full of them" (Psa. 127:3-5). These blessings, though they bring about grave responsibilities, give a woman the opportunity to fulfill her God-given role in life. There is nothing to replace a mother's love. It makes a child want to be obedient and pleasing, which in turn pleases our Lord and Savior. The world needs men and women of character who have a real belief in the word of God, and who will not lie or deceive. Training in the home by godly parents also benefits the house of God. These children are tomorrow's church. The role of motherhood can bring to the church men who are qualified to be elders and deacons and women who will qualify as their wives. This needs to be instilled into our children at an early age: to conduct themselves in a way so that they would qualify as adults to shepherd the church and to be a virtuous woman and wife who is pleasing to God.

Examples of Good Mothers

When we think of some of the women of the Bible, we are aware that throughout the history of mankind, there are good examples as well as bad. We can profit from both of them. The first good, notable woman we will examine is Mary, the mother of Jesus. What an announcement from the Angel Gabriel: "And the angel came in unto her, and said, Hail, thou that art highly favoured, the Lord is with thee: blessed art thou among women" (Luke 1:28). "And, behold, thou shalt conceive in thy womb, and bring forth a son, and shalt call his name JESUS" (Luke 1:31). She had been chosen out of all the women in the world to bring into the world the Son of God, who, by His birth, life, death, and resurrection, would be the savior of all mankind.

Another worthy woman who comes to mind is that of Hannah. She was childless, but fervently prayed to God that she might have a child. She wanted a man-child so much that she vowed to give him back to God. Hannah's desire was granted to her by God and she brought forth a son whom she named Samuel. She loved him so much, but kept her promise to God, taking him at an early age to live in the temple with Eli, the priest. Each year, she lovingly made him a new coat and took it to him, when they came to offer sacrifices. He became the high priest of Israel and is known as one of the greatest leaders Israel ever knew.

One great example in the New Testament of dedication to their child is that of Eunice and Lois, the mother and grandmother of Timothy. As a young preacher of the gospel, Paul writes to him saying: "When I call to remembrance the unfeigned faith that is in thee, which dwelt first in thy grandmother Lois, and thy mother Eunice; and I am persuaded that in thee also" (2 Tim. 1:5). What a joy it must have been to these women to see Timothy in this point of his life, receiving such a commendation regarding his faith and knowledge of the gospel from the great apostle Paul. As a mixed religion family, his father was a Greek, we see no crisis here, because his grandmother and mother had taught Timothy the gospel. We can also see that these two women were a good example to him, as he followed in their footsteps. We must be good examples to our children and grandchildren.

Mothers need to raise their children to be pleasing unto the Lord. The future of the Lord's church depends on the training of our young. What they have been taught will either sink or float the church through another generation. The Israelites were instructed to teach their children the law. "And these words, which I command thee this day, shall be in thine heart: And thou shalt teach them diligently unto thy children, and shalt talk of them when thou sittest in thine house, and when thou walkest by the way, and when thou liest down, and when thou risest up" (Deut. 6:6, 7). This tells us that we must spend time trying to cram their sweet little heads with the words of wisdom given us by the Almighty God. In Proverbs 22:6, the wise Solomon tells us to: "Train up a child in the way he should go: and when he is old, he will not depart from it." Mothers and fathers have the responsibilities of training their children spiritually, mentally, morally, and physically. As parents, we have the biggest impact on them through our examples as he/she watches us perform our duties relating to the home, to God, and to each other.

Discipline Is Love

Discipline and correction fall heavily upon the mother as she spends more time with the children than the father. In this era, spanking is looked down upon, and, in some states now, it is even unlawful to discipline your children in this way. This may be the way of the world, but it is against God's commands. *Obedience* has to be learned; it is not a natural trait.

Don't teach your children that your "no" really means, "yes." As parents, we must be aware that *when we say "No," that we mean "No."* If they whine and whine and we finally give in to their demands, we have just taught them that *"No" really means, "Yes."* Once this is learned, they continue the pattern from then on, and it becomes harder and harder to "undo" what has already been allowed to be learned. In Matthew 5:37, we read: "But let your communication be, Yea, yea; Nay, nay: for whatsoever is more than these cometh of evil." What the Lord has told us, He means and no amount of whining will change it. In like manner, should we teach our children. *Consistency* is also an important rule for mothers and fathers. Every time you say a command, stick to it and follow through with it no matter what. If you give in and don't stick with what you already said, the child will realize that you will let him get his way, if he tries real hard. This will become the pattern for future demands. Parents, be aware that there must be a positive in order to correct a negative. Children cannot exist with only negative responses. Encouragement and praise go hand in hand with correction. Make their faces come alive with as much praise for the good things they do as you can. This will help the negative tendencies to fade and make the positive actions worthwhile.

Teaching our children that God "knows all we do and think" is of utmost importance. *We cannot hide from God!* We need to conduct ourselves as if Jesus were sitting on our shoulder. When children do something wrong, the question needs to be asked, "Would God be pleased with the way you are acting?" Psalm 139:4 tells us, "For there is not a word in my tongue, but lo, O Lord, thou knowest it altogether." Verse 8 goes on to say that "God is in heaven and hell, behold thou art there." Verses 9-10: "God is in the sea and he is in the darkness, but there he is the light." We cannot escape from God!

We actually have much instruction for disciplining from the wisest king who ever lived in his book of the Proverbs. "In the lips of him that hath understanding wisdom is found: but a rod is for the back of him that is void of understanding" (Prov. 10:13). This tells us that a spanking is approved of God. "He that spareth his rod hateth his son: but he that loveth him chasteneth him betimes" (Prov. 13:24). Here God is letting us know that we actually hate our children, if we fail to correct them. As our ultimate example, we see where God corrects us because He loves us. Proverbs 3:12 says, " For whom the Lord loveth he correcteth; even as a father the son in whom he delighteth." All parents would like to have delightful children at all times, who everyone loves and adores. This is possible through godly enforcement of His commands. "Foolishness is bound in the heart of a child; but the rod of correction shall drive it far from him" (Prov. 22:15). "The rod and reproof give wisdom: but a child left to himself bringeth his mother to shame" (Prov. 29:15). So, we can see by these passages how important correction is in the lives of both our children and ourselves. If a child is left to his own devices, no one can stand him and he will bring shame, as he grows older, to his parents. Think of all the juvenile delinquents in our society today. This depicts a crisis in the way children are being raised along with the downfall of the home and family. None of us likes to be corrected, that's human; but through correction we become better people. "Correction is grievous unto him that forsaketh the way: and he that hateth reproof shall die" (Prov. 15:10).

There are so many good things we can teach our children in order to be pleasing in His sight. Children need to learn to fill their minds with good things. "Finally, brethren, whatsoever things are true, whatsoever things are honest, whatsoever things are just, whatsoever things are pure, whatsoever things are lovely, whatsoever things are of good report; if there be any virtue, and if there be any praise, think on these things" (Phil. 4:8). Communicate these things to your children. All children need instruction on how to trust in God. When they see us pray to God, they learn that we can ask God to help us in all that we do. Our example speaks to them. Children need to learn concern for others. Children need to be concerned for their parents. Ephesians 6:1-3 says, " Children, obey your parents in the Lord: for this is right. Honour thy father and mother; (which is the first commandment with promise;) That it may be well with thee, and thou mayest live long on the earth." Our children need to know that, when they obey us, they are obeying God and we definitely want to make Him happy above anyone else on this earth.

If your child runs with the wrong crowd, they will corrupt him. Think of this illustration and how it depicts this happening. Take a handful of clean, white wooden matches in your hand, strike only one and let it burn down, then rub it with the clean matches left in your hand. When you open your hand, all the matches will be black. Paul tells us in 1 Corinthians 15:33: "Be not deceived: evil communications corrupt good manners." While he is young and immature, give him your counsel while there is hope.

3. Be Sober Minded. As we have already discussed two of the subjects in Titus 2: 3-5 (to love our husbands and children), let us move on to another item in our scope of work to build a strong home. To be "sober" is *"to be marked by moderation, temperance, restraint, or seriousness"* (*Nelson's Three-in-One Bible Reference Companion*). "But let us, who are of the day, *be sober*, putting on the breastplate of faith and love; and for an helmet, the hope of salvation" (1 Thess. 5:8). We need to be of sound mind at all times, never given to the influence of intoxicants such as wine and strong drink, which takes away our capacity to be in control of ourselves. Proverbs 16:32 teaches that self-control is necessary to be pleasing and successful. "He that is slow to anger is better than the mighty; and he that ruleth his spirit than he that taketh a city."

4. Be Discreet. The meaning of "discreet" is *to be of sound mind, cautious, to show understanding.* Proverbs 2:11 says, "Discretion shall preserve thee, understanding shall keep thee."

"As a jewel of gold in a swine's snout, so is a fair woman which is without discretion" (Prov. 11:22). We all know that it is useless to have a ring of gold in a pig's snout, as they do not understand the value of it and will just root with it in the dirt. It has no meaning to the pig. A fair woman, who is pleasing to look upon, can be as uncaring and shallow minded as the pig. Beauty sometimes is only "skin deep."

Isaiah 28:26 informs us that God instructed us to be discreet. "For his God doth instruct him to discretion, and doth teach him." "My son let not them depart from thine eyes: keep sound wisdom and discretion" (Prov. 3:21).

5. Be Chaste. *Vine's Expository Dictionary of Old and New Testament Words* explains "chaste" as "pure from every fault, immaculate, modest." "Lay hands suddenly on no man, neither be partaker of other men's sins: keep thyself pure" (1 Tim. 5:22). As wives and women, we are to keep ourselves as pure as we can and untouched by the world.

6. Keepers at Home. God's ideal place for the woman is that she be a "keeper at home." Today's world looks down on a woman who "just stays at home." She does not make a big impact on society. Yet, she can be content, knowing that she is being the woman God wants her to be. She can be a big impact upon her children and husband, which is important to society as a whole. The Greek authorities say that the word translated "homemakers" in our text means "caring for the house, working at home" (Thayer). This means "working" and "at home." Managing the home requires a lot to keep it neat and attractive, creating an atmosphere that the husband and children will love to come home to. Caring for a family involves much work. There is the laundry, ironing, grocery shopping, meal planning, meal fixing, dishes, cleaning, vacuuming, children to tend to, school activities, and, if you live in the country, there are the chores, animals to care for, yard to keep up with, etc. Keep in mind all that the virtuous woman did in Proverbs 31. She was a very busy lady but she, too, was a keeper at home. In all of this, it is extremely important that we remember who this is really pleasing. God has planned it this way and we should follow His plan.

I can remember folding diapers one day (I know that I'm dating myself) and complaining that it was one of my least favorite jobs. I had two small children in cloth diapers. My husband's wise come back was, "Some day you will look back and wish you had diapers to fold again because the kids will be grown up and you'll never get this time back again." Oh so true! Gone are those days. My children are grown and are having babies of their own. You young mothers, try to savor your children at this young age, even when you grow weary of the work before you. They are precious bundles of love and nothing can take their place. Love them with all your might as you only get them for a short while and you never know when you may hear that last "I love you Mom" and never see them again. The rewards of being a keeper at home cannot be bought.

7. Good. "Good" as defined in *Webster's Dictionary* means "morally excellent; virtuous; righteous, a good man; satisfactory in quality, quantity, or degree." "Now the name of the man was Nabal; and the name of his wife Abigail: and she was a woman of good understanding, and of a beautiful countenance: but the man was churlish and evil in his doings; and he was of the house of Caleb" (1 Sam. 25:3). Abigail was a woman of good understanding with great wisdom. She knew her husband was in the wrong and had put her and their entire household in danger of death. She took it upon herself to "right the situation" between King David and her husband, Nabal. As the story goes, her husband died and David took her for his wife.

8. Obedient to Our Own Husbands. To be "obedient" means, "to be in compliance with, or submissive to authority." As wives, we must show a righteous submissiveness to our husbands as is commanded by the Lord. As this subject has already been addressed previously we will say no more.

9. So That the Word of God Be Not Blasphemed. "Remember this, that the enemy hath reproached, O Lord, and that the foolish people have blasphemed thy name" (Psa. 74:18). If the younger women are not in compliance to all of the virtues shown to us in Titus 2: 3-5, then they blaspheme

Women's Role in the Church

the Word of God by resisting His words. We want to strive to "obtain favor of the Lord" as we are told in Proverbs 8:33: "Hear instruction, and be wise, and refuse it not. Blessed is the man that heareth me, watching daily at my gates, waiting at the posts of my doors. For whoso findeth me findeth life, and shall obtain favour of the Lord. But he that sinneth against me wrongeth his own soul: all they that hate me love death." We do not want to be accused of being "foolish people" or that we "hate God."

State of Women

We can find examples of godly women in the Bible who are married, single, widowed, old, and young. All women have a role in the church, no matter what state or age of life they are living. A single woman can teach and be a great influence to the younger women and children as well as a widow or an older woman. They have the same command to teach the gospel as anyone else does.

One great example from the Bible of a woman who made a difference is that of Lydia, the seller of purple. The Bible does not specifically tell us, but it seems likely that she was a widow. She and her household had gone to the riverside, a customary place of prayer, when Paul came along. Because of her open, receptive heart, she and her household obeyed the gospel preached to them by Paul. She then became the first recorded convert to the gospel in Europe, starting the first congregation in Philippi, which met in her home. "And a certain woman named Lydia, a seller of purple, of the city of Thyatira, which worshipped God, heard us: whose heart the Lord opened, that she attended unto the things which were spoken of Paul" (Acts 16:14).

When we think of the role women have in the church, we must recognize how important the church is to the God of heaven. John 3:16 reads: "For God so loved the world, that he gave his only begotten Son, that whosoever believeth in him should not perish, but have everlasting life." We also are instructed in Acts 20:28: "Take heed therefore unto yourselves, and to all the flock, over the which the Holy Ghost hath made you overseers, to feed the church of God, which he hath purchased with his own blood." This should impress upon us how important our individual role is. Each one is blessed with certain abilities and opportunities as we go through life. We should do all we can to put forth our best effort to improve upon our abilities. We should not allow ourselves to be caught up in the "I can'ts" and the "I don'ts" as to the work we can do in our local church. There is plenty to be done and there is no rest for the weary. Brother Rody Gumpad, who preaches the gospel in the Philippines, said it well when he said, "There will be plenty of time to rest in heaven."

The Local Congregation

How would God perceive the local congregation where you are a member? The church is made up of individuals like you and me and each one makes a difference in the state of the church. Our vocation is being a Christian, and our efforts to please the Lord should be foremost in the body of God's people where we are members. Those in the world already belong to Satan and he would like nothing more than to create a crisis in the church. We must do all in our power to prevent such from happening and *it all starts with each individual person in our own congregation.* It is so very important that we evaluate the state of our local place of worship where we attend.

In the last book of the Bible, Revelation chapters 2-3, we are told about seven churches of Asia. Only one out of seven was truly pleasing to God and He recorded why the other six were a disappointment. When God looks upon us, will He say we are "deficient in love" as the Ephesians were? Will He compare us to the "poor but rich church" of Smyrna? Will we be found as "heretics" with some holding to unauthorized doctrines and ways, as was Pergamos? Will He say that He knows our works but has a "few things against us" because we "condone a false prophetess," as did Thyatira? Will He see a "stagnant, dying church with no works," like Sardis? As was in Laodicea, will He see us as a "self-satisfied" church, which is "lukewarm"? Or, will we be identified along with the good church in Philadelphia, which was a "loyal church that kept His words and did not deny His name"?

How are we representing the Lord's body where we worship? Are we honoring the roles God gave us? Are we following closely to His authority for all we do and say? Do those who enter in know us as a "warm and friendly congregation"? Or are we "luke warm," cold, unwelcoming, and unfriendly? God prefers the "warm and friendly" congregation and it is up to each one of us to make good choices to create this atmosphere. "A new commandment I give unto you, That ye love one another; as I have loved you that ye also love one another. By this shall all men know that ye are my disciples, if ye have love one to another" (John 13:34-35). Can others see Christ living in us through our love for one another?

God has provided both hindsight and foresight. We can see those things preserved behind us and before us He has told us there will be a day of judgment, which we will not be able to elude. "The Lord is not slack concerning his promise. . . . But the day of the Lord will come as a thief in the night; in which the heavens shall pass away with fervent heat . . . Seeing then that all these things shall be dissolved, what manner of persons ought ye to be in all holy conversation and godliness?" (2 Pet. 3: 9-11).

Christ's church is in critical need of godly women, godly wives, and godly mothers. May we always put God first, diligently study and seek the truth, be ever watchful of the scriptural role women have in the church and at home, teach our children God's laws, be always on guard for Satan, look to Him for strength, and just do our individual best, as we are flying swiftly towards eternity. May God bless us all.

Bibliography

Adams, James W. *Words Fitly Spoken*. Bowling Green: Guardian of Truth Foundation. 1988.

Craig, Darlene. *A Worthy Woman*. Louisville: Religious Supply, Inc. 1983.

Ferguson, Everett. *Women in the Church*. Chickasha (OK): Yeoman Press. 2003.

Harkrider, Robert. *Building Strong Homes*. Russellville (AL): Impressive Image Production. 1997.

Kellogg, Hallie Adams. *The Woman of God*. Austin: Firm Foundation Publishing House. 1962.

Meadows, James. *Some Thoughts on Women's Role in the Church*. Nashville: 21st Century Christian.

Rader, Donnie V. *Women Professing Godliness*. Bowling Green: Guardian of Truth Foundation. 2009.

Random House. *Webster's Universal College Dictionary*. New York: Random House, Inc.; Gramercy Books. 1997.

Thompson, Ruth. *That They May. . . Train the Young Women*. Bowling Green: Guardian of Truth Foundation. 1980.

Great Women I Have Known
Bobby Adams

What does it mean to be great in the Kingdom? Remember when the mother of James and John asked that her sons be given special privileges in the Kingdom? What was our Lord's reply? "Whoever desires to be great among you, let him be your servant" (Matt. 20:26). Unselfish service to others and to the Lord is what makes one great.

Mary, Mother of Jesus

The Scriptures give us many examples of great women who lived long ago. Time will not allow us to examine all of them, but I would like to look at a few. The first that comes to mind is, of course, Mary, the mother of our Lord. We are told very little about her, but we must reach the conclusion that she had to be the godliest of all women because God chose her to carry, deliver, love, cuddle, teach, and train His Son. The angel said, "Rejoice, highly favored one, the Lord is with you; blessed are you among women!" (Luke 1:28). When Jesus was twelve years old and was in the temple sitting in the midst of the teachers, both listening and asking them questions, his mother "kept all these things in her heart" (Luke 2:51). All great women have kept the sayings of Jesus in their hearts.

Sarah

Sarah was a great woman. Was she perfect? No. But neither is any human,

---

Bobby Adams was born on May 15, 1928 in Hopewell (Ohio County), Kentucky. In 1947, she married Thomas Hughes of Cleveland, Ohio. To them were born three daughters and three sons. Tom was both a teacher and an elder in the church in Berea, Ohio until they moved to Louisville, Kentucky in 1974. He died in 1982, and she married Connie W. Adams in 1986. She has taught children's classes of all ages. She travels with Connie in his full-time meeting work. She has taught classes for ladies in many states, Canada, Norway, Spain, Germany, South Africa, Italy, and the Philippines.

no matter how great. Sarah amazes most of us when we read that Abraham came in and said, "We are moving." She said, "Where?" He said, "I don't know. Wherever God tells us to go." She packed up and went with him and we do not read of one complaint. They kept moving and she "obeyed Abraham, calling him lord, whose daughters you are if you do good and are not afraid with any terror" (1 Pet. 3:6).

Ruth and Naomi

Ruth and Naomi were great women. In the book of Ruth, we read how Naomi evidently was a kind and loving mother-in-law and had taught Ruth to believe in Jehovah. Ruth loved her so much that she followed her and provided for her when she was old. Ruth is mentioned in the lineage of Jesus and was the grandmother of King David (Matt.1:5).

Elsie Shull

The first great woman in my life was my mother, Elsie Shull. There is so much that I could say about her. She loved the Lord more than anyone or anything. She grew up in Western Kentucky in a crossroads called Cool Springs and then moved to Wysox, another crossroads, when she was sixteen. At sixteen, she carried the mail for her father in a buggy pulled by a horse. She loved to read and the horse knew the route so well that he would stop at each box and she would put the mail inside. She married my father, Justus Shull, at nineteen. He was not a Christian, but she insisted on never missing a service and he went with her. I remember the night he was baptized. I was seven and it was so cold outside. In those days, we had no phone so guests would just come to visit when they felt like it, whether you knew they were coming or not. I remember one Sunday when guests showed up and we missed church. Mother told Dad after they left that she was *never* going to miss church again, even if it was his relatives. And we never did.

Mother taught me the Bible and there is no greater blessing in the world. We had a Bible drill at church and during the week, as she was washing clothes (on the old scrub board and breaking her back), she would prompt me with my memory work. We memorized whole chapters, some of which I still remember. She was a hard worker. She kept a spotless house even in the country, was a good cook, helped the neighbors, and did everything she could to make life comfortable for my father. Daddy was a good, honest, hard working man but he was not a Bible student. Mother was. She studied every day and knew the Word.

Mother loved good preachers and good preaching. She tried every way she could to encourage and support them. She had no tolerance for, as she said, "soft and mushy" preaching. She taught children of nearly every age in Bible classes. When she died, nearly all of the people who came by the casket told me of something she had taught them. What a wonderful thing to hear. When she was around eighty-five, she asked the elders if she could teach one class to the ladies. She had never taught a ladies class, but she wanted to tell them many things she had learned and exhort them to be the kind of women the Lord expects them to be. Fifty women came to hear her and she did a great job.

Mother was also very strict with us (I have two brothers). I remember "finding" a penny in our neighbor's yard and brought it home with me. She took me back, switching my legs all of the way. She said, "If it is not yours, you have stolen it." I never forgot that lesson. She taught me how to behave with young men when I was old enough to date and that kept me out of great trouble that so many have today. Mothers, are you teaching your little girls how to keep themselves pure? I am so grateful that my mother taught me. I also thought she was the most beautiful woman I ever knew.

As mother got older she loved to go with Greg Litmer, who preached for the Expressway church, to visit the "old folks" and shut-ins. She went nearly every week. She and Greg were great buddies and the love was mutual. She loved his preaching. I believe she went the week before she died of a heart attack. Greg wrote a wonderful poem when she died. He also wrote one in his book *That Ye May Grow Thereby* which I am going to share with you. I highly recommend that book. I finished it last year and loved it.

Elsie Shull

You probably didn't know her
Her name was Elsie Shull
And of all the sisters I have loved and lost,
I think I miss her most of all.

Elsie was in her 80's.
Her hair was white but she was ramrod straight.
"Come on, Greg, there's work to do,
Time's a-wasting and we can't be late!"

She could read me like a book,
She knew how I was feeling somehow.
With a simple word she could wipe away the tears.
Oh, Elsie, I need you now!

> Maybe soon the Lord will return,
> And you and I will reunite and once again embrace.
> I have done all that I know to do,
> And now I long to see your face.

In December of 1997, she baked seven Italian Crème Cakes to give to others. If you ladies have baked those, you know how much work it is. She would lie down between cakes as her back hurt so badly. She died the following January, one month before she would have been ninety. Connie and I were teaching in South Africa when she had the heart attack. She died before we got home. I shall always regret not being there for her and holding her hand to comfort her, but I will always be grateful that she "kept His sayings in her heart" and taught me to do the same.

Mosella Stotesberry

I have been asked to talk about great women that I have known. I want to say a few words about a great woman that I only know from hearing the memories of Connie and his mother. Her name was Mozella Stotesberry, lovingly called Grandmammy. I wish I could have known her. She grew up in North Carolina and, as were most of the farmers at that time, was very poor. Her husband died and left her with four children. The day of his funeral, she had to come home and cook dinner for the children. No one, not even family, provided food or comfort. That must have been very hard. Connie's mother, Nollie, was the oldest and, while her mother worked in the fields, she was responsible for taking care of the younger children. Grandmammy's work was hard and she sometimes hired out to other farmers to make enough to provide for her children. She was a member of the Christian Church, but always studied the Bible and was a good student. She taught her children. She lost two of those in death and had to deal with the grief alone. She moved to Hopewell, VA and ran a boarding house where she had to work very hard. She had a wonderful sense of humor and I loved to hear "Mama," Connie's mother, tell some of the things she said. As she grew old, she lived with Connie's family. It was a wonderful experience for him. She taught him to hunt, fish, play checkers, work picture puzzles, and, most important of all, the Bible. Every night she would say, "Son, get the Book" and she would read to him. Later, as he grew older, he would read to her. When she heard a preacher teach the pure word of God, she knew it was the truth because she was familiar with the Word. She, along with Connie's family, left the Christian Church and became simply New Testament Christians. She was great because "she kept His sayings in her heart."

Nollie Adams

Connie's mother, Nollie Adams, was a great woman. She would have been mortified if she had heard me say that. That is the lovely thing about great people. They do not think they are great. Mama, as we all called her, never taught a class, but she taught many people. She raised two sons, who have spent their lives preaching the gospel, and a daughter, who married a preacher, who preached until his death at forty-nine years old. She has three grandsons, one grandson-in-law, and two great grandsons who are all preachers of the gospel. Most of the grandchildren are Christians. That is a pretty good legacy. Mama loved the Lord, loved to worship, and opened her home to hundreds of preachers, soldiers from Ft. Lee, Virginia, and many, many others. She always felt she did not have things nice enough for company, but she served anyway. She had a sense of humor and I loved her dearly. She became very crippled with arthritis, but she never missed a worship service. Many of the young ladies in the church at Chester, Virginia came to her house and sat with her just to ask her to tell them how she did such a good job and how they could raise good families. She was happy to help them. When Connie's Dad became very ill and his mind became unstable, the doctor told her she would have to put him in a nursing home and could not take care of him at home. She said, "You just watch me!" She and Aunt Beulah took care of him at home until he died. She was great because "she kept His sayings in her heart."

Beulah Adams

Connie's Aunt Beulah, whom they called "Booby" because one of the babies could not say Beulah, was another great lady. She was the youngest of six children and her mother died when she was a very little girl. In those days, relatives helped to raise the children when they lost a parent. She was passed around from relative to relative and she said none of them wanted her. She said she often heard them arguing over whose turn it was to keep her. She was not a pretty child and had crossed eyes. She was terrified by men, so she never married. She did not tell me, but I had the feeling that she had been abused. She was the epitome of "servant of people." She spent her whole life serving others. I never heard her complain and she was so grateful for anything that was done for her. She had nearly always helped family and friends who needed her, so she had little income when she was old. I loved to take her to lunch, get her a permanent, or something new because she was like a child. She loved the Lord and knew His word. She had little education but was very bright and knew when error was taught. She lived in Connie's home most of his life and helped his mother when she became crippled. She was great because she was a humble servant who "kept His sayings in her heart."

Joan Carroll

When my children were growing up, we would ask them who they thought was the godliest woman they knew. Of course, I had always hoped they would say me, but they always said Joan Carroll. Joan truly is a great lady. She reminds me of 1 Peter 3:4—"rather let it be the hidden person of the heart, with the incorruptible beauty of a gentle and quiet spirit, which is very precious in the sight of God." She taught our children in Bible class and they loved her. Her husband later became a preacher and she helped him in her quiet and gentle way. He has gone to his reward and she now lives alone in Ohio. I am quite sure she is still teaching because she is great and has "kept His sayings in her heart."

Connie and I have been together in meeting work for twenty-four years and I could not count the great women we have known. It is very hard to choose the ones to mention.

Billie Gibson

One great lady that often comes to my mind is Billie Gibson. I especially like her because she also has a boy's name. When the institutional problem was raging, her husband, Earl, went to Akron, where Connie was preaching, and studied the problem with him. He was an outgoing, eager Christian and wanted to be right and to teach everyone who would listen. They always attended our meetings, if they could possibly get there. Billie quietly supported Earl and kept his home as long as he lived. She helped to raise four boys and one beautiful girl. Two of her sons, John and Marc, are gospel preachers and doing a good job. Her daughter, Jane, is married to Mike Vierheller, also a preacher. Billie did not give up and feel sorry for herself when Earl died, but has kept busy and never misses a meeting or worship service. She is a talented artist who paints beautiful china. The word "meek" means "strength under control" and she, indeed has a gentle and meek spirit. She is great because she has "kept His sayings in her heart."

Jane Vierheller

I just mentioned Jane Vierheller. She, too, is a great lady. We have spent many weeks in their home while in meetings in Cambridge, Ohio where Mike preaches and is an elder. Jane has so many good qualities I hardly know where to start. We are so welcome in their home. She is a great homemaker, lots of fun, great cook, and submissive and respectful to her husband. She is a good Bible student and teaches. They have three beautiful daughters who are married to Christians and working hard to teach their children to love the Lord. We have been in their home since those girls were very small and we saw them grow up. When they were teenagers I believe they were the godliest young ladies I have ever known. It takes a great mother to do that kind of job and Jane is just that. She truly has "kept His sayings in her heart."

Lucy Massey

As I am writing this, I am thinking of another great lady. Her name is Lucy Massey. She is terribly sick but she never misses a worship or Bible study unless she simply cannot get out of bed. She had a stroke some years back and, with sheer determination and faith, she overcame it but has not been in good health since. That does not stop her. She worships at Hebron Lane in Louisville where we worship and, before and after service, people gather around her like bees to honey because she is so sweet and everyone loves her. She truly has a gentle and quiet spirit. I love her for the care she gave some years ago to Nana, Connie's first mother-in-law. Lucy helped her with so many things and, when we were gone in meetings, she would stay with Lucy much of the time. Lucy loves the Lord and has "kept His sayings in her heart."

Donna Halbrook

Donna Halbrook is a very great lady. I first knew her when she and my Donna were in Florida College. She is married to Ron Halbrook and they worship with us at Hebron Lane church. I do not know of anyone who works harder for others than Donna. As some of you know, Ron spends much time in the Philippines where he is doing a great work teaching and grounding preachers, as well as baptizing many. Donna is his loyal supporter. I have never heard a complaint from her. She packs his clothes, makes all of his travel plans, and helps him in hundreds of ways. She has no self pity and, though she has a gentle and quiet spirit, she will let you know in a hurry that she supports his work. Some have questioned whether his being gone so much was good for their children. I heard her say emphatically, "Our children knew who their Daddy was." They have two sons and one daughter who are all faithful Christians. They have five very small grandchildren and Donna spends hours helping with the care of those children. She loves it and they love her. In spite of the many things she does to help others, she always seems to have time to have people in their home for dinner and those from out of town always have a place to stay. I don't know of anyone who entertains more than she does. A visitor rarely ever gets out of our assembly without Donna meeting and welcoming them. She very quietly does what we all should be doing because she has "kept His sayings in her heart."

Tessie Gumpad

I wish you could all know Tessie Gumpad. She is truly a great lady. She lives in Tuguegarao City, Philippines. I have stayed in her home two different times and she has been in ours. They have a hard life compared to the comforts that we have, but Tessie is happy and goes about her work singing. She is a joy to be around. She has six children, most of whom are grown and married, and they raised a niece, also. Every time an American preacher goes there to preach, they literally have hundreds of people come and she, with some help from her daughters and sisters, buys, prepares, and serves food to all of those people. She does not have the kind of kitchen that you and I have. The Americans pay for the food as the Gumpads could not possibly do so. When we were there, I think there were about 300 present. Twice each year they have a preacher training class for about twenty to twenty-five men for two weeks and she is responsible for feeding them. They have built a barracks type of building in back of their property in which to house them.

Her husband, Rody, has some support from America, but it is never enough because they help so many other people. He said that they never eat a meal but that someone does not come to the door and is hungry. Their children are trained to take their plates to another room and give the guests their place. Tessie told me that, when their money runs out before the end of the month, she sometimes has pulled the leaves from the trees and cooked them. She is not complaining, just stating facts. She is a hard worker and a good Bible student. I love her as though she were my daughter because she has "kept His sayings in her heart."

Pauline Carroll

I knew a great lady many years ago whose name was Pauline Carroll. She lived somewhere in the south and was very poor. I can't remember how many children she had, but I think it was seven or eight. She was a faithful Christian and had no transportation so she and the children walked to church. Her husband was not a Christian and was not a good man at that time. He sometimes would make her and the children stay home from church and work in the field next to the road on Sunday, while others passed by. That was so humiliating to her as no one worked on Sunday in those days. But she knew the Word. "Wives, likewise, be submissive to your own husbands, that even if some do not obey the word, they, without a word, may be won by the conduct of their wives, when they observe your chaste conduct accompanied by fear. Do not let your adornment be merely outward, arranging the hair, wearing gold, or putting on fine apparel, rather let it be the hidden person of the heart, with the incorruptible beauty of a gentle and quiet spirit, which is very precious in the sight of God" (1 Pet. 3:1-4). They moved to Cleveland, Ohio and that is where I met them. Her husband was converted to Christ and later became an elder of the church. Her youngest son became a gospel preacher. She has long ago gone to her reward and I am glad I was privileged to know her because she "kept His sayings in her heart."

Bonnie Lewis

Bonnie Lewis who lives in Barnesville, Ohio is one of my favorite people and is a great lady. She is kind and gentle. We have stayed in the Lewis's home many times and she always makes us feel so welcome. She is a lot of fun and a hard worker. They built their house with a large living room so they could entertain the brethren. They had a table especially made that has so many leaves that, when put together, it reaches the entire length of the room. That was bought so they could have "pot luck" dinners in their home. They love the brethren and love being in their company. Bonnie loves serving others. They have four children who are Christians and have married Christians and, as far as I know, all of the grandchildren who are old enough, are Christians. Bonnie is another of those faithful women who has a quiet and gentle spirit, loves her husband, her children, and the brethren. She has truly "kept His sayings in her heart."

Connie Maravilla Harber

Connie Maravilla Harber is another great lady whom I have known. Connie grew up in Texas and became a nurse. She met a Filipino, Levy Maravilla, who was a doctor and they fell in love. He was not a Christian when they married and her mother was not very happy that she married a non-Christian from a foreign country. After they married, they moved back to the Philippines. I have been there and that had to be quite a challenge. I'm sure at that time they did not have the conveniences and comforts that we have. She was a tall, blonde with fair skin. Most of them are short, dark skin, and black hair. (When they start to get gray, they dye their hair black.) You can just imagine the curiosity that she caused among the people of the village. She has told me of many things that are funny now, but were not so funny at that time. I believe Levy's family had more money than most of the Christians we know, but it is still nothing like our lifestyle.

Connie is amazing. She learned to adapt and to understand her husband. When language is different there can be many misunderstandings, even when you are saying the same things and do not realize it. Levy was also a great man and doctor. They moved back to the States and he had a good practice in St. Louis. She worked in his office as his nurse. However, she never neglected her home and children. I don't know how she did it. Because she knew the Scriptures and remembered the teachings of Peter (1 Pet. 3:1-4), Levy was converted to Christ. Their home was always open to visitors.

Our daughter, Kimberley, was working in St. Louis, where they lived. She was having a difficult time. Her dad had died two years before and I was not always available to her, as she adjusted to all of the changes. Connie took her into her home and she lived there about seven or eight months. After she moved to an apartment, Connie took care of her when she had her wisdom teeth all extracted and she helped her to choose her dress for my wedding when I married Connie. I will let Kimberley speak for herself.

> If you can, could you please add Connie Maravilla for me. She was a wonderful second Mom for me . . . and in some ways made all the difference in my life by just being there and being a good Christian wife. I don't think I would have all the patience with my good Filipino man if I hadn't had the chance to watch her with hers. Love, Kimberley.

You see, Kimberley also married Wally Babierra, a wonderful Filipino. I love him dearly and could not have picked a better husband for her. My husband, Connie, baptized him shortly after they were married.

Connie is the mother of David Maravilla who writes for *Truth Magazine* and has been heavily involved in the new song book which we hope will soon be available. David preaches in Republic, Missouri. He has a brother, Mike, and sister, Donna. All are faithful Christians. Our good friend, Levy, died some years ago and we still miss him. Connie subsequently married Bob Harber who had served as elder along with Levy for the church at Hazelwood, Missouri. Bob is battling cancer, which we pray fervently that he wins, and she is having some memory problems. I will always be grateful for the love that they showed our Kimberley, and so many others whose names I do not know. I gladly add her to the "Great Women I Have Known" and I know our loving God has done the same. She has loved and served, honored and obeyed her husband, she loves her children, she took care of her aged mother for years, she loved the brethren and served them, and she has the quiet and meek spirit that God loves. She "kept His sayings in her heart."

Dr. Teresa Toreja

Doctor Teresa Toreja is not only a great woman, she is amazing. She is a medical doctor in a very poor section of Manila called Kapitbahayan. She runs a medical clinic in the first floor of her house called Kapitbahayan Medical Clinic. Her family lives in the upstairs apartment. If anyone ever burned the candle at both ends, it is she. When we think of a doctor in this country, we think that they have above average income. Not so with her. Her patients are so poor that she cannot charge high fees. In the Philippines, they need not go to a doctor or a hospital unless they have the cash to pay for it. I asked her what the people do if they have no money and she said, "They die." As a result, one Saturday every month she has a free clinic and she works from dawn until into the night trying to care for as many patients as possible. Unemployment is so high in that country that her husband, Jerry, has had great problems with employment and has had to go to other countries to find work. He only got to come home some weekends and that is very hard on a marriage. Teresa has worked hard to be the loving and supportive wife and has tried to keep the home fires burning. Ron Halbrook told me, in January, that Jerry now has a job in Manila and we are all rejoicing.

When her three children were small she had to hire a "Yaya," which is a nanny and house keeper. She would go upstairs between patients to oversee how her children were being cared for. They are about grown now. She has always taught children's classes and, when I was there and teaching a ladies class, she closed her clinic and translated for me. She did a great job. She said I was the first American woman who had taught ladies classes in that area and she felt that women needed more teaching. For years, the men have had Bibles and classes, but the only teaching the women got was from the men. They loved the classes and we had large groups who came any way they could get there. We had to buy Bibles for them. After we left, Teresa started teaching ladies classes in several places and is trying to encourage other women to teach. I do not know how she works in all of that with two full-time jobs, but she does. Ron Halbrook said, "Teresa is amazing. I do not know how she does all she does for everyone."

Teresa is very humble. Many of the women wear pants to church. Most are so poor that they wear whatever they have. I wore a dress to church and to teach classes. After we had spent much time together, she asked me, "Do you ever wear pants to church?" I said "No." She asked "Why?" I replied, since she had asked, "Worshipping my Creator is the most important thing I ever do and I try to dress for the occasion. I wear pants to clean my house, travel, go to the grocery, and work in the yard but I do not feel they are appropriate to worship my Lord" (1 Tim. 2:9-10). She cried! I was stunned and felt terrible and apologized for hurting her. She said, "No, I have dresses but it is easier (and it is) to wear pants. I have just been lazy and I will never wear pants to worship again." That is humility and I felt humbled just being in her presence. Teresa has "kept His sayings in her heart."

Shirley Bunting

The first time I met Shirley was shortly after Connie and I were married. He and his first wife, Bobbie (that's right, I am Bobby 2), had lived in Norway for two years and established the first sound church in that country. He wanted me to see it and I was eager to do so. Shirley and her husband, Tom, were living and preaching there and they invited us to stay in their home. They made us most welcome and we thoroughly enjoyed the trip.

After Connie and Bobbie left Norway, the church did pretty well, for Norway. The mindset of the people makes it a very hard area to find any who are interested in the gospel of Christ. Shirley and Tom moved to Norway to work in the Kingdom in the late 1960s. They stayed for two years and things were doing fair. By the time they returned in the mid-seventies, the work had fallen on hard times with deaths, members moving, and lack of leadership. They had to start from scratch and, for two years, they were the only two who worshipped on a regular basis. Can you imagine how discouraging that would be? They were determined to find some souls who wanted to go to Heaven and they did. It grew to about 24-25 with the help of their son, Terrell, and his family. Tom and Shirley have three sons, all who preach. They spent much of their lives in Norway and speak the language fluently. Terrell and his family stayed in Norway and worked with the church for about twenty years.

We went back for two meetings while Tom and Shirley were there and it was delightful. The cost of living in Norway is astronomical and Tom was not allowed by law to work, so Shirley got a job teaching school to supplement their income. She was always cheerful and so much fun to be with. She is a good cook (I have some of her recipes) and a good homemaker. Norway has very long days in the summer and very short days in the winter. We were there in February for a meeting and it starts to get dark about 3:00

P.M. Shirley always made her home so cheerful with candles and lighting a fire in the fireplace. In fact, she gave me a large box of candles and I am still using some of them.

I believe they stayed in Norway about eighteen or nineteen years, in all. That is a long time to be away from parents, family and the conveniences that we have in the good old USA. Believe me, I have traveled enough that I can tell you, there is *no* place like the USA. It takes great courage, patience, determination, and love of God to make that kind of sacrifice. I sometimes meet young preacher's wives who will not move to the next state with her husband if it means leaving her "Momma." I say one like Shirley is a *great* lady.

After they moved back home and had planned to revisit the church in Norway whenever they could, Tom had a stroke which left him paralyzed from the waist down. She now pushes him around in a wheelchair and they still have fun together. We just saw them recently and they are still doing all they can to serve others and the Lord. Shirley is still "keeping His sayings in her heart" like all great ladies have done.

Conclusion

Do you see a pattern of behavior that flows through these great women? Do you see love for the Lord and His Word, sacrifice, patience, service, cheerfulness, and other good things?

Here are a few of the "Great Women I Have Known." There are many other great women whom I have known, but these are some who have made the most lasting impression on me. And, there are many great women whom I have never been blessed to know intimately, but whom the Lord knows are serving Him in His kingdom. Each of these great women have influenced the lives of others—their children, other children, friends, neighbors, co-workers, etc. God knows their good works, even though I don't. Not all godly women serve in the same way, but God appreciates every good work that every woman who serves in her own way does. May God bless each of you.

Ladies, if we desire to be great in His Kingdom we must forget ourselves and serve others with love, patience, gentleness and kindness. May God help each of us to "keep His sayings in our hearts."

Addenda

Addendum I
The Process of Appointing Officers
Ron Halbrook

I. The Things Written on Church Government Are to be Followed as a Pattern.
   A. Whatever God said on a subject is the pattern. What Paul wrote about elders and deacons constituted a pattern for Timothy to teach to the churches. See 1 Timothy 3:14-15. Notice that Paul's written instructions had the same authority as instructions given under his personal presence.
   B. Four passages deal with the process of appointing officers: Acts 6:1-7; 14:23; Titus 1:5; 1 Timothy 5:22-25. These passages constitute a pattern for appointing elders and deacons.
   C. The religions of men make little attempt to follow God's pattern on church government and organization. A human hierarchy appoints officers not found in the Bible and omits those revealed, or local churches vote on some human form of organization.
   D. Two offices are revealed in the pattern for the New Testament church:
      1. A plurality of elders leads each local church. They are called "elders" (or presbyters) for their spiritual maturity, "bishops" (or overseers) for their duty to manage all activities of the church, and "pastors" (or shepherds) for their work of leading the church as a shepherd leads a flock of sheep.
      2. Deacons are appointed servants of the church who serve under the guidance of elders.

II. Acts 6:1-7 Teaches Us about the Process of Appointing Officers.
   A. We must distinguish what the Apostles did and what the other brethren did.
      1. The Apostles guided the saints to select officers:

a. Called brethren together
   b. Explained the problem and the need for special servants of the church
   c. Offered solution to select special servants
   d. Gave qualifications for these servants
   e. Prayed for and appointed the servants selected by the church
   2. The local church selected its servants:
   a. Came together
   b. Listened respectfully to Apostles' instruction
   c. Pleased with inspired solution (did not protest, argue, seek another solution, etc.)
   d. Looked for qualified men within the congregation
   e. Chose or selected qualified men
B. We need to carefully distinguish the process of selecting men (in which the whole church participated) and of designating or appointing them to the work of their office (done by the Apostles who oversaw this process).
   1. See the records of the selection and appointment of judges for Israel in Exodus 18:21 ("thou shalt provide . . . able men") and v. 25 ("Moses chose able men") with Deuteronomy 1:9-18 (v. 13, "Take you wise men . . . known among your tribes, and I will make them rulers over you").
      a. "Instead of selecting the men himself. . . , Moses directed their nomination by the people, and only reserved to himself the investing them with their authority" (*Exodus* in *Pulpit Commentary*, II: 93). "In Exodus, Moses is said to have chosen these functionaries (18:25); but what many do under the direction of one may be said to be done by him" (*Deuteronomy* in *Pulpit Commentary*, 6).
      b. Moses chose judges or rulers by instructing the people to select men who fit the qualifications, and then appointed them to their duties.
C. To lay hands upon someone was a customary means to designate someone for a certain work, office, or purpose. When the Apostles laid their hands on these seven men to appoint them to their new office or service, a miraculous gift also may have been given to aid these servants in their duties and to confirm God's approval of this new arrangement. Such gifts were supplementary to the office and temporary to the apostolic age (see also Jas. 5:14-15).

The Process of Appointing Officers

III. Acts 14:23 Teaches Us about the Process of Appointing Officers.
   A. When the text says Paul ordained elders, the term "ordain" is *cheirotoneo* in Greek, literally "to stretch forth the hand," which came to mean "to simply appoint, choose, or ordain" by any means. The Holy Spirit used a word which means to choose without regard to the details of method. This term tells us the final outcome but not the intermediate steps. See 2 Corinthians 8:19 where the same term is translated "chosen" in referring to messengers "chosen of the churches." Acts 6:3 and Titus 1:5 use the synonym *kathistemi*, meaning "to appoint a person to some position or service" without regard to the means.
   B. This passage tells what the Apostles did in overseeing the process just as was done in Acts 6. The Apostles taught each church God's pattern of organization including the offices and qualifications for service, then the church selected men who met the qualifications, who in the end were appointed to the office. Paul did not simply appoint men of his own choosing. The churches selected qualified men and Paul set them into the office.
   C. Fasting was a voluntary custom associated with deep sorrow or deep devotion to prayer (see 1 Cor. 7:5), just as washing feet was a customary way of extending hospitality. Such customs are natural to the cultures in which they exist but are not legislated by God. The process of teaching the church about the work and qualification of officers, of selecting men to serve, and of appointing them should include constant and fervent prayers for the guidance of God. The mention of fasting simply shows the fervent spirit of these early saints.

IV. Titus 1: 5 Teaches Us about the Process of Appointing Officers.
   A. The evangelist did not have oversight of the church, but could carry out what an Apostle instructed him to do. The job of the evangelist was to teach what God said on church government and urge people to obey it (Tit. 2:15).
   B. Here again we must distinguish between the selection process and the final appointment.

V. 1 Timothy 5:22-25 Teaches Us about the Process of Appointing Officers.
   A. Like Titus, Timothy could teach the church what God said to do, urge people to follow it, and designate the men selected by the

church. No miraculous gifts were given because only the Apostles, and not evangelists, had the power to give such gifts (Acts 8:18).

B. An evangelist must use due caution in designating men to the office, lest he share in sinful consequences resulting from the appointment of unqualified men. In v. 22, "neither be partaker of other men's sins," follows the admonition, "Lay hands suddenly on no man." This term "neither" (*mede* in Greek) "constantly introduces an extension or development of what has immediately preceded; it never begins a new topic" (Nicoll, *Expositor's Greek Testament*, IV: 137). The need for caution in selecting and appointing men is indicated also in 1 Timothy 3:10. Time is needed to teach, to reflect, and to investigate so that the end result will be proper.

VI. Concluding Observations:

A. The particular means of selecting or looking for qualified men is not specified. That is a matter of expediency. Some format must be chosen for gathering the names of men to be considered, for setting those names before the congregation, and for assessing whether each man meets the qualifications.

1. Here is a suggested format for churches wishing to select officers:

   a. There should be thorough teaching about the work and qualifications of officers.

   b. A period of time may be set for members to submit the names of prospective officers (perhaps two weeks). The preacher or a couple of other men might be designated to receive the names.

   c. Each person whose name is submitted should be approached to know whether he believes he is qualified and whether he wishes to be considered.

   d. When the final list of prospective names is announced to the church, a time frame should be set for everyone to consider these men. If someone has a question or objection about a man's qualification, that person should go to the man or seek the help of some mature brother in approaching him. Objections should be based on Scripture, not on personal whims, likes, and dislikes. Hopefully, the matter will be resolved by withdrawing the objection, or by the prospective officer withdrawing his name from consideration.

   e. Unresolved objections will need to be considered by the

The Process of Appointing Officers

men, who will make the best decision they can based on Scripture and information available about the dispute. The parties to the dispute should yield to this decision, or remove themselves from the congregation. If either party to the dispute presses his objection to the disruption of the church, after appropriate admonitions the church should withdraw from this factional person rather than being held hostage to him. Then, the matter should be laid to rest and the process should go forward.

    f. When the period of consideration is finished, a day should be set for the formal announcement or appointment of officers. This may include a final lesson by the evangelist about the relationship between the church and its officers, and the newly appointed officers may wish to express publicly their commitment to serve in keeping with Bible principles.

B. If a church already has elders and wishes to appoint more, the present eldership would take the lead in this process as in all other matters. This does not mean the elders will singlehandedly select and appoint men without involving the whole church in the process (see Acts 6).

C. The work of the preacher is to proclaim God's will, but he cannot singlehandedly select men to serve as officers, though he participates in the selection process with the whole church. His primary duty is to provide guidance through teaching (Tit. 2:15).

D. Political devices, means, and methods contradict the nature of the kingdom of God. They can have no place in any part or stage of the process of appointing officers in the church.

  1. The nature of a spiritual kingdom limits all of our work to moral persuasion.

  2. There can be no politicking for office. See 2 Samuel 15:2-6 on Absalom's ambitious but ungodly methods. There is no place for campaign promises, lining up groups for personal support, putting out rumors for or against someone, and yielding to chronic complainers and malcontents who will say and do almost anything to block the attempt to appoint officers. All such political tactics are carnal and frustrate God's plan for scriptural church government.

  3. No petition signing movements, balloting or voting, or any other attempts to use majority rule are scriptural. In the

selection of names to be considered, names may be submitted in writing without treating the results as ballots. The focus must be on the *qualifications,* not the *popularity* of men. A man's lack of qualifications cannot be overridden by his popularity. If someone's name is suggested only once when names are submitted for consideration, it indicates a lack of confidence in that man, and he cannot lead as a shepherd without the confidence of the flock. Recognizing this fact does not reduce the process to balloting.
4. The election methods, with stated terms of office and bids for re-election, used among many Christian Churches is further evidence of a spirit of apostasy and worldliness.

Addendum II
Elders and Communication
Ron Halbrook

Let the elders that rule well be counted worthy of double honour, especially they who labour in the word and doctrine (1 Tim. 5:17).

One of the most vital functions of an effective eldership is good communication with the church. A survey of scriptural duties of elders demonstrates that good communication is imperative in every phase of their service. Wise elders get input from the congregation in the course of making decisions, which means they need a good communication process in gathering information from time to time. Obviously, if the elders wish to challenge the church to reach higher goals in various ways, they must be able to communicate those goals and the path to accomplish them. Also, a good flow of communication between the elders and the church helps them to evaluate particular needs, programs, and activities in the life of the church.

I. Elders Must Communicate with the Church

Elders must be good communicators. This is necessary in order to be "apt to teach" and able "to exhort and to convince the gainsayers" (1 Tim. 3:2; Tit. 1:9). Some are especially gifted and given to public preaching and teaching-laboring "in the word and doctrine" (1 Tim. 5:17). Not only must an elder be sound in the faith, but also he must be able to speak and teach clearly and effectively.

Yet, an elder's leadership is not limited to public teaching. If he is to pastor and oversee the church, he must be a leader of men with the ability to communicate clearly and effectively in setting goals, in expressing mature judgments on a wide range of matters, and in generally giving direction, encouragement, and counsel. That lesson can be learned from the terms which define the essence of the office: elder (or presbyter), pastor (or shepherd), and bishop (or overseer). This is essential if elders are to "take care of the church of God," "rule well," and "watch for . . . souls" (1 Tim. 3:4-5; 5:17; Heb, 13:17).

There are some men in the church with hearts of gold but who cannot communicate with others in the public teaching of the word. Such men cannot scripturally serve as elders though they can find other ways to serve the cause of Christ. They are no less vital to the Lord's work, and no less due our love and respect, than are elders. Other men can prepare and teach a public lesson but do not have the ability to express themselves clearly so as to be able to lead in matters of direction, judgment, and counsel. Some do not have the patience to consider different options in decision-making, or else are not sufficiently decisive and firm in reaching a decision. In such cases, real guidance and leadership will be missing if such men are appointed elders. It is a sign of maturity for such a man to find other ways to serve and glorify God, rather than aspiring to a work for which he is not suited.

Sometimes men who are fully and truly qualified are appointed as elders, but they do not fully utilize their opportunities or do not fully develop their potential for leading the church. They may even do an excellent job in teaching the word. Their failure to provide strong leadership may be in the area of communicating with the church in matters of direction, judgment, and counsel.

Neglect in this area can lead to stagnation in the church's program of work – evangelism, edification, or benevolence. Another result may be that some person or persons in the church with strong opinions and dominant personalities will in effect steal away the reins of leadership from the elders. When elders conduct all of their work "behind closed doors" and neglect avenues of open communication with the church, they cut themselves off from the help of good brethren and stunt their growth while also giving some Diotrephes plausible grounds upon which to lead a rebellion. Elders everywhere need to be convinced of the importance of good communication with the church.

It has been my good fortune through the years to work with elders who wanted to improve their work and who were open to suggestions in the area of communication. There are many means and methods by which elders can properly communicate with their brethren, and no one plan of procedure is final and absolute. Shortly after I moved to West Columbia, TX in 1984, the elders (Osby Weaver, Charley Alexander, and James Moore) requested that we study and discuss how to improve the communication process within the church. As the result of this consultation, we outlined "A Plan

Elders and Communication

of Communication Between Elders and other Brethren" and distributed it to the church. It provides for a flow of communication through several avenues and in both directions – i.e. elders toward the brethren and vice versa. The plan worked well for us and it is submitted here in the hope that other brethren may consider making similar efforts.

A Plan of Communication Between Elders and Other Brethren

Elders' Work
1. General Oversight
2. Decision Making
3. Communication

Announcements

Reports
Suggestions
Questions
Discussion
Encouragement

All Other Brethren

The Elders Want to Keep the Following Avenues of Communication Open:

- Regular Announcements. By making the regular announcements most of the time, the elders can have most direct communication with brethren. People who have announcements which need to be made will know to bring them to one of the elders. This will also give the elders regular opportunities to offer to the church exhortation and encouragement.

- Meetings with the men. These meetings will be planned on a quarterly basis. Each meeting will be announced in advance. The elders will give reports and exhortations, then open the floor to suggestions and discussion. To help the elders in planning profitable meetings, brethren who want to discuss some point would be wise to write it out briefly and hand the written note to one of the elders well in advance of the meeting. This will help the elders to have any needed information on hand.

These meetings will be planned and conducted in such a manner as to cultivate communication in both directions, from the elders to the men and from the men to the elders. The elders will not shirk their duty to make final decisions nor will they try to settle matters by having a vote taken. The meetings are designed for communication and not for decision making.

- Elders Meetings. The elders are meeting at least once a month and more often when needed in order to oversee the work of the church on a constant basis. If the elders need to meet with someone or if someone wants to meet with them, the elders will always be ready to arrange such meetings. Anyone is free to make suggestions to the elders at any time.
- Elders and deacons to meet. The elders plan monthly meetings with the deacons in order to work with them as closely as possible.
- Elders and teachers to meet. The elders plan quarterly meetings to encourage the teachers and to share communication with them.

It should be noted that this plan is not designed to replace the divine pattern for oversight and rule by elders with some form of democratic government. This is purely a matter of communicating as elders. As we continued our work to improve the communication process, three letters were prepared and distributed at the direction of the elders on "Gathering Information for a Decision," "Setting Higher Goals," and "Evaluating a Program."

II. Gathering Information for a Decision

In an effort to improve their communication with the church, the elders of the church at West Columbia, TX requested that the letter published below be sent to each family. The idea of some schedule changes discussed in the letter had been offered at a meeting of the elders with the other men of the congregation. Sometimes elders hesitate to conduct open meetings of this kind because they have bad memories of brethren bickering and haggling in open meetings conducted before elders were appointed. Such meetings can be productive if the elders preside and lead them properly. In the thirteen years I labored with the church at West Columbia, there was not an untoward incident of any kind in our open meetings. When brethren are accustomed to such meetings properly conducted on a regular basis, rather than being called only when the kettle has reached a boiling point, even criticisms and complaints can be handled in a more orderly fashion. Suggestions may be offered in these meetings which help to solve problems

Elders and Communication

while they are small and before they reach the size where they provoke confrontations, bitterness, and factions.

This letter makes it clear that the elders are not forfeiting their God-given duties to the changing whims of a ballot box. The letter also makes it apparent that the elders are trying very hard to take into account the needs and wants of the church as a whole. There is no desire – or even appearance of a desire – to impose an arbitrary decision purely to suit the whims of the elders. When the elders announced their decision, it was obvious to those who agreed and to those who disagreed with the new schedule that the elders had been fair and open in the process of reaching a conclusion. Such a letter is certainly not necessary in making every decision, but it can be a valuable tool of open communication from time to time.

Letter from the Elders to Each Family in the Church at West Columbia

Dear Brethren,

The elders are continuing their efforts to maintain good communication with the church. This letter is being sent to every family in order to gather information on a suggestion offered by some of our men in the recent quarterly meeting. It was suggested that we might change the time of some or all of our assemblies.

This letter is not a ballot and the elders are not going to make decisions by asking you to vote. The decision will not be based on "majority rule" or "minority rule" but upon what we believe to be in the best interest of the church as a whole. As one part of gathering information before we make a decision, we want a response from each family and so we are asking you to return this letter. We want to consider the preference and convenience of the church as a whole. We want to know whether a change in the time of a service will work a hardship on anyone or make it impossible for them to come.

With each change suggested by some of the men, you will see the reason given. When you indicate your preference, please give the reason listed fair consideration and then feel free to indicate a reason for your preference if you wish to.

1. Some suggest an earlier time for Sunday morning services is better. They feel fresher and more alert earlier, which helps them get more out of the services. Children might do better if services did not run close to the noon meal time. There would be more time left for afternoon visits, trips, etc.

Check Your Preference for Sunday Morning Services:

_____ 9:00 A.M. Bible class, 10:00 worship

_____ 9:30 A.M. Bible class, 10:30 worship

_____ 10:00 A.M. Bible class, 11:00 worship.

If you wish to, give reasons for your preference:

2. Those who wish to will gather for a special 30 minute session on Sunday evenings before the regular worship period. One week the time will be devoted to memory work and other training for children (seated on the first two or three rows); the next week, the time will be used for our men to work on Bible reading, short lessons, leading songs and prayers. We will alternate these sessions week after week.

Check Your Preference for the Sunday Evening Services:

_____ 5:30 P.M. session, 6:00 P.M. worship.

_____ 6:00 P.M. session, 6:30 P.M. worship.

Some of the men prefer 6:00 P.M. session and 6:30 P.M. worship along with 9:00 A.M. classes and 10:00 A.M. worship to give a longer afternoon and time for supper before services. If you wish to, give reasons for your preference:

3. Someone suggested that since it gets dark earlier now, we might consider having Wednesday service at 7:00 P.M. through the winter, but this might make it hard for some people to attend after work. Check One: _____ 7:00 P.M.; ____ 7:30 P.M.

Thank you for your cooperation and suggestions! Please sign.

III. Setting Higher Goals

One of the steps taken by the elders to strengthen the church at West Columbia, TX in 1985 was an effort to reach the weak and erring before they fell away from Christ completely. When some new deacons were appointed, the specific assignments made to various deacons were discussed and reviewed, and a new task was divided among them all. A peg board was already in use to keep tabs on attendance patterns; at each service, every member pulled his peg and dropped it into a box, and a deacon recorded each member's attendance on a chart in a notebook. The members' names were divided among the deacons as a new step, so that each deacon was responsible to check on anyone on his list who was absent. An announcement was made and the lists were posted matching the deacons with the other families in the church. Additional members were added to the lists

Elders and Communication

as they joined themselves to the disciples (Acts 9:26). If a person knew in advance he would be absent, he could call the appropriate deacon.

When a problem or pattern of absence appeared, not only did the deacon try to help and encourage the person involved but also the matter was discussed in the regular meetings of elders and deacons. As a result, counsel was shared on how to best approach the matter and visits were made in an effort to resolve the problem and to help the person grow.

The deacons perform a wide range of tasks, many of them involving physical aspects of the work, but the fact is that there is an interplay between physical and spiritual aspects of the Lord's work (study Acts 6:1-7). Deacons are selected on the basis of qualifications which reflect spiritual maturity (1 Tim. 3:8-13; Acts 6:1-7). Their office and work cannot encroach upon that of the eldership, but wise elders will find the skills and counsel of deacons to be a great asset in every aspect of the Lord's work. This does not mean that deacons are "junior elders," sharing the oversight and rule. Deacons are servants and helpers who minister under the oversight of elders. Elders need the help of such godly men to make their own leadership more effective.

Communication was vital to the effort to identify problems and strengthen the weak. The whole church had to understand the importance of this goal. In addition to public statements, teaching, and admonition, a letter was sent to each family seeking their help and prayers. The letter admitted neglect by the elders in some aspects of dealing with the weak in the past. They wanted everyone to know that they were setting higher goals for themselves in the role of overseers, as well as for the whole church.

The result of communication with and through the evangelist, with and through the deacons, and with each family in the church was that everyone knew exactly what the goals were, what the plan of action was, and what was expected of everyone. The whole church began to pull together and the elders continued to do a more effective job in helping the weak. This does not mean that all weak Christians among us suddenly matured. It does mean that everyone knew the elders were trying more earnestly to help them grow and to reach them before they fell away completely.

The letter which the elders sent as one phase of communicating higher goals in this area of their work is published below.

Letter from the Elders to Every Member
of the Church Here at West Columbia

Dear brother and sisters in Christ,

As elders, overseers, and shepherds, we bear two heavy responsibilities according to Hebrew 13:17. "Obey them that have the rule over you, and submit yourselves: for they watch for your souls, as they that must give account, that they may do it with joy, and not with grief: for that is unprofitable for you."

First, we must "watch for your souls." That means to watch with love and care for the well-being of each soul here. We watch for signs of growth and progress so that we may encourage you to continue in that direction. We also watch for signs of weakness and wavering so that we may help you to change your direction for the better. Every effort is for your profit and for your gain spiritually.

Second, we are responsible to give an account of our efforts to Christ Himself. There will be great joy when we tell the story of the progress of those who are growing. We will have grief and sorrow when we must tell of those who wavered and then fell away. On that Last Great Day, we cannot profit you any longer.

We are constantly looking for ways to profit and help you more. As you know from your home life and other relationships, some acts of love are difficult and painful to perform, but they must be performed if the bonds of love are to grow. This letter speaks of some difficult and painful duties of love, but it will bear fruit for the good of us all if we can be united in doing what God teaches us to do. We ask for your prayers, your moral support, and your help in every possible way.

As elders we confess our neglect in following to completion God's plan to strengthen the weak and to restore the fallen. There is the need for greater diligence in following every step of God's plan, including the final withdrawal of fellowship. With God's help and your help, we want to be better leaders in this area.

One of the danger signs in a Christian's life is a lukewarm attitude toward the duty of assembling with the saints each time they meet (Heb. 10:25; Rev. 3:15-16). Such things as old age, sickness, and job requirements are not sinful; we do not have them in mind. But willful absence is sinful. Willful absence sears the conscience (1 Tim. 4:2), sets the wrong example (Matt. 18:6), and leads to other kinds of unfaithfulness (Gal. 5:19-21). After much exhortation and warning, the church must "withdraw from every brother that walketh disorderly" (1 Thess. 5:14; 2 Thess. 3:6).

Elders and Communication

We want to do a better job and encourage everyone to help us in calling, visiting, teaching, admonishing, and rebuking those who are willfully absent. When we see a Christian missing from our assembly, let us inquire where he is and contact him to see if he needs our help in any way. Please expect someone to contact you when you are absent. You can help by getting the word to one of the elders or deacons if you get sick or when you know in advance you cannot be here. Any time you learn that a person is absent only a few times or is habitually absent, please help us to be more effective in reaching that person.

Some of you can help us by being more careful to pull your peg on the attendance board. With the appointment of new deacons shortly, we will divide the names or our members among the deacons so they can help us to stay in better touch with you about your attendance.

When a person obeys the gospel, he is asking Christ and the people of God to follow God's plan completely if he begins to stumble or if he falls away. We fail in our duty to God and to our erring brother if we fail to do everything the Bible teaches in an effort to reach the erring. The church must continue in the relationship, fellowship, and process of working with these people until the point of a final withdrawal of fellowship. Final withdrawal is designed to bring the erring to repentance (1 Cor. 5:5), to assure the removal of the leaven of sin from the church (1 Cor. 5:6-7), and to cause others to fear (1 Tim. 5:20). Final withdrawal is a part of God's plan and must not be neglected.

The church at West Columbia continues to have a great potential for good in the service of the Lord. Let us unite in love and patience toward the weak and the erring. Let us work closely with them as long as they show any desire to grow and to correct their lives. If there are spiritual problems in your life and you are willing to talk with us, please contact us and we will get together with you. If you have any suggestions on this matter, let us know. May all of us unite in following every step of God's plan regarding those who stumble or fall away. We ask the prayers and the help of every deacon, of all our teachers, of the evangelist, and of each member of the church.

With our love and care for each of you,

Signed Elders

IV. Evaluating a Program

Effective leaders evaluate every phrase of their work from time to time to see if changes and improvements need to be made. Traditionalism – we do this or that because we have always done it – leads to stagnation. When changes are made just for the sake of change, there is no real leadership involved. Such cosmetic action is superficial and immature. The process of review and evaluation will reveal the need to keep some things as they are, to make minor adjustments in some areas, and to discard programs that have proven ineffective.

In the process of evaluation, elders are wise in seeking various forms of responses and various kinds of suggestions from many sources which are at their disposal – deacons, evangelists, class teachers, and other members. As a part of its program of evangelism and edification, the church at West Columbia, TX began purchasing the *Guardian of Truth* for each household in the church in 1985. A little over a year later, the elders decided to examine the use being made of this teaching tool in order to judge whether it was making a significant contribution to our overall work or not. The potential for good was there, but was it being realized?

As a part of this process, the decision was made to seek direct response and evaluation on the part of all those who were receiving the magazine. The elders asked that a letter be prepared clearly presenting the goals and values of this program so that people would understand what they were being asked and why. Were these goals being met? Were these values being obtained by the readers?

The response was positive beyond our hopes! Two aged people said they were no longer able to read anything at all. One man said that he doubted he got much out of it because he was so busy with other things. Everyone else said, yes, they read some of the articles, benefitted from it, and desired for this material to continue coming into their home. This program was helping us far more than we realized.

Some interesting comments were added in the space provided for that purpose. Several stated that they read every article in each issue. "It has helped us tremendously to grow as Christians. Thank you." One lady said she read the paper while riding her stationary bicycle. "Some articles have stimulated conversations and discussions besides just benefitting me." Another person inquired as to how she could send the paper to her relatives in liberal churches in other towns. Several said they stop whatever they are doing when the paper comes in the mail and sit down immediately to read it. The input of the readers was invaluable in the elders' decision to continue using the *Guardian of Truth* in the church here.

Other programs and phases of the work were evaluated. The adult class program was revamped so as to provide three subjects on Sunday and three on Wednesday, and new classes were offered each quarter. The children's classes at one time had been left to individual teachers and lacked any overall progression or continuity. Now they study the *Truth In Life* series on Wednesdays and *Walking With God* on Sundays. So that our teachers would stay fresh, no one was saddled with a class for eternity but changes were made on a regular basis. The elders communicated with the preachers we supported in other places from time to time to evaluate our work in this area. In order to encourage personal contact between our members and the men we supported, we periodically passed out a list of these men's names and addresses. We constantly worked to develop new teachers in our midst, and preachers as well. At times, we had a young man work with us for the summer. Andy Alexander, one of our own, prepared himself and began full-time evangelistic labors in his mid-30s in 1988.

The church in West Columbia did not claim perfection but constantly aspired to improve its work. We wanted to press forward and grow in every phase of our work and service unto God! The point of this material is simply this. Open lines of communication are vital if elders are to lead the church in an effective way. We have tried to reinforce that lesson with illustrations taken from the experience of the West Columbia church. Our elders included Osby Weaver, Charley Alexander, James Moore when these steps were first taken, and after Osby moved away Jimmy Dale Harris was added in July 1987. Our deacons were Ferg Frederick, Hollis Harris, Earl Hathorn, Raymond Maxwell, Joe Sutherland, and Charles Kelley, all dedicated saints. Men and women of all ages used their talents and abilities in many ways. The church helped and encouraged me to grow in my work as an evangelist. My whole family grew spiritually. We were thankful to be a part of a church with such good leadership.

The letter used by the elders in evaluating the church's use of the *Guardian of Truth* is reproduced below. They discussed with me the ground they wanted the letter to cover and asked me to draft it, then they finalized it as follows:

Evaluating the Church's Use of a Gospel Journal

A word is in order on behalf of the elder's effort to evaluate our use of the *Guardian of Truth*. A good eldership not only initiates plans for evangelism, edification, and benevolence, but also evaluates those plans. They periodically evaluate the men being supported in evangelism and every other phase of the church's work. The church here has been purchasing the *Guardian of Truth* for our members for over a year now and having it mailed into our homes. The elders ask each of us to consider our use of this gospel paper and to help them in evaluating this program of work.

There is no financial problem with our use of the *Guardian of Truth*. For the amount we pay, especially with the group discount, we could not put out a good bulletin, as I know from having edited a bulletin for five years. Neither could we provide in a bulletin as much good material by mature writers from around the country as we get in the *Guardian of Truth*. So the cost for what we are getting is minimal at $1.00 per month per household. That is a bargain for the sound, spiritual teaching which goes into each home. But nothing is a bargain if it is not used. If it costs only $1.00 a year for the whole church to get it, and we were not using it or benefitting from it, we don't want to waste even a dollar. The elders need to know whether or not we use it and benefit from it.

They are not asking if you read every article and line of every issue. I don't always get to do that. At home, we take several newspapers and secular magazines – we don't read every line of every issue of any of them. We use them as we can. If we never read or benefit from one, eventually we stop taking it. The elders are not trying to make you feel guilty if you do not get to read every line of every issue. We are all simply being asked to evaluate the usefulness of the journal in our own home. We are being asked to circle "Yes" or "No" in answer to this question: Do you read some articles in the *Guardian of Truth* as you have time, benefit from it, and desire that it continue to come into your home?

The point is this. If you never read or benefit from it, if you prefer not to receive it, do not hesitate to circle "No." Your candid judgment is needed. If you scan and read articles of interest to you, if it helps and encourages and benefits you spiritually, if you would miss it and want it to keep coming, circle "Yes." Feel free to write down any additional comment you wish to make.

This is an effort to have good communication and accurate information, so that this phase of our work can be properly evaluated. No idea of voting or majority rule is involved. The elders may decide to continue this program or to drop it. Also, the paper can be easily stopped where it is not wanted. It is not forced on anyone. After their evaluation, the elders will let us know their decision.

Purpose and Value of the Present Program

Sometimes we initiate plans and programs but fail to explain their purpose or value. Why do churches sometimes use gospel papers? Why have we been using the *Guardian of Truth*? It is an expediency to provide admonition, edification, and gospel teaching in general just like class literature, tracts, newspaper articles, correspondence courses, and other printed materials. All such expediences are authorized by every passage which authorizes the church to preach and teach the word of the truth of the gospel (1 Tim. 3:15; Col 1:5). Whether a specific aid is expedient or not at a given time is a matter of judgment (1 Cor. 6:12).

The simplest way I can express the value of gospel journals after reading them for 25 years is this: It is like having several gospel preachers coming into my home from time to time to stimulate my study, to increase my zeal, to provoke my thought, to widen my horizon about trends and efforts (good and bad) in other places, and to deepen my love for the Lord and all things spiritual. When men like Bill Cavender, Irven Lee, Harold Fite, Larry Hafley, Hoyt Houchen, Steve Wolfgang, and Mike Willis come into your home to sow the seed of the kingdom, it will do you good if you have an honest heart. If you cannot get all the seed they have to sow every time they come, whatever amount you do get will do you good! That is why brother Alexander recently reminded us to take note of the articles in this magazine, adding that they are some of the finest he had ever read.

A journal can be used in connection with personal study, to generate discussion with a family member or friend about a particular subject, to aid family devotions, to improve Bible class preparation, to pass Bible lessons on to other people (saints and sinners), to save for reference material for future use, or to prepare talks, invitations, remarks at the Lord's supper, and sermons.

Let me make a personal observation on such expediencies properly used, drawn from 25 years of gospel preaching. I can go to heaven without Bible classes, class literature, or gospel journals. I can even use such aids on an individual basis whether the church includes them in its program or not. But, such aids are used by fewer people when left to the individual alone to provide his own. We may get busy or lack initiative and overlook the opportunity on our own. But when the challenge to reach a little higher is laid before us by those who watch for our souls, we often rise to that challenge and make the effort which brings a blessing to our lives.

I have learned that a church which includes classes in its program gains an added layer of strength and depth. I have preached where class literature was rarely provided by the church and where it was regularly provided. When a church includes literature often in its classes, another layer of growth can be seen after a time. I have preached where the church sent a religious journal into each home and where it did not. When a church included a gospel paper in its program, I have seen in time without fail an additional layer of strength, depth, and growth. Some of you confirm in your development what I am saying, because you have grown as a direct influence of the *Guardian of Truth* since the church has been using this aid in its teaching program. Several have expressed this from time to time.

The more we are surrounded with spiritual tools, activities, and influences, the more we grow and bear fruit in the Lord!

May God bless elders in every place who sacrifice their time and talent in watching for the souls of saints (Heb. 13:17). May God bless elders to strive for effective communication in leading souls to serve Him for time and for eternity.

[This material is a slight revision of four articles published in 1990: "Elders and Communication (1-4)" *Guardian of Truth* XXXIV 17-18, 21-22 (Sept. 6-20 & Nov. 1-15, 1990): 522-523, 557, & 648-649, 678-679 respectively.]

www.ingramcontent.com/pod-product-compliance
Lightning Source LLC
Chambersburg PA
CBHW070608170426
43200CB00012B/2619